Books by

C·W·CERAM

THE MARCH OF ARCHAEOLOGY (1958)

THE SECRET OF THE HITTITES (1956)

GODS, GRAVES, AND SCHOLARS (1951)

These are Borzoi Books
Published in New York by Alfred·A·Knopf

THE MARCH OF ARCHAEOLOGY

THE MARCH OF

 BY

Translated from the German by Richard and Clara Winston

ARCHAEOLOGY

C·W·CERAM

NEW YORK ALFRED·A·KNOPF 1958

INTRODUCTION

This picture book was planned in conjunction with my first book on the history of archaeology, *Gods, Graves, and Scholars.*

To my surprise, I discovered that although there were any number of picture books which show the riches of past civilizations as revealed by archaeology—the bookseller sets them on his shelves under the general heading of "art books"—there was not a single one whose subject was the history of archaeology itself.

Archaeology, considered in its full import as the study of antiquity, includes far more than the often dusty and sometimes monotonous process of excavation. There is the drama and beauty of the important find. And every find is followed by the far more important process of interpretation. And in the course of interpretation there takes place that wonderful, methodical re-

creation of the past which our civilization alone has practiced and which makes it clear that archaeology is among the "conquering sciences of the nineteenth century," to borrow a phrase from Adolf Michaelis, who was the first to deal with the history of archaeology. In this larger sense, archaeology is a complete science of which excavation is but a part, and it leads to a wealth of fascinating pictures among which only a few are of a man with a spade. Perhaps the failure to grasp this is the reason why there has been no previous pictorial history of archaeology.

How our view of the ancient world was born, how it changed, and how it is still changing—that, then, is the real theme of this book. (The reader will find a small selection of essential texts on this subject in the introduction to the list of sources.)

In devising a format for this book I soon

realized that the time-honored method of assembling a collection of pretty pictures with such captions as "No. 17; carved cosmetic palette; late predynastic period; height 3.4 inches" would be useless for the sort of book I had in mind. Similarly, the manner of most picture books, of referring the reader to the appendix for additional information, has always seemed to me something less than encouraging. In fact, it is the fate of such collections of pictures to be merely leafed through (except by interested professionals, of course); they are seldom looked at intently. Similarly, their texts are not particularly readable. I therefore chose a format in which picture and text are so welded together that the one cannot stand without the other. If the result has been a picture book that can be read—it is not my province to judge—then I have achieved my aim.

The pattern of the book deliberately follows the structure of *Gods, Graves, and Scholars* because I have sought to trace the historical and cultural continuity that extends from Sumeria through Babylonia, Assyria, Crete, Greece, and Rome down to our own times. This, to me, is a more natural presentation of the facts than any attempt to draw in the over-all archaeological scene. The excursion into Middle America is justified only as an express and conscious digression. For the reader who wishes to apprehend at least the outlines of the general scene, the chronological tables offer a chart highlighting the major events in the history of archaeology, from the first stirrings of interest in antiquity to the present-day triumphs of specialists.

Many of the illustrations are reproduced here for the first time. Several of the quotations are here published from manuscript for the first time; many others are reprinted here for the first time after having fallen into oblivion for two, three, or even four hundred years. Thus, even the specialist will find some pictures and texts new to him. The conjunction of pictorial and written documents has resulted in a work absolutely independent of *Gods, Graves, and Scholars*, even though it follows the same broad historical track.

There are such vast treasures of pictorial material that I was forced to cull them boldly to keep the book to a manageable length. I can only ask the forbearance of those who might have chosen a little differently, and hope that critics will notice the particular and significant order in which the material has been presented.

The 326 pictures have for the most part been photographed anew, from the originals. Similarly, all the quotations in the text have been drawn directly from the sources. Wherever translations were necessary, they have been done anew; condensations and cuts have been noted in every case. Thus the material in this book is documentary in the strict sense. The detailed list of sources will enable the interested reader to pursue various subjects farther.

A word of explanation: This book, like

Gods, Graves, and Scholars and *The Secret of the Hittites*, is not basically a scientific but a literary work. I am not a scientist, but a writer. In my presentation of the history of archaeology I have acted upon a literary principle: reality seen through a temperament. I simply followed the method that guided the naturalistic novelists when they described the world of priests, bankers, or coal-miners, subjecting themselves to the exceedingly severe obligation of studying very closely, before writing, theology and Church history, the stock exchange, or the social conditions of miners.

May I also, then, in this book, take my farewell *as a writer* from a subject that has fascinated me to the utmost for more than ten years, but toward which, after ten years of study, I have lost my naïveté. That my efforts have been successful and have won some recognition among professionals must not be allowed to turn a writer's head and keep him ever bound to the same theme.

ACKNOWLEDGMENTS

My expressions of gratitude, which ordinarily are but a matter of custom, here are a necessity. It is due only to the patience and labors of the publisher, Walter Neurath, and his associates at Thames and Hudson that this book, technically so difficult to produce, and requiring years of preparation, can be made accessible to a larger public. The readiness of museums, libraries, and numerous scholars to aid in the production of this book was extraordinary.

I owe particular thanks to the following institutions: American Museum of Natural History, New York; Ashmolean Museum, Oxford; British Museum, London; Germanisches Museum, Nuremberg; Griffith Institute, Oxford; Kunsthistorisches Museum, Vienna; Metropolitan Museum, New York; Musée du Louvre, Paris; Musée de l'Homme, Paris; Museum am Kupfergraben,

Staatliche Museen, Berlin-Dahlem; Museum für Völkerkunde, Vienna; Museo Nacional de Historia, Mexico; Museo Regional de Oaxaca, Mexico; Peabody Museum, Harvard University, Cambridge, Mass.; Staatliche Kunstsammlungen, Weimar; Vorderasiatisches Museum, Berlin; Victoria and Albert Museum, London; Biblioteca Civica, Parma; Biblioteca Laurenziana, Florence; Biblioteca Nazionale, Naples; Biblioteca Nazionale Centrale, Florence; Biblioteca Vaticana, the Vatican; Bodleian Library, Oxford; Newberry Library, Chicago; British School at Athens; Université St. Joseph, Beirut; Warburg Institute, London.

For assistance in assembling the pictures I am indebted to: Professor C. W. Blegen; M. Philippe Diole; I. E. S. Edwards, Esq.; Dr. Johannes Friedrich; Dr. Zakaria Goneim; Dr. Siegfried Grotefend; Mrs. Seton Lloyd; Professor Amadeo Maiuri; Dr. Ernst Meyer; the executors of the estate of Sir Arthur Evans; and Miss Ann Petrie, who also gave permission for the inclusion of a paragraph from the book by her father, Sir Flinders Petrie, *Pyramids and Temples of Gizeh*. I am grateful to Sir Leonard Woolley for allowing me to quote from his books *Digging Up the Past* and *Excavations at Ur*, and to Penguin Books for permission to use a passage from Aubrey de Selincourt's translation of *The Histories* of Herodotus.

C·W·C

May 1958

LIST OF COLOR PLATES

I.   ZEUS ABDUCTING GANYMEDE.   *faces page* 14
(*Photo Professor Max Hirmer.*)

II.   GREEK TEMPLES WERE COLORED.   15
Engraving from Semper: Über Anwendung der Farben in der Baukunst, Dresden, 1836. *Photographed especially for this book.*

III.   VASE PAINTING: ATHENE BEARING ARMS.   30
(*By permission of the Trustees of the British Museum.*)

IV.   ROMAN WOMAN PLAYING THE CITHARA.   31
(*By permission of the Metropolitan Museum, New York.*)

V.   EGYPTIAN DEATH SHIP.   126
(*By permission of the Trustees of the British Museum.*)

VI.   PHARAOH TUTANKHAMEN.   127
(*Photo George Allen, Esq.*)

VII.   A DEAD MAN'S PRAYER.   142
(*Photo George Allen, Esq.*)

VIII.   ENTRANCE TO THE TOMB OF AN EGYPTIAN QUEEN.   143
(*Photo Professor Max Hirmer.*)

IX.   BILLY GOAT AT THE TREE OF LIFE.   174
(*By permission of the Trustees of the British Museum.*)

X.   MODEL OF PERSIAN WAR CHARIOT.   175
(*By permission of the Trustees of the British Museum.*)

XI.   PERSIAN DRINKING-HORN.   190
(*By permission of the Trustees of the British Museum.*)

XII.   HEADDRESS OF A QUEEN OF UR.   191
(*By permission of the Trustees of the British Museum.*)

XIII.   AZTEC SKULL OVERLAID WITH MOSAIC.   286
(*Photo Irmgard Groth-Kimball, by permission of the Trustees of the British Museum.*)

XIV.   RITUAL AX FROM CENTRAL AMERICA.   287
(*Photo Irmgard Groth-Kimball, by permission of the Trustees of the British Museum.*)

XV.   MAYA ATTACK THEIR NEIGHBORS.   302
(*By permission of the Peabody Museum, Harvard University, Cambridge, Mass.*)

XVI.   AZTEC SHIELD WITH MOSAIC OF FEATHERS.   303
(*Photo Conzett and Huber, Zurich, by permission of the Museum für Volkerkunde, Vienna.*)

TOPICS OF THE BOOK

BOOK I

The Birth of Classical Archaeology

Introduction	xv	Winckelmann and the birth of "art	
The girl of the Via Appia	2	archaeology"	8
Laocoön misunderstood	5	Antinous—favorite and god	9
Raising the statue of Livia	6		

Pompeii and Herculaneum

"Even for gods this was going too far!"	10	The youth from the ashes	21
The bronze horse "poured in a single		The Pompeian bar and the "little	
mold"	11	donkeys"	22
Cavaceppi's workshop	14	Electioneering	23
Antiquity in a romantic light	15	Verecundus the felt-maker	24
The skeleton in the laundry	17	"The house of the moralist"	25
The plaster corpses	18	The "villa of the Mysteries"	26
Mazois and "the slow, best method to		Father Piaggio and the papyri	28
proceed with an excavation"	20	The mysterious magic square	30

Schliemann's Venture in the Dark

The hill called Hissarlik in 1809   32
Schliemann as a wholesale merchant   33
Table: Schliemann the entrepreneur   34
Table: Schliemann the excavator   35
A page from Schliemann's diary   36
The great tower of Ilium   38
Sophia and "Helen of Troy's jewels"   39
Trojan excavation sites   41
Foe and friend   42

Schliemann's letter to the Prime
    Minister of England   45
Sketch map of the west coast of Asia
    Minor   46
Sketch map of Greece   46
The grave circle of Mycenae   46
What was the "Homeric Age"?   49
Gold and science   50

New Light on Crete

The nearsighted Englishman   52
Table: Chronology of Cretan-
    Mycenaean culture   53
Authentic view of Cretan architecture   54
The problem of "restoration"   57
The "prince in the field of lilies"   58
The "bull-dancer"   60

The "snake-goddess"   61
Cretan miniatures   63
The disc of Phaestos   64
Ventris deciphers Cretan script   64
Restoration of the temple gate of
    Baalbek   66

BOOK II

The Egyptian Sphinx

Female or male   70
Flaubert greets the Sphinx   72
Its *grand charactère*   73
The riddle   74
Napoleon and Denon   76
The *Description*   77

The forgotten expedition   78
Poetry and truth   80
On the merits of photography and
    drawing   81
Belzoni transports a colossal statue of
    Ramses   82

The "strong man" and plundering
   excavations   83
Champollion   84

The Rosetta Stone   86
Hieroglyphs   89
Obelisks   90

Geometry in Stone

Pyramids are tombs   91
The interior of the Cheops pyramid   93
Early views of it   94
Archaeology and gunpowder   95
Lane in the burial chamber   97
Self-portrait of E. W. Lane   98
Camera-lucida view of the Great
   Pyramid   100

"Bible in stone"?   101
Flinders Petrie   102
Cross-sections of three pyramids   105
Borchardt's reconstruction of the pyra-
   mids at Abusir   107
Goneim's discovery in 1954   108
The pyramids speak   110

Mummies

"Mumia is . . ."   111
Mummies as medicine   112
Grave-robbing   112
The dancing mummy   113
Herodotus describes embalming   114
The mass grave of sixty warriors   116
Robbers with Maspero and Brugsch   119
The mummy of Ramses II   120
Maspero unwraps Sethos I   121

Flower-decked Amenophis I   122
Queen Isimkhobiu   123
Tau-a-quen's death agony   124
The best-preserved mummy   125
The first portraits in history   127
X-ray photograph of Wah's mummy   128
Mummified animals   130
Women in archaeology   132
Thais   133

The Valley of the Kings and Relics of Ordinary Life

The Hay Expedition again   135
The valley   136
View of the tomb of Tutankhamen   138
Treasures of the antechamber   140

Carnarvon and Carter open the burial
   chamber   142
The golden sarcophagus   144
The graceful goddesses   147

Jewelry 148
Problems of transportation in antiquity 150
What tools did the Egyptians have? 152
Stonemasons at work 153

Funeral furnishings 154
Death ships 156
The Book of the Dead 159

BOOK III

Early Travelers to Babylon and Persepolis

Two views of the Tower of Babel 162
"Dangerous adventure" 164
Sitti Maani 166
Persepolis 167
Sketch map: Between the Mediterranean and the Persian Gulf 171

A jeweler turns archaeologist 172
Kanavas Khan's gala reception 173
Engelberg Kämpfer at Xerxes' throne room 174
The human-headed bull—as Chardin and De Bruin saw it 175

The Decipherment of Cuneiform Script

From right to left or from left to right? 177
Copy of cuneiform script by Kämpfer 178
Niebuhr survives 180
The development of cuneiform script from picture-writing 182
Grotefend makes a wager 183
Portrait of Grotefend 183
The decipherment 184
Portrait of Rich 187
Rich's map of Babylon 188
Portrait of Sir Robert Ker Porter 189
Four artists—four different conceptions 190

Rope trick along the wall of a precipice 191
Birs Nimrud 193
"Take your steamship on your back" 194
Moving ships across the desert 195
Shipwreck 196
Niebuhr draws Nineveh 198
Botta digs in Nineveh 199
Place ventures river shipment 201
Two examples of Assyrian art 202
The Darius relief 204
The Behistun inscription 206
Riddle of cuneiform script 208
Four decipherments agree 209

Layard in Nineveh and Koldewey in Babylon

Two portraits of Layard	211	Riot in Nippur	223
Layard at work	213	Obituary on Koldewey	225
"Nimrod himself"	214	View of ancient Babylon	226
The winged bulls	215	Thus it rose out of the rubble	229
The black obelisk	216	The Ishtar Gate	229
The "sleeping lioness"	217	The dragon of Babylon	230
The gate of Balawat	219	Reconstruction of the Tower of Babel	231
30,000 clay tablets	220		

Methods and Results of the Excavation at Ur

Woolley on trifles	232	Salvaging the "silver harp"	240
Baksheesh	233	The Mosaic standard of Ur	242
Baking cuneiform tablets	235	A ruler of Sumeria	245
1,800 graves	236	The Flood is historical	248
The "death-pit of Ur"	238		

BOOK IV

First Accounts of the Conquest of Mexico

The archaeology of Middle America began with war	250	The gifts to Cortés	254
What did Cortés really look like?	252	Albrecht Dürer's opinion of them	257
Mexican art in Europe	253	The first Indian in Europe	257
		Indians playing with rubber balls	258

In the Service of a New Science

Priests burn and one priest saves	259	The angel of the Annunciation approaches from left to right	264
Eight examples from Sahagún's book	261	Human sacrifices	266
"The Jupiter of these wretched people"	264	The "tenth Muse of Mexico"	267

Humboldt's "singularly beautiful voyage"   268
"The gods disapproved of this building"   269

The pyramid becomes a Mount Calvary   271
Kingsborough dies in debtors' prison   271

Conquest of the Jungle Cities

The feathered serpent   273
Dupaix's expedition   274
Ruins burned over   275
Palenque   277
Waldeck publishes his most important book at the age of one hundred   278
The ruins of Uxmal   278

The "Temple of the Sun"   279
Stephens discovers Copán   280
Stelae behind barbed wire   282
Catherwood's "moonlight in Izamal"   284
Transportation in the jungle   285
Abbé Brasseur sacrifices his career in the Church   286

New Problems in Mexico

A Mexican fable   288
The sacred well   290
Thompson dives for gold   290
Eduard Seler   293

Elephants in Middle America   295
Are Middle American pyramids also mausoleums?   297
The discovery of the "colored walls"   299

BOOK V

Retrospect and Perspective

Archaeology today is global   302
The Empire of the Hittites   302

Underwater archaeology   304
Aerial archaeology   305

Appendix

Chronological table   307
Bibliographical note and list of sources   316

Index   follows page 326

I

BOOK I

The Birth of Classical Archaeology

Pompeii and Herculaneum

Schliemann's Venture in the Dark

New Light on Crete

Along Rome's Via Appia, in April 1485,

laborers uncovered a sarcophagus whose contents shook the minds of men. Exhibited in the Palazzo dei Conservatori in Rome two days later, the find attracted so vast a crowd that it was as if indulgence from all sins were being given. Within the sarcophagus was the body of a girl of Ancient Rome, well preserved and extraordinarily beautiful. After twenty thousand persons had come to see it on a single day (lured also by the rumor that an oil lamp miraculously still alight had been found beside the body), Pope Innocent VIII issued an unusual order. The body was taken in the dead of night to a deserted spot outside the Porta Pinciana and there reburied in secrecy. The picture shown here is the only contemporary one that has survived; it was a tinted pen drawing appended to a letter written in Latin by a Florentine humanist to a friend of the famous Medici, Lorenzo the Magnificent. The letter reads:

"Bartolommeo Fonte greets his friend Francesco Sassetti. . . . You have asked me for tidings concerning the woman's body recently found on the Via Appia. I can but hope that my pen is equal to describing the beauty and charm of this body.

Cæterum hoc corpus cum .XVIII.
cal. maij anno à natiuitate Christi
millesimo quadringentesimo octogesimo quinto
Innocentij uero Papæ octaui anno
eius pontificatus primo repertum
sit apud casale fratrum sanctæ
mariæ nouæ in uia appia ad sextu
ab urbe lapidem : biduo post dela-
tum est in capitolium maximo po-
puli concursu iussu conseruatorum
urbis.

Had we not all of Rome for witnesses, the story would indeed be incredible. . . . Close to the sixth milestone on the Via Appia laborers looking for marble were extracting a large block of the stone when they suddenly broke through a brick vault twelve feet deep. Here they found a marble sarcophagus. When they opened it, they discovered a body lying on its face, coated with a greasy but fragrant substance to the thickness of two fingers. When they cleared away the perfumed coating—they had begun at the head—they looked upon a pale face with features so clear that it seemed as if the girl might have been buried that very day. Her long black hair, which was still firmly attached to the scalp, was fastened in a knot and parted in a manner suitable to a maiden; it was also covered with a snood of silk and gold.

"Tiny ears, a delicate forehead, black eyebrows—and finally eyes of a curious shape, with the whites showing under the half-open lids. Even the nostrils were unimpaired, and so soft that they yielded to the slightest pressure of a finger. The lips were red and slightly parted, the teeth small and white, the tongue scarlet almost to the palate. Cheeks, chin, throat, and neck seemed warm as life. The arms hung from the shoulders in such perfect state that they could be moved in any direction. On the lovely, long fingers of the outstretched hands, the fingernails were firmly rooted; no pulling could have detached them. Breast, abdomen, and loins, however, had been pressed to one side, and disintegrated after removal of the aromatic coating. The back, hips, and buttocks, on the other hand, had retained their shape and their wonderful curves; likewise thighs and legs, which during life must have displayed even greater beauties than the face.

"In short, here was a sublimely beautiful girl of noble family from the days when Rome stood at the pinnacle of her glory.

"Unfortunately, the imposing monument above this burial vault was destroyed many centuries ago, and the inscription was not preserved. The sarcophagus, too, bears no markings—we know neither this maiden's name, her origin nor her age. . . ."

This mummy, ripped from its grave in 1485 and a few days later returned to the earth at some unknown spot, is certainly not the one discovery from which we can date the beginning of archaeology—it was too haphazard a find for that. But up to that time such finds had kindled the imagination and aroused delight in only a few connoisseurs and collectors. Now, in the age of rebirth of interest in classical antiquity, people were learning to think, to feel, and to create anew in its spirit, albeit they sometimes misunderstood it.

A wonder-struck populace stood ready to imbibe the very breath of remote times. Their excitement suggests that something new was truly in the air. The past of which the Roman maiden was envoy had come to life again and was to remold the culture of the West.

"When as a boy I was in Rome for the first time,"

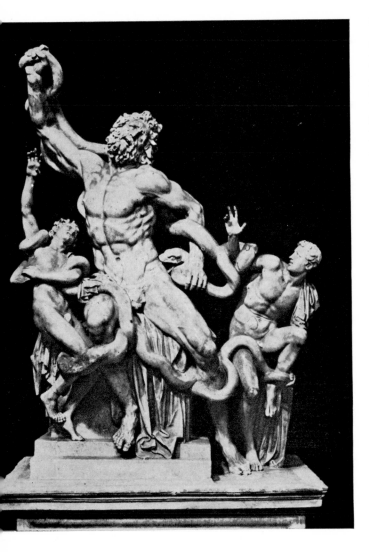

the aged sculptor Francesco di Sangallo recalled in 1567, "news was brought to the Pope of some remarkably fine statues just discovered in a vineyard near Santa Maria Maggiore. Then the Pope sent forth a servant: 'Go and tell Giuliano di Sangallo to hasten to the place and look.' So my father went; but since Michelangelo Buonarotti was living with him, he asked him to come along. . . . When we reached the place where the statues were standing, my father said at once: 'This is the Laocoön mentioned by Pliny!' . . . After we had seen what there was to see, we returned home for our supper."

Thus, we have a terse account of Michelangelo's confronting for the first time a work of art which was to exert the most powerful influence upon the sculptors of the Renaissance. Two centuries later the piece of sculpture could still inspire Gotthold Ephraim Lessing, the celebrated German writer, to write his *Laocoön: an Essay upon the Limits of Painting and Poetry.* "Everyone in Rome considers it the most wonderful statue that was ever created," a contemporary of Sangallo wrote. And another: "So valuable was it reckoned by all who would possess it that the owner, Felice de' Freddi, kept it in his own room beside his bed."

The group was carved (according to Pliny) by the Rhodian sculptor Agesandros and his sons Polydorus and Athenodorus (1st century B.C.). It represents the Trojan priest Laocoön (who warned the Trojans against drawing the wooden horse into their city) being strangled by serpents rising out of the sea. The reception given to the Laocoön group is an excellent example of the way a new consciousness of history tends to take up a single chance discovery and exaggerate its importance, with the result that a highly one-sided picture of an alien past is transmitted to succeeding centuries. The century of humanism (whose artistic manifestation was the "Renaissance") turned passionately toward pagan antiquity, but it was nevertheless profoundly Christian. What it saw in antiquity was indubitably an ancient world, "but inwardly illuminated by the Christian Faith. That world never existed as they pictured it . . ." (Huizinga).

Naturally, at the time the Laocoön was found, other significant discoveries had already been made, as the Chronological Table shows (see page 307). But none had such an instant and compelling effect. In spite of the efforts of a few persons genuinely interested in the art of antiquity, certain scarcely commendable practices long remained the rule. Fanatics broke the heads off newly unearthed statues because these were naked and pagan. Treasure-hunters pillaged and destroyed graves. Because Christianity needed churches, princes needed palaces, and vine-growers needed terraces, ancient buildings were used as quarries for worked stone.

The man who was to revolutionize the whole approach to antiquity was not born until 1717.

In the early days of archaeology

all excavations were viewed as tasks requiring merely the application of sufficient force. In the drawing made by Giovanni Permoli around 1760, a classical statue of Livia, wife of Emperor Augustus and mother of Tiberius, is being crudely raised with levers. This marble statue was found near the North Italian city of Parma in the early eighteenth century. Permoli intended his drawing as an illustration for a work that never reached print—on monuments "brought to light from the depths of the city of Velleia, with some reflections thereon." The manuscript, precious for its early and extremely vivid descriptions of archaeological finds, is now in the Palatine Library at Parma.

This man, whose unfortunate propensities

were to bring about his death, has been called "the Father of Archaeology." More accurately, Johann Joachim Winckelmann (1717–1768) was the father of archaeology insofar as it resurrected the art of antiquity. He brought order into the interpretation of art. Son of a German cobbler, he was the first to discriminate among styles. Only to this extent was he an archaeologist. A poet hid under his scholarly mantle. Some of his descriptions of ancient sculpture are close to ecstatic hymns. Phrases in his *Sendschreiben . . . (Open Letters)* and his *Geschichte der Kunst des Alterthums (History of the Art of Antiquity)*, phrases such as "noble simplicity and tranquil grandeur," "noble harmony," and "men like gods," were taken up by his contemporaries and applied to the whole of Greek culture and civilization. Thus fundamental misunderstandings were propagated, and these persisted into the nineteenth century.

His work gained fame in all Europe, and after his conversion to Catholicism he was accorded high offices in Rome. At fifty-one he was murdered in an inn in the Adriatic port city of Trieste by a stranger with whom he had unwisely taken up.

The cobbler's son was not only a scholar and poet; he was at times a conceited ass. "Mr. Hamilton," he wrote, "the English Minister at Naples, who is the greatest connoisseur of painting among living men, declares that he has never seen a handsomer head than mine; and he is right!"

This portrait, dated 1768, is by Anton von

Maron. Winckelmann is wearing his Russian wolf's pelt; in the left background is a Bacchus, to the right a bust of Homer—and before him on the table lies an engraving of the statue he loved best: that of Antinous.

"... Thence he led me with marked gravity

to the gem of the collection, the head of
Antinous, in low-relief, of white marble.
Even an Iroquois, I reflected, would have
to apprehend the beauty of this statue.
... But how beautiful the entire relief
must have been. For Winckelmann asserts
that this is only the upper part; ... presumably the whole figure was represented
as standing on a chariot. This he surmised,
he said, from the preserved hands, of which
the right seems to be holding one end and
the left the other end of the reins. In restoration a bunch of flowers was placed in
the left hand" (Christian Traugott Weinlig
in *Briefe über Rom* [*Letters on Rome*],
1782).

The relief dates from the period between
A.D. 130 and 138, the dates of the deaths
of Antinous and Hadrian. The heavy-
hearted boy from Claudiopolis was Emperor Hadrian's favorite companion. In a fit
of melancholia, and perhaps also with the
idea of proving the magnitude of his devo-
tion to the Emperor, Antinous drowned
himself in the Nile A.D. 130. Hadrian had
him deified.

In 1735, when this Antinous was found
in the Villa Hadriana, the first excavations
near Naples were beginning. Within three
years they had brought to light the wonderful discoveries that were to send Winckelmann into raptures. Herculaneum and
Pompeii rose out of the graves in which
they had lain for almost 1,700 years.

(9)

"Even for gods this was going too far,"

said the poet Martial. On August 20, A.D. 79, Vesuvius gave vent to a low growl; birds stopped singing, and the cattle tugged at the chains in their stalls. On August 24 a terrible thunderclap crashed into the peace of a radiant morning. The sun was suddenly obscured; the peak of Vesuvius split open; fire and smoke leaped toward the sky. Rain streamed down upon the rich cities of Pompeii and Herculaneum, and rivers of lava poured into the streets.

Herculaneum, in the midst of its bustling life, was overwhelmed and covered by a river of lava which in places congealed to a thickness of fifty feet. Pompeii was buried under hot ashes and lapilli, small fragments of volcanic stone. Dense fumes of sulphur descended on both cities, suffocating all living creatures. On the third day, when the sun rose again, the earth all around Vesuvius was covered by a vast shroud of white ashes under which the cities of Pompeii and Herculaneum had vanished.

Here is a photograph of a model of the excavated city of Pompeii as it looked about

1900. In the foreground are the large and the small theaters, on the left the Forum Triangulare. "The tiny dimensions of Pompeii astonish everyone . . . less a town than a model for one," as Goethe put it (a remarkable statement from one who lived in the tiny ducal-court town of Weimar). The first successful excavations began in 1748 under the direction of Rocco Gioacchino de Alcubierre, an engineer in the employ of King Charles III of Naples. On April 6 the first wall painting was found. From that date onward excavation has continued, with interruptions, to the present day. Three fifths of the city have been uncovered, and wonderful works of art brought to light.

In April 1943 Allied reconnaissance patrols flying over the city thought they had detected a German panzer division hidden in the ruins. (There was none.) The first bomb struck the Forum. It was followed by 150 more bombs. Damage was enormous. The monuments and buildings that had been reconstructed with so much toil were once again demolished and covered over.

Herculaneum lay buried under stony lava,

unlike Pompeii under its soft pumice. For that reason General Emanuel Moritz, Prince d'Elboeuf, had enormous technical difficulties to overcome before he could make his way from a peasant's well-shaft into the darkness of the city. We may assume that he was actuated in equal degrees by love of art and greed for treasure. Among a variety of fragments he found first an inscription on marble, then three splendid classical statues of women. These were damaged, and parts were missing. Believing that only perfection could be valuable, he secretly removed the statues to Rome, where second-rate sculptors "restored" them to their "ancient beauty"—without knowing in the slightest what such beauty was.

So began systematic archaeological restoration—a practice that only rarely served a useful purpose, and that usually led to the strangest reconstructions and misconceptions.

A still more amazing case of "restoration" occurred after the next sizable excavations in Herculaneum, under the direction of Alcubierre. Working at the Theatrum Herculanense (and thus following the trail of d'Elboeuf, who by chance or instinct had dug point-blank into this storehouse of statues), Alcubierre came across numerous fragments of what had obviously been a mighty bronze horse. He reasoned that this had belonged to an extremely imposing quadriga, or four-horse chariot. The sculptor Joseph Canart, who was entrusted with the restoration, simply melted down many of the pieces. Either he thought them beyond using, or was unable to recognize them as belonging to a greater whole. From the metal so easily obtained he made chandeliers for chapels and a statue of the Madonna. Years later the rest of the pieces, which had meanwhile been scattered widely, were assembled and patched together into a single whole: the bronze horse here reproduced. It still stands in the Naples National Museum, and to the casual eye looks as if it were poured from a single mold.

Since even Winckelmann saw nothing wrong with such treatment of fragments, let us glance into one of his favorite workshops.

Naples gave Winckelmann nothing but trouble,

and yet offered him the challenge that moved him to arrange the art of antiquity along rational lines of development. It was in 1756 that he made his first journey to the city—he was thirty-nine and not yet famous. But although he was known for his just-published, three-volume *Gedanken über die Nachahmung . . .* (*Thoughts on the Imitation of Greek Works in Painting and Sculpture*), he encountered the most annoying barriers whenever he wanted to examine finds. The nineteenth-century concept of a museum—as a collection of beautiful and significant objects accessible to everyone—was quite absent in the eighteenth century. Charles III, who had accumulated a sizable collection, kept jealous

watch over these works; unasked visitors were unwelcome, and to break the ban was to court severe penalties. Winckelmann, aggrieved and therefore crafty, succeeded in the course of time in inspecting many of these works of art. When he published his account of them, he fell into disfavor in the highest quarters.

A quotation from Weinlig, the German traveler who was at Portici in October 1768, summarizes the situation:

"It is scarcely permissible to look at an object long enough to form an impression, let alone to take out a pencil. I had the bright idea of using the stem of my lorgnette to scratch a few of the patterns of the mosaic floor into the lining of my hat, and even this had to be done with great caution. I believe the custodian would have cut out the hat lining if he had noticed."

Winckelmann was on a friendly footing with a restorer, Bartolomeo Cavaceppi, and had great faith in his skill and conscientiousness. Undoubtedly too great faith, as we can see today in the catalogue from which our picture was taken. The man in the foreground on the right, who is "restoring" a bust with the aid of a heavy mallet and a foot-long chisel, would horrify a contemporary restorer.

We shall return to the question of restorations, reconstruction, and condition of finds in our section on Crete. For the present it is important to see, by a few examples, how the spirit of the age viewed these finds.

I. **Zeus abducting Ganymede.** Peloponnesian terracotta, *c.* 470 B.C. Fragments of the group were found scattered in several places at Olympia by various German expeditions operating there between 1878 and 1952. The sculpture, which shows unmistakable traces of having once been colored, now stands in the Olympia museum.

II. Greek temples were colored. Entablature of the Parthenon in Gottfried
Semper's colored restoration. Hand-colored engraving.

Probably the earliest picture of resurrected Pompeii.

It shows the Via di Sallustio, which leads to the Herculaneum Gate, and is a pen drawing by Giovanni Battista Piranesi (1720–1778), a prolific sketcher of classical architecture. Piranesi was a romantic. His depiction of the so-called Accademia of the Villa Hadriana at Tivoli (right) shows an ancient world so overgrown by ivy and woodsy vegetation that it is a wonder the buildings still stand. This is a good example of the then dawning conception of classical architecture as "picturesque ruins." Only a few decades later the custom arose of viewing the Colosseum at Rome by moonlight.

(15)

(Francesco, who died in 1810), reproduced here from a drawing by Desprez, contrasts by its clarity—although it is, if we will, the "clarity" of a Late Baroque tableau. It is amusing to see the groups of strollers among the ruins—people were already organizing Sunday-afternoon outings to the world of classical antiquity. (The engraving shows the Temple of Isis adjacent to the theater at Pompeii.)

It is astonishing that the numerous masters of architectural drawing in the period so completely missed the human aspect of many of the Pompeian finds. Where it was recognized, the artists indulged not in romanticism, but in the baser practice of romanticizing.

The skeleton in the laundry.

This is a scene that might have climaxed a nineteenth-century *grand guignol* drama. It would be perfectly in order for the lady on the left to recognize, from an amulet, the skeleton of her murdered mother. Nevertheless, such spectacles were actually encountered at Pompeii. The English antiquary Sir William Hamilton, writing in 1777, narrates: "Skeleton of the washerwoman (for anatomists say it is that of a female); she seems to have been shut up in this vault, the staircase having been filled with rubbish, and to have waited for death with calm resignation, and true Roman fortitude, as the attitude of the skeleton really seems to indicate. It was at my instigation [*sic*], that the bones were left untouched on the spot where they were found."

The next picture, a photograph, reveals the gulf between an early nineteenth-century artist's version and the unvarnished reality registered by the modern camera's eye.

Here, crushed by lapilli and suffocated by sulphur fumes,

the first Pompeians collapsed. The figures on the right are of a young girl and an older woman into whose arms she crept for refuge. During excavation archaeologists came across hollows that they recognized as the forms of bodies preserved by the petrified cinders. They poured plaster into the hollows—thus obtaining these reproductions of bodies dead 1,700 years but still imbued with a ghostly reality.

These are the famous skeletons and plaster casts of the House of Mysteries, which was again destroyed by the bombing of

1943. This technique of making plaster casts from hollows, incidentally, enabled archaeologists to determine that the palaestra, the great stadium of Pompeii, had been surrounded by tall plane trees before the disaster. The trees themselves had vanished completely, but the space left by their root systems could be filled, and the nature of the roots indicated the size and variety of the trees. The palaestra yielded nearly one hundred human skeletons. Among them was a doctor, for beside one body lay a remarkably well-equipped bag of instruments.

Nor did the animals of Pompeii escape

the fate of the humans. Here is the plaster cast of a dog that had probably been on a chain. The body shows the convulsive effect of the poisonous fumes.

"Though slow, this is the best method

to proceed with an excavation: the work being done by women and children, who carry away the earth by small basketfuls. During the French occupation the government assigned a regiment of engineers to the work, and I saw as many as 1500 soldiers employed. But they were so destructive that their activities had to be restricted to excavating the city wall and the amphitheater. Nowadays the excavations are let to entrepreneurs for so and so much per double cubic yard. The disadvantages are plain; to mention but one, the heavy ox-carts moving constantly through the ruins cause disastrous cave-ins. . . ."

These words were written by François Mazois (1783–1826), court painter for the short-lived Kingdom of Naples, whose king was Napoleon's general Murat and whose queen was Marie Caroline Bonaparte. The engraving above comes from his book *Les Ruines de Pompéii*. . . . Such was Mazois's passion for the ruins that he was able to stir the interest of the new and therefore enterprising royal couple. He persuaded them to finance extensive excavations. While he was in Paris, however, preparing publication of his first series of pictures, Napoleon was overthrown. Murat was shot by a firing squad, and the "Bonapartist" Mazois was not granted a passport to go back to Naples. In 1816 he thought of a stratagem by which he was able to return. The Neapolitan Bourbon prince had applied for a papal dispensation. Mazois managed to have himself appointed the carrier of this document. Thus highly honored as a papal envoy, he returned to his beloved ruins.

The excavator, never knowing

what the earth will yield,

stumbles on a prize. In May 1925 this
youth was brought to light—one of the finest copies of early Greek sculpture to be
salvaged from the ashes of Pompeii. The
statue is nearly five feet tall. The broken
legs were easily restored; the bronze eyes
were intact; iris and pupil had no doubt
been inlaid in color, but were missing. Various factors suggest that this statue, on
which a high value must have been placed
at the time, was moved at the beginning of
the eruption from its original site in a garden to a semi-sheltered porch.

(21)

Here, at the corner of the Via di Stabiae and the Via dell'Abbondanza,

the Pompeians could buy themselves a bowl of steaming mulled wine before they went upstairs to be welcomed by Aegle, Maria, and Smyrna, those charming ladies of easy virtue who were called "little donkeys" (*asinellae*).

The bar had been marble-topped. Scattered on the floor were found coins dropped by the last customers. The names of the girls were scratched into the wall.

"The talisman by which the archaeologist reanimates long-dead civilizations," writes that great antiquary Ernst Buschor, "is made of the tangible property left by men of the past. . . . Such things run the entire scale of value, and are of varying significance, but to the eye of the true archaeologist each one has something to tell." Only in Pompeii and Herculaneum, however, is this "tangible property" still warm from men's hands, so to speak; only here do we feel so vividly the living presence of the human beings who inhabited these cities. To make a coherent story of the following pictures we may, for example, imagine a certain Mr. Pompeius. He has drunk his bowl of wine at the bar, exchanged a few words with the proprietor on the dreadful political situation . . .

And after turning into the Via dell'Abbondanza

he is prompted to pause in front of Trebius Valens' house, the wall of which is covered with advertising inscriptions in red and black letters. They are election slogans—and no wonder, for Trebius is related to many politicians. Pompeius reads the candidates' names and the praises of their virtues (second rectangle from the left): Q[*uintum*] *Postumum modestum*; he reads (middle of the wall and at right) the announcement of gladiatorial combats and athletic games sponsored and paid for by Lucretius Satrius, who evidently hoped to win popularity in this way.

(The wall reproduced here is about thirteen feet long. It was excavated in 1913–14. Many houses would be covered with election slogans at the time of the annual elections in March. After elections a painter came along and covered the inscriptions with a coat of fresh whitewash.)

Mr. Pompeius walks on. Suddenly it occurs to him that he has promised to drop in on Verecundus, the draper, and inquire about the long-promised blankets.

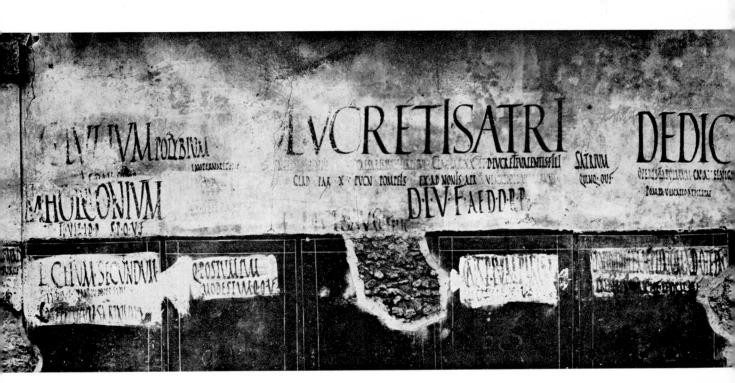

Marcus Caecilius Verecundus is by trade,

as the inscription on the lower frieze of this painted store front advertises, a dealer in cloth and a manufacturer of wool and felt. If our friend Pompeius cares for painting, he will like looking at the upper frieze. It represents Venus Pompeiana, goddess of the city, bearing crown and scepter and leaning against a tiller, the symbol of a coastal city. She rides in a chariot drawn by four elephants. On the left is Fortuna, scattering good luck and rolling along with the globe; on the right is the Genius Coloniae with cornucopia and drinking-bowl.

If our Pompeius is partial to Pompeian modern art, he may be delighted by the deceptive reality with which the painter has done the apparently three-dimensional frame that separates the upper from the lower picture.

Pompeius enters the shop, whose activities we can reconstruct from the frieze. He watches the nimble fingers of the wool-carders who, seated on stools, the scraping-block between their feet, are working on the raw wool with big wooden combs and scrapers. They are demurely dressed in long, bright-colored skirts, while the felters beside them are bared to the waist as they toil over their steaming vats. They dip the vinegar, which serves to bind the felt, from a basin and pour it into the two triangular tubs in which the felt is made by constant shaking and reheating. Arms outstretched, Master Verecundus displays the finished blanketing to Pompeius.

Before Pompeius goes home,

he may drop in at a friend's. As he is a creation of ours, he cannot object to our making this friend stern Arrius Crescentius, whose private dining-room (*triclinium*) in the Casa del Moralista is shown here. Arrius has had this room inscribed with mottoes which must have seemed a little captious in gay Pompeii, so that archaeologists have called his home "the house of the moralist." "If you cannot refrain from quarrels and disputes, you had better go home," we may read on the upper left. And in the center: "Do not look with longing eyes upon another's wife." And in the panel to the far right he actually tells his guests to wash themselves and to keep their host's linen clean.

Arrius had room for four guests—as these are not benches but couches; the Romans, like the Greeks, ate and drank in a reclining position. Undoubtedly the stone was covered with cushions. The wall paintings—alternate red and black rectangles—are extremely plain: simple borders surrounding a small wreath or bird. Standing on the table are the utensils Arrius used: glass bottles and bronze jugs, a ladle, a lamp with a chain, and the big mixing-bowl on its high bronze pedestal. The house was bombed in the Second World War.

Apparently a Greek named Zosimos

was the last owner of the splendid building (excavated 1909–10 and 1929–30) that we now call the Villa dei Misteri. Let us have our imaginary Pompeius, upon leaving the "moralist," end his round of visits in the private chapel of this villa, which contains one of the finest examples of classical painting we possess.

In twenty-nine life-size figures the fresco shows the initiation of a bride into the Dionysian Mysteries—a sectarian form of religious ceremony whose abuse led to such excesses that it was outlawed by the Roman Senate. The climax of the ceremony, the bride's hailing of the male symbol of fertility, is dimly depicted at the extreme right.

For the age of Winckelmann, Pompeian paintings were only sensational aesthetic discoveries. There was some discussion of their artistic form and mythological content but not of the questions that now concern us, such as the relationship of this ubiquitous painting to the Roman house as an architectural whole, and to its inhabitants. For this Roman painting was more than mere decoration. It fulfilled a new function in domestic architecture: it *extended* the house, "created aura and atmosphere" (Karl Kerényi), employed perspective devices to create the illusion of large spaces. In this, it was the true forerunner of the Renaissance.

(27)

Father Piaggio, who unrolled
the charred rolls of papyrus

with skillful hands and the aid of ingenious devices and thereby made them readable, while Winckelmann looked on. These two men represented the meeting of two hitherto separate sciences that have ever since been indissolubly linked: the science of monuments and the science of documents.

In Herculaneum in 1753 a treasure trove of manuscripts was found in the villa that had belonged to Philodemos, the philosopher. But the rolls of papyrus were all charred and gummed together. It seemed impossible to do anything with them. A cer-

tain Camillo Paderni undertook the work of salvage. He rolled up his sleeves, tied a rough apron around his waist, and with his Genoese razor went boldy at the papyri. Cutting a slash the length of the roll, he extracted the core, gutting the roll so completely that a single smooth sheet remained from the outer layer—all the rest was reduced to chips and was thrown away as rubbish.

Antonio Piaggio, the Franciscan father, proceeded differently. Outside of Italy, little had been known about him, except for what Winckelmann had written.

An ingenious apparatus made by Piaggio

by means of which he succeeded in unrolling the papyri with relatively little damage. He must have been a rather crusty
character—he spoke ill of the King and
slanderously of Alcubierre, who did not sufficiently appreciate his work. To satisfy his
spite, he supplied the material for Winckelmann's *Open Letters*.

Recently a letter of Sir William Hamilton's was found in the British Museum
which at least enables us to calculate the
year of his birth. "He is now 87," Hamilton
writes in 1794, "and no longer able to work."
We possess also a letter written to the Royal
Society in 1755 which not only provides the
first description of his technique, but also
shows a proper appreciation for it.

"It is incredible to imagine what this man
[Piaggio] contrived and executed. He made
a machine which, by the means of certain
threads which, being gummed, stick to the
back of the papyrus where there is no writing, begins by degrees to pull (with screws
fitted into a horizontal bar above the scroll),
while he loosens one leaf from the other
with a sort of engraver's instrument (which
is the most difficult part of all), and then
makes a sort of lining to the back of the
papyrus, with exceeding thin leaves . . .
and with some spirituous liquor, with which
he wets the papyrus, by little and little he
unfolds it. All this labour cannot be well
comprehended without seeing. With patience superior to what man can imagine,
this good father has unrolled a pretty large
piece of papyrus. . . ."

The first papyrus Piaggio unrolled, shown
on the left, was, in fact, the famous treatise
On Music by Philodemos.

The mysterious magic square.

Professor Matteo Della Corte, one of the most successful Pompeian excavators of the twentieth century, found scratched upon one of the pillars of the stadium an inscription of twenty-five letters which yielded the same five words no matter which way they were read. Moreover, the center word, TENET, when outlined made a cross. As the letters could also be arranged to form the beginning of the Paternoster, the discoverer concluded that this had probably been the secret sign of a Christian sect. After all, a Christian cross had been found scratched into a wall in Herculaneum.

This is a controversial question. Whether the magic square really was intended to represent a Christian cross is not yet established. Heretofore, the oldest evidences of a Christian cross dated from the second century A.D. It is unlikely (but by no means impossible) that even before A.D. 79 there were Christians in Pompeii who used the sign of the cross.

The magic square has been the subject of endless discussion. Recently a new interpretation that seems reasonable has been presented. Hitherto, the word AREPO has always given trouble; no such word is known, whereas the others are common Latin words. Ludwig Diehl, studying the matter, suggested that the square should be read BUSTROPHEDON ("as the ox plows"—the mode of writing employed by scribes of Hieroglyphic Hittite, for example)—in other words, the first line from right to left, the second from left to right, and so on. In this case the central word, TENET, must be read twice. The result is then:

SATOR OPERA TENET; TENET OPERA SATOR

The meaningless word AREPO is thus eliminated. The translation, in spite of the repetition, has a convincing sound: "The great Sower [God] holds in his hand all works; all works the great Sower holds in his hand."

There have been other surprising minor finds at Pompeii, and no doubt there will be more in the future. In October 1938, in the so-called "House of the Four Styles," was found an ivory statuette of Lakshmi, the Hindu goddess of love and wife of the god Vishnu.

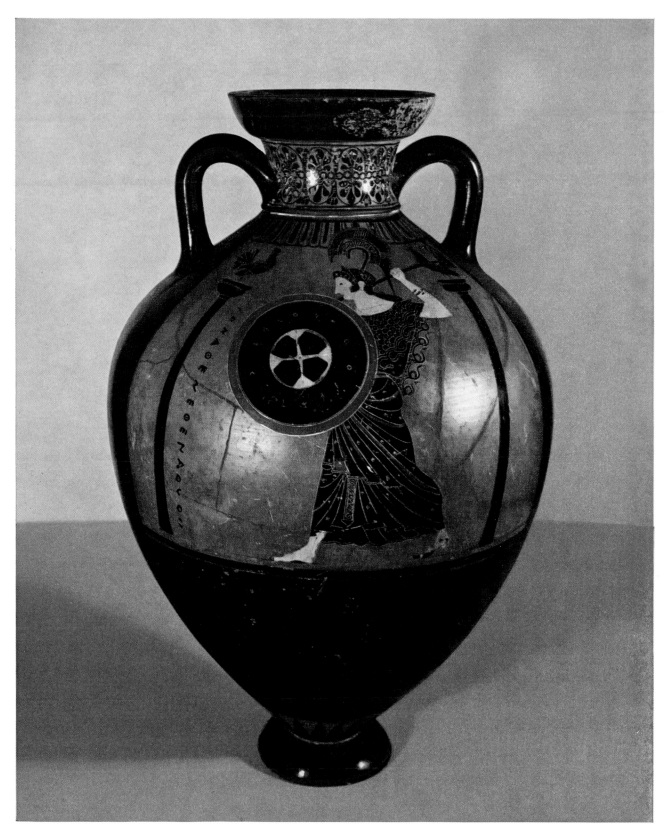

III. Athene bearing arms. Greek vase painted in Athens (late sixth century B.C.).

IV. **Roman woman playing the cithara.** Wall painting in a villa at Boscoreale, near Pompeii (first century A.D.).

A new era of intelligent excavation

began at last in 1861 under the direction of thirty-seven-year-old Giuseppe Fiorelli—with a crew of 512 men. Arrested during the revolution of 1848, and confined to prison, he wrote there the first pages of his description of Pompeii (*Pompeianarum antiquitatum historia*). Jobless afterward, he happened by chance to prevent the Count of Syracuse from being swindled when he discovered that several "well preserved heads of antique bodies," which someone was about to sell the Count, were fakes made of wax. Ultimately he obtained the appointment as director of excavations at Pompeii (replacing the French novelist Alexandre Dumas, to whom the post had been awarded as a sinecure by Garibaldi). Fiorelli introduced a number of important innovations in the technique of excavation. He not only dug; he protected. It was he who first had the hollows left by skeletons filled with plaster.

Professor Amadeo Maiuri

finally placed the work upon a thoroughly modern scientific basis. He has been digging and conducting research in Pompeii and Herculaneum since 1911. The picture above shows him looking at recently discovered Roman tombs. He has made many significant finds, and published exemplary accounts of them. During the Second World War, with the troops advancing and the dangers of needless destruction and perhaps of pillaging daily mounting, he waged a stalwart defense of his life work. He remained at the site until he was within range of small arms, and finally fled on a bicycle, wounded by a machine-gun bullet.

Excavation continues in Pompeii and Herculaneum. Professor Maiuri is now furthering an extraordinary project. He wants to install a cable railway to transport the highly fertile lava-ash, which has been removed from the ruins for more than two hundred years, to unfertile soil, thus enriching all the land around Naples. A great deal might be said about the symbolic significance of such an undertaking.

Meditatively circling this curious hill

in the spring of the year 1869, the middle-aged man in European dress looked something of an anomaly among the camels of this unpromising scrubland. This man, whose success equaled his energy, blazed new paths in archaeology, leading the way to such extraordinary insights that his professional colleagues refused to follow him.

"My claims are most modest," he was to say later—although he was in fact outlining a program that went far beyond the prevailing school of art archaeology. "I do not hope to find works of plastic art. From the start the sole purpose of my excavations was to find Troy. . . . I should be content if I have succeeded only, by my work, in penetrating into the profound obscurity of prehistoric times and in enriching science by the discovery of a few interesting pages from the most ancient history of the great Hellenic nation."

With the *Iliad* tucked under his arm (in striking contrast to all the other scientists of his day, he regarded Homer's work as a precise description of actual events), and with a watch in hand, he walked around the hill called Hissarlik. He needed the time-piece to determine whether it was humanly possible to circle the walls of the city three times in the heat of battle, as Homer reported Achilles and Hector did. These facts established, he pronounced the site to be that of ancient Troy—once more countering the general view that Troy, if it ever existed, should lie beneath a mound near Bunarbashi, which he had previously tested in the same manner.

This picture is taken from a travel account by the Count of Choiseul-Gouffier (published in 1809), who until the beginning of the French Revolution was France's ambassador to the Sublime Porte. The hill had in no way changed eighty-odd years later when it was seen by the Homer enthusiast.

Heinrich Schliemann,

wholesale merchant of the Imperial Guild of St. Petersburg, hereditary honorary free-man, Judge of the St. Petersburg Commercial Court, and Director of the Imperial State Bank in St. Petersburg. (The photograph was taken around 1860.) This is the man who wrote to his father as early as 1854: "Here in Moscow I am considered the slyest, most cunning and most capable of merchants. . . ." In 1868, at the height of his success, a millionaire many times over, he retired from business to pursue the dream of his youth: to dig up Troy.

A simple-hearted pride speaks in the lines he wrote on June 24, 1870, to his son Serge, who was then at school: ". . . You ought to try to follow the example of your father who in whatever situation always proved what a man can accomplish by unflagging energy alone. During the four years in Amsterdam from 1842 to 1846 I truly performed wonders. My achievements there have never been equaled, and never will be equaled in the future. Later, when I became a whole-sale merchant in St. Petersburg, I was the most brilliant and at the same time the most astute dealer on the stock exchange. When I began to travel, I was a traveler par excellence. No St. Petersburg merchant has ever written a learned book, but I have written one that has been translated into four languages, and generally commended. At the moment, as an archaeologist, I am the sensation of Europe and America because I have discovered ancient Troy, that Troy for which the archaeologists of the entire world have searched in vain during the past two thousand years. . . ."

Schliemann the entrepreneur.

1822 Birth of Heinrich Schliemann, son of a poor pastor in Neu-Bukow, Mecklenburg, Germany. Until

1831 the family lives in the village of Ankershagen, about whose ruins, hills, and ponds many ghost stories are told. These stimulate the child's imagination, as do his father's tales of the doom of Pompeii and the struggle of the heroes at Troy. In

1829 he receives the then popular *Universal History for Children* as a Christmas present. In it he finds a print depicting the mighty Scaean Gate of Troy, and expresses his opinion to his father that such monuments cannot possibly have vanished utterly. "And by and by we agreed," he says in his autobiography, "that someday I should excavate Troy."

1831 His mother dies, leaving seven children. The family comes to know neglect and poverty.

1832 He writes his first Latin composition on Troy as a Christmas present for his father.

1836 Aged fourteen, he becomes an apprentice in a grocery store in the small town of Fürstenberg in North Germany. For five and a half years he works eighteen hours a day behind the counter and in the warehouse. His most momentous experience is an encounter with a down-at-heels student who in return for three glasses of brandy recites Homer in Greek to him.

1841 He has to give up this job because of illness. He goes to Hamburg on foot, is able to take only temporary jobs, and signs on as a cabin boy on the brig *Dorothea*. The ship is wrecked on the night of December 11 off the Dutch island of Texel. After nine perilous hours the crew is rescued.

1842 Destitute in Amsterdam, he finally finds a job in a merchant's office, and begins to devote every free minute to the systematic study of foreign languages. "After three months I could with ease recite . . . twenty printed pages of English prose word for word if I had read them through attentively three times." He learns English, French, Dutch, Spanish, Italian, and Portuguese—spending only six weeks on each of the last four languages.

1844 He enters the firm of B. H. Schröder & Co. as correspondent and bookkeeper. He learns Russian.

1846 He goes to St. Petersburg as agent for his firm. Before the end of his first year he does so well in the indigo trade that in

1847 he is admitted to the guild of wholesalers.

1850 He goes to California in search of a missing brother. While he is there, the entrance of California into the Union automatically gives him American citizenship.

1852 He sets up a Moscow branch of his St. Petersburg company for wholesale trade in indigo.

1854 He learns Swedish and Polish. By now he has a fortune of 150,000 taler, which he doubles in the course of the following year (during the Crimean War).

1856 At the age of thirty-four he learns modern Greek in six weeks, and ancient Greek in another three months, in order to read Homer in the original. He reads exclusively ancient Greek literature. Meanwhile, his fortune keeps increasing, even during the depression of 1857.

1858 He perfects his knowledge of Latin, and

decides to retire from business. Travels take him to Sweden, Denmark, Germany, Italy, and Egypt as far as the second cataract of the Nile. "Here I made use of the favorable opportunity to learn Arabic." He travels on to Jerusalem and takes a quick look at Syria.

1859 He visits Smyrna, the Cyclades, and Athens, falls ill, and because his business runs into difficulties without his guiding hand, has to return to St. Petersburg.

1860 The value of the goods he imports within six months amounts to some two and one half million dollars. Up to

1863 he makes a series of such remarkably profitable deals in cotton and tea that he finally decides to liquidate his companies completely and devote his time to his youthful dream of excavating Troy. First, however, "in order to see more of the world," he embarks in

1864 on a tour of the world from Egypt through India, China, and the United States. On the fifty-day crossing from Japan to San Francisco he writes his first book, *La Chine et le Japon*—in French.

1866 He settles in Paris "to devote myself permanently to the study of archaeology."

Schliemann the excavator.

1868 "At last I was able to realize the dream of my life, to visit with requisite leisure the realm of action and the homeland of the heroes whose adventures had delighted and sustained me in my childhood." Schliemann journeys through Ithaca, the native island of Ulysses. In December his book is published: *Ithaka. Archäologische Forschungen* (*Ithaca: Archaeological Researches*).

1869 He visits Troy, Mycenae, and Tiryns, and in a new book announces his theory that the ruins of Troy lie beneath Hissarlik, and that the graves of the Atrides should be sought inside rather than outside the fortress wall. Nearing fifty, he marries an eighteen-year-old Greek girl, Sophia.

1870–3 Excavations in Troy, eleven and one half months in all, with from 100 to 150 workmen. Schliemann discovers much evidence, especially in the form of ceram-

ics, of a pre-Greek Aegean culture upon this site hitherto unknown to science. In the charred rubble of the second and third strata he believes he has found the palace of Priam. In June 1873 he finds "Priam's treasure."

1874 First survey in Mycenae.

1875 Refusing to deliver half of his finds at Troy to Constantinople, he is fined 10,000 francs. Instead of paying the fine, he makes a gift of 50,000 francs to the Turkish government, and receives permission to continue digging. When in spite of this the local pasha obstructs his work, he writes a letter to *The Times* of London (July 24, 1876) "in which I submit the conduct of Ibrahim Pasha to the judgment of the civilized world." As a result of this publicity, the pasha is transferred by the central government.

1876 Besides his travels in Greece (where he

keeps his journal in Greek), he goes to England, Germany, and Italy, and begins one excavation in Sicily which he abandons because the finds date only from the fifth century B.C., and another near the Sea of Marmora. In August he begins excavations in Mycenae; in November he finds five graves with skeletons bedecked with gold and jewels; he decides that these are the bodies of Agamemnon and his companions. The finds include types of art which have not been encountered in Troy; Schliemann has discovered true "Mycenaean" culture.

1877–8 Schliemann busies himself preparing the publication of his book *Mycenae* in German, English, and French.

1878–9 Resumption of excavations in Troy. Now fifty-six, Schliemann regularly every morning before sunrise rides out to the coast, a good hour away, takes a dip in the sea, and is back at the site of the excavations before his workmen have awakened. Rudolf Virchow, the famous physician and amateur student of prehistory, and the French scholar Emile Burnouf publicly come out in support of Schliemann's views; other scientists remain skeptical.

1880 Excavations in Orchomenos; discovery of the Treasury of Minyas.

1882 The young architect Wilhelm Dörpfeld comes to assist Schliemann in digging at Troy. Henceforth deliberation and method rather than wild enthusiasm govern the conduct of the excavations. The patterns of the various Trojan strata are recognized.

1884–5 Uncovering of the Cyclopean palace walls of Tiryns. Small finds establish beyond any doubt the interrelationships of a pre-Greek culture around the Aegean Sea, which we now call Minoan-Mycenaean.

1886–7 Schliemann goes to Cuba on business, then to Egypt.

1888 He makes a survey of Crete, but does no digging. However, he recognizes the "Palace of Minos," which is later excavated by Evans.

1890 Schliemann's last excavation at Troy. On Christmas Day Schliemann dies in Naples. He collapses on the street, and the bystanders wonder who is to pay for the cab to the hospital—until someone recognizes the modestly dressed foreigner.

A double page from Schliemann's diary (April 14, 1873)

wherein he records that he employed 157 workers for digging that day, and discovered several small pots, ornamented urns whose

resemblance to owls would make them emblems of the tutelary goddess of Troy. Among the decorative motifs he was most impressed by the ancient swastika, which, raised once more to a symbol, was to gain a grim notoriety during the thirties and forties of the present century.

It is high time the nonsense about Schliemann's "dilettantism" were corrected. It is true that he made many mistakes—but what pioneer does not make them? The errors perpetrated by professional scientists, especially in regard to pre-Homeric Greece, fill far more volumes than Heinrich Schliemann wrote. The excavation of clay tablets in the manner adopted three decades later (when archaeological methods had been greatly refined) by the bona-fide "scientific expert" Hugo Winckler, at Boghazköy, was an outright scandal compared to Schliemann's rough-and-ready work at Troy. The charge that Schliemann was no professional stems from that academic conceit which rates proper degrees, even if secured by the most mediocre minds, above genius. Schliemann, with his phenomenal memory and gift for languages, devoted from four to five years to intensive study of antiquity (delving in museums and libraries, and conversing with the foremost scientists of his age) before he went to Troy. Moreover, he was, although the fact is little known, a legitimate holder of the title Doctor of Philosophy. He received his degree from the University of Rostock, Mecklenburg, for an account of his travels in the Peloponnesus, and for a dissertation written in classical Greek.

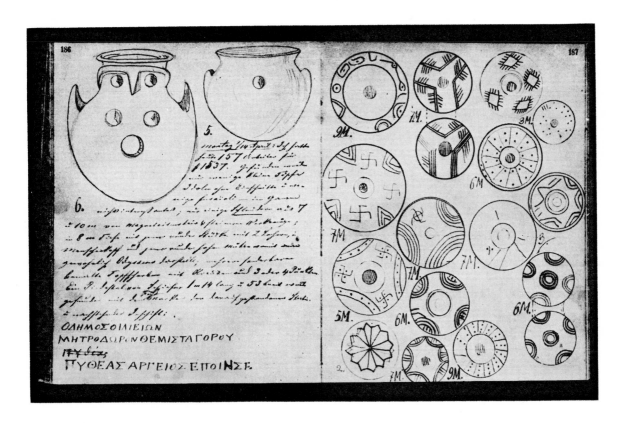

The great tower of Ilium.

"There was and is at the site of Troy no sublimer place than this," wrote Schliemann in his earliest account of the excavations in 1874. Homer enthusiast that he was, his imagination immediately animated the ruins. "And I therefore presume that it was Ilium's great tower to which Andromache climbed because she had heard (*Iliad*, VI) that the Trojans were sore oppressed and that mighty was the power of the Achaeans." On the brow of the hill we see the barracks of Schliemann and his laborers; the nature of the excavation, as we may see at lower left, suggests that the work was not without its dangers.

He made the find that stirred the world just one day before the end of the 1873 season. He was with his second wife, whom he had acquired in a highly curious manner.

Sophia Schliemann, née Engastromenos,

Schliemann's second wife, is here wearing the golden ornaments found in the second stratum at Troy. Schliemann's ardent imagination straightway decided that these jewels had belonged to that beauteous Helen whose face had launched a thousand ships. As he considered the second stratum the castle of Priam, he did not hesitate to speak of "Priam's treasure." The incredible accumulation of diadems, earrings, finger rings, buttons, and so on—all in all, he and Sophia took a total of 8,750 small fragments of gold jewelry from under the dangerous overhanging rubble—certainly prompted the conclusion that he had discovered a mythic treasure house.

To return to Sophia: his plan to marry a second time, after his first wife refused to follow him on his archaeological quests, was set forth in two letters of very different tempers. On May 18, 1869, he wrote to his father: "The Archbishop of Greece . . . has sent me the portraits of several Athenian women for me to choose from. Of these, I have selected Sophia Engastromenos as the most charming. . . . It seems . . . that the Archbishop, before he was advanced to the higher clergy and while he still thought he would be able to remain a sinner, had intended to marry her. In any case I plan . . . to go to Athens in July in order to marry her. . . . For since the growth of my passion for the Greek language, I believe I can be happy only with a Greek woman. I will take her however, only if she has an interest in sciences. . . . A pretty young girl can love an old man in such a case only if she cares deeply for the sciences in which he is so far ahead of her."

To his brother-in-law, however, he wrote on July 30, 1869, a far more crass description of his enterprise: "I intend to go to Greece in a fortnight in order to look around for another wife, for there I have the tremendous advantage that the girls are as poor as church mice. . . . Thus I can cold-bloodedly and at leisure get to know the ladies there very well, and if I should find a Greek girl whose age still offers hope of progeny . . . and who moreover is enthusiastic about classical Greek language and literature, as well as ancient history, archaeology and geography . . . I shall marry her, but *only in that case*, and you may be sure that I will not be overhasty. . . . Thank God, the choice in Greece is large, and the girls as beautiful as the pyramids of Egypt!"

Strangely enough, the marriage proved an extremely happy one. Sophia actually became her husband's best assistant, and bore him two children: Agamemnon and Andromache.

Not far from the "Great Tower of Ilium"

the foundation walls of a house, in places still ten feet high, were found in 1873. Schliemann could not at the time suspect that he would find "Priam's treasure" at this spot. But the walls alone sent him into transports because here for the first time he saw the outline of a Trojan house. He called it "the most interesting object I have been able to find in the past three years." This exultation at a purely scientific discovery should prove that Schliemann was anything but the gold-seeker so many critics later branded him. The first detail from a drawing by Lempesis (lower left) of the excavation gives some impression of the tremendous masses of earth Schliemann's men moved—with only picks, shovels, and wheelbarrows for tools.

In the second detail from this drawing (upper left) Dr. Schliemann is handing his wife a pot that has just come to light.

Here Schliemann is digging in Stratum II. Shortly after Schliemann's death Dörpfeld began to wonder whether this was actually the Homeric stratum. In 1932–8 Professor William T. Semple of the University of Cincinnati carried out another thorough study of the ruins. The results of this work were published after Semple's death (1950) by Professor Carl W. Blegen, the scientific director of the expedition. The photograph shows one of the strata at the eastern wall. This is the level on which, it is now believed, Priam's fortress stood. The matter probably cannot be settled with absolute certainty. The Hissarlik mound has been thoroughly sifted, and affords no further information.

Foe and friend.

HISSARLIK
WIE ES IST.

Fünftes Sendschreiben
über
Schliemann's
Troja
von
ERNST BOETTICHER.

Auf Grund der Untersuchungen
vom 1. bis 6. Dezember 1889.
und
im Frühjahr und Sommer 1890.
(Nebst Protokoll der Zeugen.)

Mit 14 Plänen und 21 Abbildungen.

Berlin.
Als Handschrift gedruckt im Selbstverlage
des Verfassers.
1890.

Schliemann's bitterest adversary, as obstinate and hidebound as they come, was a German army captain named Ernst Boetticher. He insisted that the finds at Hissarlik were the remains of an ancient crematorium—a view which even the most casual glance refuted. In 1889 Schliemann invited him to come to Troy to see for himself. Once on the site, the stubborn captain did not quite dare to oppose the verdict of the many scholars who were present. But no sooner had he returned home than he published a new pamphlet, *Hissarlik as It Is,* repeating his old contentions (see title page left). Schliemann's adviser in the battle against Boetticher was Wilhelm Dörpfeld (1853–1940), the stanch friend who moderated his sometimes excessive enthusiasm. Schliemann had met him at the site of the exemplary excavations at Olympia, and, impressed by his work, had promptly retained him as an architectural expert. Dörpfeld, who made priceless contributions to our knowledge of ancient architecture, continued the excavations at Troy in 1893–4, with financial support from Sophia Schliemann and the Kaiser. So energetically did he labor that Professor Semple, whose 1932–8 expedition he advised, could avow: "By the time the 1894 season ended, all in all more than half of the mound had been excavated, and perhaps four fifths had been at least superficially investigated." The photograph shows Wilhelm Dörpfeld between Professor Semple and Mrs. Semple in front of their house at Troy in 1935.

Before we leave Schliemann we must glance at his second important excavation: his equally sensational and scientifically still more rewarding exploration of the graves of Mycenae. For it pointed beyond the palace at Tiryns to the oldest leading culture of Europe, that of Crete.

Your Excellency's

kind letter of 9ᵗʰ January and the review of the famous Ethnological Essays I duly received and read with paramount interest. Y. Exc opinion that the Trojans spoke greek is now outdone by Professor M. Haug's cuneic translation of my Trojan inscriptions, one of which he has already published in the Augsburg gazette: Θείω Σίγω. He has explained at the same time that this name (Sigo or Siko) is contained in the name of the Σκαιαι Πύλαι, of the Σκάμανδρος, and of Σίγειον. I would add that it is also in Σίγια, the site of Alexandria Troas, according to Strab, and in Σκηψίς, of which, according to the Iliad, Echepolos a Trojan and son of Anchises was king.

Professor Haug gives me the translation of 5 more of my inscriptions, all of which are written in ancient Cyprus characters, except one, which is in very primitive phoenician and reads l'Gokap or l'Gokef (to gokap or gokef). The phoenician alphabet not being older than the 13ᵗʰ century B.C., and the phoenician inscription having been found in a depth of 10 metres or 33⅓ feet, Prof Haug declares the chronology of Troy's tragic fate in 1180 B.C. to be approximately right. In all other inscriptions occurs the name Sigo or Siko, which stands even twice on a coin. Very often on the Trojan antiquities Y. Exc sees the sign Ⅲ alone, with the meaning (according to Haug) of Si, the first syllable of Sigo, very much like the ΣI on the medals of Sigeum (Σίγειον). The inscription on the vase, translated by Mr Burnouf with the chinese alphabet, and at first declared by Max Müller and Haug to be no inscription at all, is now reacknowledged by the latter to be in very primitive Cyprus characters; but he has not deciphered it yet. Neither has he succeeded yet in making out the inscription on table 190, which is in phoenician. Prof Haug is going to publish a second article on the inscriptions. He acknowledges with immense enthusiasm the discovery of the Homeric Ilium.

Max Müller having provoked me in the Academy to prove that Juno had been a cowheaded monster (sic) I solicited from the ministry the permission to make excavations at Mycenae and without awaiting for an answer, which I have even not got until this hour, I started for the capital of Agamemnon, where, under the pretext merely to make some soundings I succeeded in exploring the premises thoroughly; to dig at 34 places — the acropolis and

This is one of Schliemann's first reports

on his excavations in Mycenae—a letter dated March 15, 1874, addressed to British Prime Minister Gladstone, who later wrote the foreword to the Schliemann book *Mycenae*. Parts of the original letter are reproduced here.

In Mycenae Schliemann uncovered a culture whose existence had hitherto been unsuspected by scholarship—a culture exhibiting a wealth of artistic and architectural forms such as was developed in Greece proper only a thousand years later (around 500 B.C.). By excavating the citadel of the Atrides (where Perseus, Atreus, and Agamemnon ruled, where Aegisthus committed threefold murder, where Clytemnestra became an adulteress and Orestes a matricide), Schliemann threw archaeologists into the situation of a museum curator who, prepared to arrange a single room full of new acquisitions, suddenly finds a dozen vast halls confronting him.

After preliminary investigations, the regular excavation

of Mycenae began in August 1876. Schliemann had studied the account of the great Greek traveler Pausanias (second century A.D.), and had come up with a translation and interpretation that differed startlingly from the general opinion of scholars. He started digging directly behind the famous, long-known Lion Gate—a procedure his professional colleagues regarded as utterly futile.

The result: at the outset he found five graves containing skeletons bedecked with jewelry. These he held to be the remains of Agamemnon and his companions; today we know that they are older, dating from the sixteenth century B.C. On the upper right we see the area after Schliemann's excavation; the illustration is taken from his book *Mycenae*. Below is the same area seen from another angle; this is a photograph of its present state. By 1877–8 the Greek overseer Panagiotes Stamatakes had discovered a sixth vault; later Chrestos Tsountas carried on the work, and sketched the first relatively realistic picture of Mycenaean culture.

GRANARY RESTORED PLANS

FIRST FLOOR

GROUND FLOOR

RAMP HOUSE
RESTORED PLAN

GROUND FLOOR

BASEMENT

LION GATE

GRANARY

WALL OF GR. ACROPOLIS

VI

V

I

II

IV

III

RAMP

B. D.
RAMP

LITTLE
RAMP

GOLDEN
TREASURE

HOUSE

N

W   E

S

HOUSE OF

WARRIOR VASE

SOUTH

HOUSE

WALL OF CYCLOPEAN

MYCENAE

LION GATE &
GRAVE CIRCLE
AREA

BRITISH SCHOOL AT ATHENS   1920 – 1923

MIDDLE HELLADIC WALLS	
LATE HELLADIC I AND II	
LATE HELLADIC III	
HELLENIC	
HELLENISTIC	
GRAVES	☠

SCALE   100 0 1 2 3 4 5 6 7 8 9 10   20 METRES

LEVELS : DATUM LINE IS 200 METRES ABOVE SEA LEVEL · APPROX

The area of the graves,

mapped in 1923 by the British School at Athens. This plan clarified some of the obscurer riddles of the site, enabling scholars to read "from the stones" alone the history of a city that has not left us a single line of writing about itself. For we must not misunderstand Schliemann's use of the words "Homeric period," and imagine that ancient Troy knew the art of writing. Homer was not the contemporary of his heroes. He came along hundreds of years after their time to sum up the traditional accounts that had come down to him. The precise time and basis of the Homeric epics is still a subject of conjecture among scholars. The prevailing view nowadays is that Homer lived (and the *Iliad* and *Odyssey* were written) between 810 and 730 B.C.; the age of the Homeric heroes must be assigned to about 1200 B.C.

The first traces of human settlement in Mycenae date from between 3000 and 2800 B.C. "Golden Mycenae" grew during the second millennium B.C. It stood at the height of its power and cultural development probably between 1400 and 1150 B.C. At this time it had been richly impregnated by Cretan civilization, and we may say that European history began at this point; we have the work of Georg Karo and Alan B. Wace to thank for the best account of the connection.

Eloquent treasures.

The seventeen skeletons Schliemann unearthed in the citadel at Mycenae had some
thirty pounds of precious metal about them,
most of it gold. This fact is not altogether
without interest to archaeology, though for
scholars the objects themselves and what
they tell are of such great intrinsic value that
the preciousness of their material becomes
secondary.

The dagger at right is a sample both of
artistic mastery and of technical skill. It
demonstrates the treatment of metals of different colors, including alloys, by punching,
engraving, cold hammering, and riveting—
more than three thousand years ago. The
scene shows a lion hunt.

The silver fragment of a drinking-horn
(upper left, opposite) tells a story, if we
examine its embossings closely: a saga of a
battle before a towering citadel, of terror-
stricken women on the wall (brick wall,
right half, center), of defenders making an
assault (only twelve can be seen on our
fragment; they are fighting toward the four
olive trees on the left), and of the use of
slingshots and bows. But there is another
important factor: the outlines of the tower,
mere primitive representation as it may
seem to the layman, reveals to the scientific
expert a similarity to the mosaics at Knossos
in Crete. The stele (middle left, opposite)
shows a charioteer; some eleven such stelae
were probably standing near the graves.

(50)

Schliemann thought this Agamemnon's mask.

All that can be said is that the royal golden mask from Grave V does have the quality of an individual portrait. The golden goblet (lower left) with three lions around the rim, crouched to spring, comes from the same grave. It is interesting that the handle of the cup is riveted on in random fashion, right in the middle of a lion's back, without regard for aesthetic principles. Such disregard for finished artistic form—which no Egyptian or Greek artist of the classical period would have permitted himself—has its counterpart only in Hittite art, where what may be called "aesthetic nonchalance" is typical.

(51)

A small, dreadfully nearsighted man

who always carried a strong cane in order to feel his way along turned up toward the end of the 1870's almost everywhere in the Balkan countries that antiquities were to be seen. And everywhere he was well known and well received, because it was not ruins alone that interested him; as correspondent of the *Manchester Guardian*, he gave active support to the Slavs in their struggle against Austrian rule.

The portrait (opposite) of Arthur Evans (1851–1941), later Sir Arthur Evans, was painted in 1907 by Sir William Richmond. Evans was destined to complete the work that Schliemann had begun in Troy, Mycenae, and Tiryns: the unlocking of that pre-Homeric culture of the second millennium B.C. which we may properly call the first European civilization. ". . . In its style, in which man remained the measure of all things, it was free of the non-European elements of giantism and bombast. . . . Everything had a delicacy of structure, as does our continent compared to the mighty, oppressive land masses of Asia and Africa" (Ernst Sittig, co-decipherer of the Cretan hieroglyphs).

Sir Arthur Evans is rightly regarded as the opposite extreme from Schliemann. He was neither a self-made man nor a self-taught scholar. The son of a wealthy manufacturing family in Nash Mills, England, he grew up in the atmosphere of Victorian learning (for generations his family had produced scholars as well as businessmen) and studied at Harrow, Oxford, and Göttingen. His great interest was initially anthropology; in 1873–4 he traveled in Finland and Lapland, then in the southern Balkans. Traces of the Celts in the Balkans awakened his interest in archaeology. At first he concentrated on numismatics, the study of coins. He pursued this interest in Bosnia and Herzegovina. In 1878 he married Margaret Freeman. When in 1881 the Austrian authorities became aware of his activities on behalf of the Slav nationalists, the troublesome foreigner was arrested and then deported from the empire.

By 1883 he was back in the Balkans with his wife—this time traveling in Greece. The finds at Mycenae fascinated him. While Margaret Evans and Sophia Schliemann chatted, Evans examined the ruins, and the question that was henceforth to dominate his life germinated: where had all this come from, since it was neither Greek nor Oriental?

In 1893 he went to Crete for the first time. His essay *Cretan Pictographs and Prae-Phoenician Script* (1896) indicates that he had begun to be interested in inscriptions. To find more of these, he returned to Crete in 1900—this time to dig for them.

And he dug up the so-called Palace of King Minos.

Cretan Mycenaean culture.

After more than fifty years of excavation, the following chronological system has been arrived at. It represents the result of awe-inspiring labor, for it has been worked out exclusively from finds in the ground (often with gaps of centuries between them), supplemented by no written evidence.

This table, which distinguishes fourteen epochs in 1,500 years, is of course only an arrangement imposed by archaeologists. Periods and styles fuse into one another; all such boundaries are fluid. It is well to remember the quip of J. D. S. Pendlebury, for many years Evans's close associate. He said: "Nowhere do we read that Minos ever stated: I am now tired of this Middle Minoan Age Number III; let us move on to the Late Minoan Age."

3500–2600 B.C.:	Transitional period from Stone Age to so-called Minoan Age.
2600–2200:	Early Minoan II and III.
2200–1550:	Middle Minoan Ia, Ib; IIa, IIb; IIIa, IIIb.
1550–1100:	Late Minoan Ia, Ib; II; IIIa, IIIb.

In Troy a new mythological world

had been resurrected. In Knossos on Crete still another rose out of even denser and more distant darkness. Here Theseus had slain the Minotaur in the Labyrinth and had made his escape by following Ariadne's thread. The ancient Cretan art that Evans brought to light, and quite quickly published, appeared to be the gay, cultivated form of expression of a highly civilized people. The Cretan architecture that he restored or reconstructed out of fragments had a bold, wholly original quality. People at the beginning of our century saw the Cretans as Evans saw them. But had he seen correctly?

The photograph of the foundation walls of the western storehouse in the "Palace of Minos" at Knossos (right) is one of the few pictures which afford us a view *in situ*— that is, of Cretan stones left where they were found and as they were found. This is, therefore, authentic Cretan architecture. More and more archaeologists today are sharply questioning Evans's restorations. Thus one of the oldest problems of archaeology has again come to the fore.

Let us take a look at some of the issues involved in restoration and reconstruction, although we must limit ourselves to only a few examples.

(55)

Evans was no dilettante, as Schliemann

was always accused of being. Evans was also no robust pioneer. He applied and elaborated modern methods of excavation and reconstruction. But does the reconstruction to the left really resemble an Old Cretan colonnade? Are these Cretan women of the second millennium B.C., and are they really in an Old Cretan salon (above)? For this is what Evans asserts in regard to the painting published in his *Palace of Minos of Knossos*, in which he reconstructed one of the inner rooms of the palace. Above are the few fragments on which he based these reconstructions.

The first sharp protest against his work made itself heard in 1930. Camillo Praschniker, an Austrian archaeologist, called Evans's reconstruction of Knossos "a movie city."

There was no doubt that Evans had per-

mitted his imagination a freer range than the finds justified (or should we not pay tribute to the great discoverer, and say vision rather than imagination?). For his reconstructions he put together elements of ancient buildings from various places; he used materials that were completely unknown to the Cretans. Many archaeologists nowadays say that he erected a "concrete Crete."

To illustrate what strong words were used in this dispute, we quote Praschniker: "Recently I had the opportunity to visit the palace once more, after a long interval, and unfortunately was compelled to recognize that my worst expectations had been far surpassed. There is so much new construction that it is scarcely possible to see old stones any longer; we walk through hypotheses of reinforced concrete which are not thereby rendered any the less shaky."

(57)

The prince in the field of lilies,

actually the priest-king, is one of the wall decorations that the painter Edouard Gillérion restored at the request of Evans. Another example of his work can be seen serving as background for the portrait of Evans on page 53. Here the elements ascribed to Cretan civilization are clearly present: fragility, noble form, serenity of expression, charm, the decadence and snobbism of *Yellow Book* art—words and concepts that had instant appeal at the beginning of the twentieth century when what was modern in

art looked to the remote past for confirmation.

But what of the facts? Below we see the actual stucco relief of the "lily prince" which the excavation yielded; opposite we see the painted stucco relief after restoration by Gillérion. The question of what was genuinely Cretan, large as it looms in the case of sizable objects, is almost as troublesome in the case of the smallest finds, such as the bull-dancer and the snake-goddess.

The bull-dancer poses one of the most interesting problems

of ancient Crete. Scholars still disagree in their interpretations of it. We do not know whether what is depicted represents sacrifice, sport, acrobatics, or military training. The stone seal reproduced above, and the cup below, show this "dancer" motif, which is found frequently on Cretan artifacts but rarely in clear form and unimpaired condition.

(60)

The difficulties of restoration.

Given these circumstances, it is plain how difficult and dubious are all restorations of the very badly damaged Cretan frescoes. Left are the remains of one such fresco identified as a bull-dancer—one of the very few wherein the head of a Cretan has been preserved. Only the left arm has been restored.

The snake-goddess with the large, expressive eyes,

rich garment, and exposed breasts has been, perhaps even more than the "prince in the field of lilies," a key figure in our conception of ancient Crete—as evoked by Evans. From her came all the talk about the "Parisian charm" of Cretan women. It is amazing that a very few specimens of this kind have been able to form our whole concept of the culture. This picture, in particular, was very widely published, especially in histories of costume, where it was used to represent women's fashions in Crete.

(61)

The drawings at left show us what was actually found. All the white portions in these drawings were reconstructed. Of the thing the painted clay figurine holds in its right hand only the upper part existed; it might have been anything other than a snake. The small fragment found apart from the figurine (*) might be anything other than a seated lion worn as a hat ornament. The entire face, the two forearms, and the greater part of the body are hypothetical. Left, front and side views of the "snake goddess," restored in glazed clay. The worn round seal, below, with the two dancing princesses, formed one of the few "proofs" of the style of exposed breasts. But—are these princesses? Perhaps they are temple prostitutes. To attempt to deduce a Cretan fashion from these "proofs" is more than daring.

Two comments by Ernst Buschor in his introduction to the *Handbuch der Archäologie* (1939) define the nature of the problem. "The falsification of monuments by deceptive restoration or reconstruction verges on the deliberate production of fake monuments, on forgery." But he also remarks: "Where only fragments of the object are preserved, or where it has been torn out of its vital context, scholarship is obligated to attempt to determine the original form. To leave everything in fragments would be to perpetrate a greater deception than the most unsuccessful reconstruction."

Yet the grace of this figure remains, for all that the tooth of time has gnawed it so cruelly. It leads us on to a few further examples of Cretan *objets d'art*.

Seals and votive figurines

of various materials display this people's sense of life and decoration better, perhaps, then the fragmentary frescoes—because the smaller things are perfectly preserved, and therefore far more authentic. Above, a stone seal in the form of an owl. One of the oldest such seals to be found, it dates from the Early Minoan Age III, between 2400 and 2200 B.C. Below that, a bird with spread wings, looking astonishingly modern in the manner in which it tensely fills its space. This dates from the same age, and the seal was a link in a chain of semi-precious stones. Center right, a jug under four waxing crescent moons (here, in reproduction, the moons appear to be waning), from the Middle Minoan Age I (2200–2000 B.C.). Then two wild goats browsing on a rocky hillside —on a stone seal of white carnelian. Middle Minoan II (2000–1800 B.C.). Lower right, finally, three clay votive figurines of women; although these appear to be much more primitive, more archaic than the seals, they belong to a more recent epoch, Late Minoan Age IIIb (1250–1100 B.C.).

Remnants of buildings, sculptures, even paintings so faded they can barely be made out, afford significant information. But true penetration into the life of an ancient civilization, into its customs, laws, social structure, ideas, and organic development, and thus its history, can only be achieved through written documents. Evans had originally gone to Crete because he was interested in scripts. But the decipherment of Cretan script presented fearful difficulties, and the task is only now being accomplished.

(63)

so called from the site at which it was found, is a clear example of a very unusual style of hieroglyphics. It is a clay disc covered by inscriptions on both sides. Norbert Wiener, one of the most noted mathematicians and thinkers of our times, and developer of electronic calculators, wrote in *The Human Use of Human Beings:* "Probably much of the greatest ingenuity which has been shown in the breaking of ciphers appears not in the annals of the various secret services, but in the work of the epigrapher."

The story of the decipherment of Cretan hieroglyphics is a prime verification of this statement. For more than fifty years a dozen scholars wrestled with this problem, until finally Alice Kober, an American authority, declared resignedly in 1948: "Let us face the facts: An unknown language written in an unknown script cannot be deciphered, *with* or *without* a bilingual text."

Evans had discovered more than two thousand clay tablets in the course of his first excavations. Helmuth T. Bossert (who recently deciphered Hieroglyphic Hittite), Piero Meriggi, Sundwall, and Ernst Sittig devoted years of their lives to studying this script—in vain. At last something happened which occurs again and again in the history of archaeology: an outsider solved the problem that had defeated the specialists. This is the sort of triumph reserved to the unbiased newcomer who leaps over the hurdles of conservatism at which the scholar shies.

Michael Ventris, the English amateur who succeeded in taking this leap, was an architect, a specialist in prefabricated schoolhouses, who during the Second World War did service as a bomber navigator and cryptographer in the R.A.F. Studying Cretan scripts, especially the so-called Linear Script B, was his hobby. His first published speculations aroused nothing but benevolent forbearance among the professionals. But in 1953 he was fortunate enough to become acquainted with a newly discovered clay tablet from Pylos. Here he found a tripod as a hieroglyphic sign, and the context was such that on the basis of his previous knowledge he felt encouraged to try the reading *ti-ri-po-de*, which suggested the Greek "tripod." After philological detail work of inordinate complexity, he ventured the leap that any professional would shudder at. Ancient Cretan, he maintained, had been a Greek dialect.

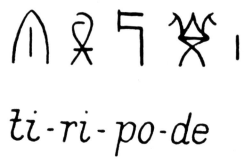

ti-ri-po-de

This assertion shook the structure of ancient history. It meant that Greek had been spoken on Crete six hundred years before Homer's time, whereas previously there had not been the slightest historical hint that this might be so. Quite the contrary. As far as scholars knew, around 1400 B.C., when Crete was flourishing, the Greeks had still been a semi-barbarian people. The heroes who fought before Troy, as Homer draws them, had been ignorant of reading and writing.

Nevertheless, Michael Ventris did not merely make assertions; he came forward with more and more proofs. The script is still as far from complete decipherment as Egyptian hieroglyphics in Champollion's day. But the road is now open. Although we know that many of the clay tablets hold virtually nothing but accounts, army rolls, and

(65)

```
ti-ri-po-de   ai-ke-u   ke-re-si-jo   we-ke      ⋈  II
2 tripods;    Aigeus the Cretan(?) brings them
```

```
ti-ri-po   e-me   po-de   o-wo-we      ⋈  I
1 tripod; with-a-single-handle(?) on one(?) foot
```

lists of tribute, what Ernst Sittig wrote of Ventris's work shortly before the Briton's death in 1954 is as true as ever: "This much is clear today: Europe—which received its name from the maiden Europa whom Zeus in the form of a white bull abducted and carried to the island of Crete, where she became the mother of King Minos—Europe must look again to that mysterious island for more clues to its cultural history."

Incidentally, this "disc" is a fine case in point of the way common sense, coupled with logic, can penetrate into the mysteries of an ancient inscription.

Evans attempted to determine where the script began. After prolonged consideration he decided that it must start from the center of the disc. This assumption was wrong. Rather, one may notice that all the signs have their feet or bases toward the outer rim, their heads toward the center. It would be absurd for the reader to place himself in the center of the disc, whence all the figured hieroglyphs would be seen standing on their heads.

Thus simple detective work, without any specialist's knowledge, can lead to initial insights into such problems.

Since restoration and reconstruction

have been discussed so often in the preceding pages, let us close with an example of timely and happy salvage. In Baalbek, Syria, stand the ruins of the mighty temple of Heliopolis, built in the first and second centuries A.D. The so-called Temple of Bacchus is probably the best-preserved example

of a monumental Roman temple. Right (the photograph dates from before 1860) we can see how dangerously the ten-foot-thick marble keystone of the lintel had dropped down—in fact, it was miraculously hanging on with a bearing surface of about two square inches against its left abutment.

In 1900 and 1901 the German Archaeological Institute took measures to save the ruin, as the cornice was meanwhile threatening to collapse. The expedition's architect, Bruno Schulz, built a provisional wall on which to stand four large screw jacks borrowed from a railroad (upper left). In one and a half days of work he raised the block back to its original position. Upper right: view of the restored gate from within the temple.

And now our scene changes. Stimulated by the Renaissance and humanism, men of the seventeenth and eighteenth centuries had reached back into the pasts of Hellas and Rome, where the roots of Western civilization are to be found. The beginning of the nineteenth century saw an expedition start out for a country that was known but not yet understood, toward which men of Western Europe felt neither intellectual nor emotional kinship. It was a land whose monuments, mute and monstrous, seemed only alien or frightening—as mysterious as the face of the gigantic image, half animal, half man, which rose out of the yellow sands of the desert: the Egyptian sphinx.

BOOK II

The Egyptian Sphinx
Geometry in Stone
Mummies
The Valley of the Kings
and Relics of Ordinary Life

The Sphinx.

December 13, 1565: "The following day we were early awake and several of us sought out the place where the great *Pyramides* stand. When we came close to these, we found firstly a large head, hewn out of a stone, towering on high, as is to be seen in this figure. . . . This statue is quite hollow inwardly, so that one can go and come to it under the earth, from far off, through a narrow passage which is lined with stone. By means of this passage the pagan priests went into the aforesaid head and spoke to the people out of the head, and so prevailed up-on the poor folk that the head or the statue were doing so with its own tongue. . . ."

In this early depiction of the Sphinx (the text and woodcut are from the diary of a German traveler, Johannes Helffrich, published in 1579), Greek myth is mingled with bad observation.

The Greek Sphinx was female, descended from one of the most dread families of Greek mythology. She was the daughter of the serpent Echidna, the sister of Cerberus the three-headed hound of hell, and sister also of the Nemean lion, the dragon Lado,

Durch diesen Gang seind die Heidnischen Pfaffen / in den gemeldtem Kopff hinein gangen / zu dem Volck / aus dem Kopff geredet / vnnd also das arme Volck beredt / als habe der Kopff / oder das Bildnis solches aus eigenen kressten gethan.

the Chimaera, and the many-headed Hydra. It was this Sphinx which propounded the famous riddle. She appeared in the vicinity of Thebes and mangled the passers-by who could not answer her question: what goes on four feet in the morning, on two feet at noon, and on three feet in the evening. It remained for Oedipus to find the answer: man, who as a child creeps on all fours and in old age uses a stick. Whereupon the Sphinx cast herself from a precipice and Oedipus became ruler of Thebes.

The most famous Egyptian Sphinx, that of Gizeh, is male; it has a lion's body and a man's head. The Sphinx of Gizeh never posed riddles or issued oracles, as Helffrich believed. Nevertheless, it remains to this day the most mysterious of Egyptian monuments. Indeed, the word *sphinx* stands as the symbol of mystery, although sphinxlike figures of both sexes are common enough in the Orient, in Christian Europe (where in the seventeenth and eighteenth centuries they did duty as baroque garden ornaments), and even in the high civilizations of Central America.

"Toward three-thirty o'clock we reach the place in the desert

where the three pyramids tower up. I can wait no longer and give my horse its head. It races forward at a full gallop. . . . A wild ride. Involuntarily, I cry out; we ascend to the Sphinx at a tempestuous pace. It grows, grows, and mounts up out of the earth like a dog getting to its feet. . . . Sand, pyramids and Sphinx appear grey, bathed in a powerful pink light. The sky is deep blue; eagles circle above. . . . We stop before the Sphinx; it looks terribly at us. . . . I am afraid of becoming giddy and try to suppress my excitement. . . .

"Its eyes seem still full of life. The left side is white from the droppings of birds. It sits precisely facing the rising sun; its head is grey; the ears are very large and protruding, like those of a Negro. Its neck is weather-beaten and has become thinner; in front of its breast is a great hole in the sand. . . ."

These are the impressions of the great French novelist Gustave Flaubert as recorded in his travel diary on December 7, 1849. And he added: "Incidentally, it was certainly of Ethiopian origin; the lips are thick."

Curiously enough, the draftsman Denon

came to the same conclusion. Denon accompanied Napoleon on his Egyptian adventure in 1798 and brought back to France the first drawings of the wonders along the Nile— including the drawing reproduced below. The headdress is pure invention. Denon could plead that he was supplying what might have been there originally. For the Sphinx had indeed suffered a great deal of damage. During the Islamic period, around A.D. 1400, an iconoclastic sheik destroyed as much of it as he could. Later a Mameluke cannon ball tore a deep gash in the skull. And through all the millennia flying desert sand ground away at the limestone of the neck. The symbolic beard and parts of the ornamentation of the brow fell off. But the picture does at least bear witness to a unique undertaking. While a French army corps set about conquering Egypt militarily, men attached to the same corps were bustling about with plumb line and drawing crayon, engaged in scientific research. Their results, summed up in one of the most monumental publications the world has ever seen (*Description de l'Egypte*, 1809–26), engendered another image of the Sphinx.

Only the Sphinx's head

was known to the first travelers. This drawing, from the *Description*, renders the headdress better, and suggests the *"grand charactère"* and the *"certaine grâce"* the French travelers saw.

The lion's body had been drifted over by the blown desert sands in the remote past. But it was not left so. A tablet erected by priests between the paws of the Sphinx relates a dream of Thutmosis IV (1450–1405 B.C.) before he became pharaoh, which troubled him when he returned from a hunt and in his weariness sank down "in the shadow of the great god."

"Look at me," a voice spoke in his dream, "and behold me. My son Thutmosis, I am your father, the god Harachte-Chepere-Re-Atum. I will give you the kingship. . . . The earth in all her length and breadth will belong to you. . . . The wealth of Egypt and the great tributes of all lands will be paid to you. For a long period of years my face has been directed toward you, and my heart likewise. I am sore oppressed by the sand of the desert on which I stand. Promise me that you will fulfill my desire. For I know that you are my son and my savior. . . ."

In the first year of his reign Thutmosis had the sand dug away. But the desert was stronger—stronger, too, than the protective wall erected in Roman times, probably during the reign of Septimius Severus, A.D. 146–211, the sole Roman emperor to die in Britain. In modern times the monument was once again completely exposed by Caviglia in 1818. But by 1886 the general director of Egyptian antiquities, the Frenchman Gaston Maspero, had to resume the struggle against the desert sands. In 1925–6 Baraize excavated once more—and this time repairs were effected, props placed where needed, to stave off further crumbling.

Hewn out of a single tremendous rock,

sixty-six feet tall, the Sphinx raises its head above the desert floor. In the whole history of man's art there is nothing more amazing than this human countenance facing eternity—at the foot of the most rational monuments of architecture ever created, the stone geometry of the pyramids. This photograph, taken during Baraize's 1925-6 expedition, shows the Sphinx from the southeast. The head and forepart of the body are chiseled out of living rock, the body and paws completed by the addition of brick. From claws to tail it measures 242.5 feet. The mouth is 7′8″; the length of the nose can be estimated proportionally at 5′8″; the length of the ears is 4′5″.

There are many sphinxes in Egypt; in fact, there are whole avenues of sphinxes. During the Middle Kingdom especially (between 2100 and 1700 B.C.) some fine sculptural work was done. We may perhaps consider the sphinx of Queen Hatshepsut as the last one on which true artistry was lavished. Most sphinxes were portraits of kings. But was the Sphinx of Gizeh also such a portrait? Archaeological evidence and written testimony indicate that it was created at the time of Pharaoh Chephren—that is, around 2650 B.C. But does it represent Chephren himself? There is some reason to believe that it was intended as the portrait of the Sun God, Re-Harachte. Or is it simultaneously god and king? Is it possibly only the watcher over the pyramid tombs? Or nothing but a gigantic whim on the part of the builders of the pyramids who thought to do something with a rock that happened by chance to be suggestively shaped?

We know a great deal about the land of the Nile, about its history, religion, art, and social order. It seems peculiarly appropriate that the largest work of sculpture left to us by antiquity, this stone figure with the mysterious look, should remain forever a riddle.

"Once the Parisians see me three or four times,"

said twenty-eight-year-old General Bonaparte after his victorious campaign in Italy,
"not a soul will turn his head to look at me.
They want to see *deeds*."

The general went to Egypt to accomplish
the deeds the Parisians wanted. In May
1798 he put to sea with 38,000 men aboard
his fleet, including 175 scholars. In the
shadow of the pyramids a victorious battle was fought, but the campaign was a
failure.

It is paradoxical that naked force was
midwife to the birth of a new science. New
Egypt, barely won, was lost again at once;
but Old Egypt was truly conquered. More
scholars followed the soldiers, and they
brought home the booty of new knowledge.

The most diligent interpreter of all the
ancient novelties was Baron Dominique
Vivant Denon, adventurer, diplomat, fine
artist—a mixture of Casanova and Caglio-
stro filtered through the French Revolution.
He was fifty-one years of age when, after
Napoleon's landing, he accompanied General Desaix to Upper Egypt in wild pursuit

of the Mamelukes. While the youth of
France fought, he made drawings. And in
his book, *Voyage dans la Haute et la Basse
Egypte*, published in 1802 in Paris, he gave
to an amazed Europe its first pictorial account of the wonderful age-old world along
the Nile.

The picture above contains his likeness.
In the romantic setting of a medieval vaulted
tomb, which served as a bivouac during the
campaign, General Belliard is having prisoners brought before him. Around him are
his staff officers. In the left foreground,
seated on the edge of the rug, near the general, is Vivant Denon himself.

Today it is apparent to us how wrongly
he saw many things (cf. the Sphinx drawing on page 72). But future archaeology
profited enormously from his work. Moreover, his labors provided essential documen-
tation for the great *Description de l'Egypte*,
which was completed by a special commission long after the Egyptian adventure had
been overshadowed by Napoleon's far more
spectacular European conquests.

This one work catapulted

a hitherto little-known world into the minds of Europeans. The preliminary labors were performed by the Egyptian Institute at Cairo. There, everything the Institute could lay hands on was collected. The collection waxed enormously, for in Egypt things that elsewhere had to be toilsomely sounded for lay right on the surface. Moreover, collecting was easy behind Napoleonic bayonets. When, under the treaty of capitulation, France had to surrender her collections to England, it turned out that the commission had acted with forethought. Plaster casts had been made of all the pieces, especially of that noteworthy stone covered with three types of script which two decades later was to provide the key to the decipherment of Egyptian hieroglyphs.

François Jomard began publication of the *Description de l'Egypte* in 1809. Here are three examples of the numerous illustrations that adorned the work. Below, a panorama of the Temple of Amon (then described as the Palace at Karnak). The artist, in conformity with the custom of the times, did not forget to place himself in the picture. The principal gate of the Temple of Luxor is reproduced on page 78. This print shows the obelisks which a few years later were sent by Sultan Mohammed Ali to France as a gift to Louis Philippe, and which now stand in the Place de la Concorde in Paris. In the lower left-hand corner of the lower illustration is the artist again; here he is standing in front of the remains of the statue of Ramses III which guards the entrance to the great colonnade at Karnak.

Two decades later a British expedition brought similarly handsome pictorial matter back to Europe. Attached to this expedition were three artists whose work practically compels discussion of the archaeological merits of drawing and photography.

A hitherto
unrecorded disaster

in the history of Egyptian archaeology was the Robert Hay Expedition. This Scottish landowner's son (1799–1863) scoured Egypt many times between 1820 and 1839, taking measurements, making drawings, and writing. The fantastic result of his labors—more than one hundred volumes full of sketches, finished drawings, architectural plans, descriptions, travel notes, and diary entries—has never been published. It reposes at present in the manuscript collection of the British Museum.

The work of Edward William Lane (1802–1876), Hay's most diligent assistant, suffered the same fate. Lane went to Egypt in 1825 seeking to cure his tuberculosis. With the aid of an ingenious device (see p. 101) he made such strikingly successful perspective drawings that only modern photography has surpassed his precision. And we must remember that for archaeologists precision ranks—necessarily so—ahead of artistic value. However, in the case of Lane—who, incidentally, could boast of being related to the Gainsborough family—quality accompanied accuracy. His planned book, *Exhaustive Description of Egypt,* was never completed because he was unable to find a technique for reproducing his drawings which satisfied his artistic demands. One single picture of his was lithographed (see page 97). The drawings on this page as well as the plates on pages 98, 99, 101 are published here for the first time. Above is the cornice and vault of the temple at Abydos of Sethos I (1317–1301 B.C.), the rest of which was then still buried under sand. Below is a view of the interior of the cliff temple of Ramses II (1301–1234 B.C.) at Abu Simbel. Staring silently into the darkness of the temple carved into rock are the gigantic statues of the god Osiris, lord of the hereafter and judge of all the dead. These statues, shown buried to their knees in sand, have since Lane's time been dug out.

"The wonderful
stone statue of Memnon"

(right), as Bernard Picart conceived it and pictured it in 1754 in his *Neueröffneter Musen-Tempel* (*Newly Opened Temple of the Muses*). "His statue . . . was of a black stone, from a mount in Ethiopia. As soon as the sun's rays touched it in the early morn, it was as if it came to life and gave forth a sweet and mellifluent twanging."

This musical sound was heard by Roman Emperor Hadrian three times one morning A.D. 130, and the event was immortalized by his court poetess Balbilla. Emperor Septimius Severus (A.D. 193–211) also heard the song of the statue. After the torso was repaired, the romantic phenomenon ceased, and we no longer know what could have caused it.

The name "Colossus of Memnon" was conferred on the gigantic statue at Thebes by the Greeks of the Ptolemaic period, who took one of the giants for the son of Eos, goddess of the dawn. For there are two colossal seated figures—only the northern one gave forth a musical tone. In reality they are statues of Pharaoh Amenophis III (1412–1376 B.C.).

The print on the lower left shows one of the colossi drawn by Frederick Catherwood, of whom more later.

It is instructive to recall how weirdly astray scholars and artists would go in their conception of ancient monuments when they had only literary sources to rely on, and direct inspection was barred to them. The dominance of philology in the study of antiquity—the result of a long tradition of textual criticism and the relatively late beginnings of serious excavation—has frequently led to grotesque absurdities. Eminent scholars, insisting on the authority of their texts, have denied what everyone could see plainly with his own eyes. But the converse has also been true: field workers have produced "results" that have had to be checked and rectified by the tedious toil of decipherers and philologists. Nowadays there can be little doubt that the diggers and the philologists are both servants to the selfsame master: the historian.

(80)

The four statues of Ramses the Great

in front of the cliff temple at Abu Simbel, drawn by Joseph Bonomi, another member of the Hay Expedition, along with Lane and Catherwood. This kind of painstaking draftsmanship has gone out of fashion nowadays, inspired as it is neither by the artist's mood, nor desire for expression, but by the object itself. For science, this is regrettable (whether it is fortunate or unfortunate for art is a delicate question), because photography, an invention hailed jubilantly by archaeologists, has proved in the course of time not to be always the ideal substitute for skilled descriptive drawing. Writing in the foreword of his friend M. B. Cookson's book on the technique of archaeological photography, Sir Mortimer Wheeler (one of the excavators of the Indus culture) bluntly called the camera "an awful liar." And Ernst Buschor has pointed out: "Drawings of architecture . . . are quite different from plans drawn before a building is erected.

They are always abstractions, phantoms of a physical structure which has extension in space. Photographs go to the other extreme; they exaggerate the manner in which the structure merges with light and air, and in any case distort the harmony, alter the color, blur the proportions, and introduce optico-pictorial elements."

Nowadays, in fact, there has developed—especially in France and Italy—a method of photographing antiquities which produces pictures of great technical and aesthetic refinement. Often these surpass the original; they always change it. But, these qualifications apart, we must keep our sense of proportion, especially in regard to the use of photography in field archaeology. The camera has by now become a priceless and irreplaceable aid, for it can yield excellent results in the hands of a man who would be unable to produce the crudest drawing.

How did the Egyptians transport these mighty colossi?

The great monuments have prompted this question for a long time. By and by we shall let the Egyptians speak for themselves on the subject. But our picture is one hint of how it may have been done in antiquity. May have been done—because the drawing below, made by the man who directed the operation pictured here, was done quite "recently," only 140-odd years ago.

This section of a statue of Ramses II was not only moved a short way along the Nile; it was also transported from Thebes to the British Museum in London.

Oddly enough, the man who organized this feat in 1816 thereafter gave up being what he had hitherto been: a professional strong man!

G. BELZONI.

This strong man

proved to be the first colorful personality in the history of Egyptian archaeology. Giovanni Battista Belzoni (1778–1823) was born in Padua. He intended to become a monk in Rome, fled from the advancing French, and turned up in Holland in 1800, in England in 1803. An imposing six feet seven, he found a scarcely less imposing spouse to share the better with him, and a great deal of the worse, for they lived in dire poverty. But their situation improved after they were hired by Astley's circus to appear in acts of strength. Belzoni played the parts of Hercules and Apollo, and later, during a tour of Spain and Portugal, of Samson. Right at the beginning of his circus career he sandwiched variety in between his strongman acts. He demonstrated tricks with wa-

ter, technical stunts which he later developed so cleverly that the idea came to him to offer Mohammed Ali, the Sultan of Egypt, a hydraulic pump for irrigating the gardens of Subra on the Nile.

Salt, the British consul-general in Cairo, smoothed the path for him. But the strong man seems to have had little success, for he was stranded in Cairo and forced to subsist as a dancer. His acquaintanceship with Salt, however, ultimately proved fruitful in another way. Through the consul he obtained a commission to transport attractive Egyptian antiquities for the British Museum. And the strong man performed his mightiest feat of strength: moving the torso of the colossal statue of Ramses all the way to London.

(83)

Thereafter, he could not shake off the fascination of Egypt. He was not a genuine scientist; rather, he was a hunter of antiquities, and he collected them with a passion that brooked no obstacles. In 1820 his book appeared in London: *Narrative of the Operations and Recent Discoveries within the Pyramids, Temples, Tombs and Excavations in Egypt and Nubia.* This was the first sizable account of Egyptian antiquities in Egypt. It contained numerous drawings done by Belzoni himself.

In 1823 the urge took him to seek the sources of the Nile. He attempted to push forward from the African west coast to legendary Timbuctoo—and died miserably near the little village of Gwato in the African bush.

Belzoni's accomplishments were sizable. He was the discoverer of the grave of Sethos I, to this day referred to in guidebooks as "Belzoni's Tomb." And he was the first European to set foot inside the second-largest burial monument in the world, the pyramid of Chephren at Gizeh. His successes were founded on his ruthlessness, and on the magic his tremendous physical strength exercised over the natives; he would take as many as four fellahin in his arms and toss them twenty-five feet into the sand, so it was said. Belzoni was a pioneer of archaeology, but at the same time the foremost representative of the earliest phase of the science: plundering rather than scholarly excavation.

But before we turn to the Egyptian "Valley of the Kings," the pyramids and the despoiling of tombs, let us pay tribute to the man who as early as 1821, without stirring from his desk, solved one of the greatest riddles of Egypt: the hieroglyphs.

Jean-François Champollion

must have heard the word Egypt for the first time at the age of seven, from his brother who had hoped in vain to go there with Napoleon. At eleven he told the former secretary of the Egyptian Institute, Fourier, that he was determined to decipher the hieroglyphs someday. At seventeen, instead of the usual valedictory, he read to the assembled faculty and students of Grenoble Academy the introduction to a book he was writing about Egypt under the Pharaohs. Shortly thereafter he saw at Fourier's a copy of the Rosetta Stone, which was to seal his destiny.

Champollion (1790–1832), who by the time he was eighteen had studied more than a dozen languages, was the scholar par excellence. Only the tumult and high passions of the Napoleonic Age tempted him to leave his study on occasion and march in the streets with banner in hand. At nineteen he was already a professor at Grenoble. After the Hundred Days he was branded a traitor, more by chance than for good reason. He put exile to good use. In 1822 he published an essay, *"Lettre à M. Dacier relative à l'alphabet des hiéroglyphes phonétiques."* It contained the key to the decipherment of the hieroglyphs.

This painting by Leon Cogniet misses the great drive and high-keyed character of the man. It shows nothing of the anxiety, the frequent despair which we encounter in his letters: the fear that he will not finish. After the consummation of his most important labors, he received many honors. In 1827 he was placed in charge of the newly founded Egyptian section of the Louvre; in 1829 the first Chair of Egyptology in Europe was founded for him at the Collège de France in Paris. (The second was created seventeen years later for Lepsius in Berlin.) From July 1828 to December 1829 he had been privileged to see the country to which he had devoted so much study: he had led an expedition to Egypt.

Champollion died in 1832. Today he is justly considered the classic decipherer. He owes this reputation to his genius and industry, of course, but also to the lucky find of an unknown Napoleonic soldier: the Rosetta Stone.

The Rosetta Stone

came to light in the course of labors by a troop of engineers near the Nile city of Rosetta in 1799. It is a slab of black basalt, about the size of a card table, but almost eleven inches thick. By lucky chance some officers were on hand at the time it was dug up. Observing the three long texts in three different scripts, they suspected its value and had it sent to Cairo. After changing owners several times, it landed in good condition in the British Museum. But before it left French hands, two specialists, Citizens Marcel and Galland, were sent from Paris on orders from the French general staff to make brush-proofs of the stone. Several of these proofs reached Paris.

Even at that early date the three basic forms of Egyptian script had been detected, if not always too clearly. In early times the Egyptians used actual picture-writing. Out of these hieroglyphs a simplified script, the hieratic, developed on the new writing materials of papyrus and clay. After the Twenty-fifth Dynasty this was further abbreviated and simplified into a cursive script, the demotic.

The Rosetta Stone contained not only fourteen lines of hieroglyphic and thirty-two lines of demotic text, but in addition fifty-five lines in Greek script and language. The Greek could be read and translated; and even before the stone left Cairo, scholars had determined that it was a document of the year 196 B.C. in which the priesthood of Memphis paid tribute to King Ptolemy V. There was every reason to assume that the content of all three texts was the same, hence by comparison with the Greek it should be possible to decipher the hieroglyphic text picture by picture.

This supposition was based upon a misapprehension some fourteen hundred years old. It stemmed from the book *Hieroglyphica* by Horapollon, an Egyptian of the fourth century A.D. (by which time hieroglyphic script was already dead). This book described the hieroglyphics as pure picture-writing; hence, ever since the seventeenth century scholars had struggled to interpret *symbols*. Their results were fantastic, and often grotesque.

A decisive step forward seemed to have been taken when the Swedish diplomat and philologist Åkerblad identified in the demotic version of the Rosetta Stone all the proper names found in the Greek version, and in addition the words for *temple* and *Greeks*. Then Thomas Young, physicist, physician, and amateur philologist, recognized the names of kings in the clusters of hieroglyphics inside oval frames. These *cartouches*, as they are called, can be seen in the sixth, twelfth, and fourteenth lines of hieroglyphs in the illustration. Finally he detected the names Berenice and Cleopatra in a bilingual stone excavated at Philae in 1815. But although Young took the bold step of assuming that some of the signs were phonetic rather than symbolic, he shrank back, like all other scholars, from the logical conclusion that hieroglyphic script was essentially phonetic and, indeed, the forerun-

ner of our own alphabet as it was later re-shaped by the Phoenicians, enriched with vowels by the Greeks, and handed down to us by the Latins. Champollion was the first to adopt this rash hypothesis. And he proved his revolutionary theory on the basis of the royal names. In the names Ptolemy and Cleopatra he established the correlation between individual hieroglyphic signs and single Greek letters. Thus the decipherment began.

The principle of this first decipherment

appears incredibly simple. But we have described only the first step. The next was correlation of the ancient hieroglyphs with the hieratic and demotic scripts. It was then discovered that the three basic scripts had not only undergone considerable wear in the course of three thousand years of evolution, but that each had developed characters of its own—depending on whether the script was used for religious or official texts, personal or governmental messages. Finally it turned out that the phonetic signs coincided with symbolic signs (a pictured face could mean both "face" and the preposition "on"), that there were word signs and meaning signs. The vast amount of written matter which now began pouring into Europe, especially in the form of papyri, contributed more to confusion than to clarification. No one knew any longer where to start.

It is testimony to Champollion's genius that he did not stop at the first step. In fact he succeeded, shortly before his early death, in demonstrating all of Young's errors and writing the outlines of an Egyptian grammar.

On the left page is the decisive plate from his *Précis du système hiéroglyphique des anciens Egyptiens*, published in 1824. The three cartouches show: No. 1, Ptolemy; No. 5, Cleopatra; No. 16, Berenice. The square (extreme upper right of the Ptolemy cartouche) is the sign for P; No. 4 gives the hieratic equivalent. The segment of a circle under the square is T; No. 6 shows the same in demotic. There is scarcely more tell-

Signes Hiéroglyphiques		Valeur selon Mr Young	Valeur selon mon Alphabet
1.		BIR	B
2.		'E	R
3. ★		I	I . É . AI
4. ★		N	N
5.		inutile	K
6.		KE . KEN	S
7.		MA	M
8.		OLE	L
9. ★		P	P
10.		inutile	Ô . OU
11.		OS . OSCH	S
12. ★		T	T
13.		OU	KH
14. ★		F	F . V.
15.		ENE	T

ing testimony of enormous evolution of Egyptian script than the hieroglyphic symbol for lion and hieratic sign No. 7—both signify L.

In the same book Champollion set a reading of his own beside one of Young's (above). A generation later there was no doubt that the real decipherer of the hieroglyphs had been Champollion.

"Nowadays we no longer decipher texts,

we read them," the Egyptologist Alexander Scharff remarked in 1939. Here is an example of hieroglyphics, probably the most impressive monumental script in the ancient world, carved on an obelisk. The stone is one of those innumerable giant slabs which for centuries were hewn out of the rose granite of Aswan, always in one piece one hundred or more feet high, then set upright as towering guards before the temples of the pharaohs. This picture shows a detail of the eastern obelisk before the entrance to the temple of Luxor. The row of three car-touches near the top contains two forms (left and right cartouches are identical) of the many names and titles of the king who erected the obelisk, Ramses II. Above the names, three times repeated, are the words: "Ruler of Upper and Lower Egypt," and below: "Son of Re."

Incidentally, there would be less solemnity in our whole approach to archaeology if we were all philologists. The familiar word "obelisk" is a Greek popular joke; it means "roasting-spit."

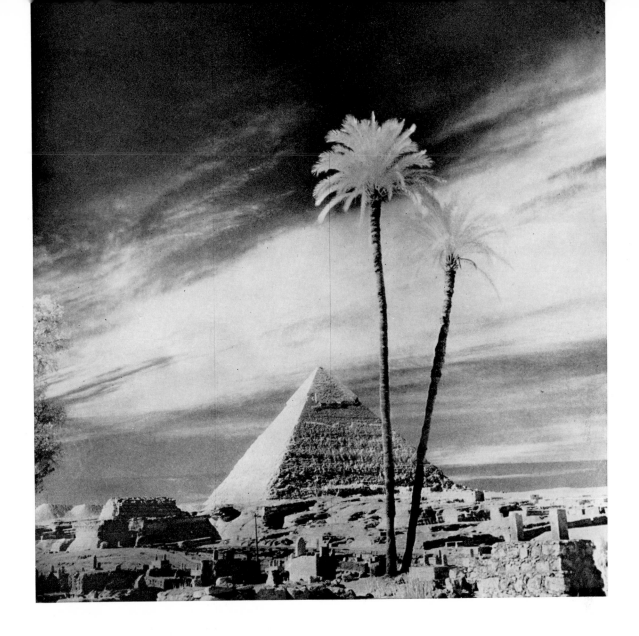

Here is the pyramid of Chephren,

the middle pyramid of the three great monuments at Gizeh, in an infra-red photograph. Pyramids are tombs, tremendous bastions erected above a small chamber containing the sarcophagus of a pharaoh. They are meant to protect the royal remains, which must be preserved if the *Ka*, the personification of the life-force and man's sole support and succor in the hereafter, is not to abandon the body.

In Egypt's very earliest days, the dead were cremated. The ashes were interred in *mastabas*, vaults at the terminus of long shafts. Gradually these came to be marked above ground as well, and ultimately they became monuments. The step pyramid of King Zoser at Sakkara (Third Dynasty, around 2650 B.C.) is the first monumental structure; there one can still trace the development of the pyramid from six mastabas heaped one upon another. The first pyramid proper was that of Snofru (around 2600 B.C.), known as the pyramid of Medum. It was never completed, and so afforded scholars an insight into the technical process of pyramid-building.

The kings of the Fourth Dynasty (2600–2480), Cheops, Chephren, and Mycerinus, built for themselves the three gigantic pyramids at Gizeh, which are surrounded by the numerous small pyramids for their wives, and by the tombs of high dignitaries. Until the middle of the second millennium the kings continued raising these monuments, the mightiest expressions of both man's power and his fear. Hundreds of thousands of men slaved to provide protection for a few corpses.

Ever since Greek antiquity the pyramids, especially that of Cheops, have been counted among the seven wonders of the world. Extensive reports, notably those of Herodotus, tell us more about them than about any other structures of the third millennium B.C. Still, in the course of time they proved to hold no fewer riddles for the probing eye of the scientist than the Sphinx. In fact, the Great Pyramid in particular has down to the present fired adventurous minds to the wildest speculations.

(92)

The man at the foot of the ladder, portfolio under his arm,

is Le Père, the architect of Napoleon's expedition. He is watching his assistant Contelle climb into a hole just beneath the ceiling of this gloomy entrance into the great pyramid of Cheops (opposite page). (This drawing and the one on this page, showing another view of the same chamber, are taken from the fifth volume of the *Description de l'Egypte*.)

On the same spot some 235 years earlier stood a man who later wrote of the pyramids: "Of this edifice some say that it was built to be the tomb of the Pharaoh who drowned in the Red Sea, wherefore said grave remained empty." Although this particular statement is open to question, the author's descriptions are sharp and clear. We continue to quote from Johannes Helffrich's journal of 1579:

"We climbed a high corridor which lay straight before us, with great difficulty, because this corridor was both wide and extremely high. On the sides the wall is set back at about half a man's height, with holes each a good pace distant from the next; we had to hold onto these and climb up as best we could."

A "musty atmosphere" greeted them, he wrote, and they became "so full of this same unhealthy air that the following night we fell into such weariness and weakness that, within two days, we could stir neither arm nor leg." It is not so bad today, but guidebooks still warn against the close, hot air.

Among the mosaics of St. Mark's in Venice

are two representations of pyramids, done around A.D. 1250. They form part of the pictorial narrative of the Joseph story in the ceiling vault of the porch. On the left (below) stands Joseph, who has sent his brothers to fetch sheaves of grain from the pyramids, which at the time of the mosaics were thought to have been granaries.

The woodcut (above, right) was done later. It comes from Helffrich's diary. Remarkably enough, his pyramids appear much the same as those represented three hundred years earlier in the St. Mark's

mosaic, although in 1565 Helffrich had actually crawled into the interior of the Cheops pyramid at Gizeh.

Thereafter, depictions of the pyramids appeared more and more frequently, often in the strangest contexts. In this preoccupation we can feel the burning curiosity of Western man to make contact with his past, and to find the essence of things behind appearances. With this in view he will subject himself to infinite mental toil and physical hardship, and stop at no means, not even brute force.

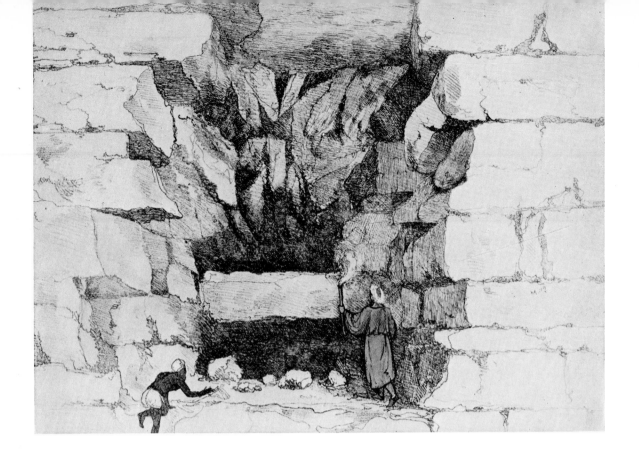

In 1646 John Greaves, a professor of astronomy,

published a book called *Pyramidographia,* a work fascinating in some respects. Like all his predecessors, he held that the pyramid of Chephren, unlike that of Cheops, was a solid structure devoid of entrance or burial vault. On March 2, 1818, Belzoni (see page 83) disproved this by smashing the stone in one section of the second pyramid (he determined the spot for his attempt by comparative measurements of the pyramid of Cheops) and so breaking in. Such methods were not unusual at the time. In 1837 Colonel Richard Howard Vyse, the successful British excavator, forced his way into the pyramids with gunpowder, and bored deep holes into the Sphinx to see whether it was hollow.

Belzoni actually found the entrance. He must have felt the pride that so many archaeologists since his time have acknowledged: the elation of being the first to enter a pharaoh's tomb since the ruler's interment. But his experience was like that of so many of his fellows: he found that others had, after all, preceded him. His great disappointment was the absence of a sarcophagus. He found a funeral vault half closed by a heavy lid, but without a mummy or those precious accompanying gifts which he had hoped for. He found only a few bones, and an inscription in Arabic.

Who had been here before him? And by what route had they made their way into the burial vault? Today we know that all the tombs of Egypt, not only the pyramids, have been the prey of robbers since earliest times, and that the enormous ingenuity employed by the ancient Egyptian architects to seal invisibly the tombs of the kings was almost always surpassed by the cunning of the thieves.

In his drawings Belzoni represented himself three times. On page 95 he is standing before the hole he had hacked into the pyramid. Below he is leading his workers toward the burial chamber, then on the left he is seen entering the chamber itself.

The Pharaoh's burial chamber

is the top chamber in the Great Pyramid at Gizeh. It measures 17 feet in width by 34 feet 6 inches in breadth and 19 feet in height. The red granite sarcophagus is so magnificently polished that Helffrich, when he saw it in 1565, thought it had been made of poured metal. No one knows whether it ever contained a mummy; robbers may have been at work here too, thousands of years ago.

The drawing on the preceding page, like the ones on these two pages, is by Lane.

Always in Arab dress,

Edward William Lane traveled up the Nile in 1826–7. Here is a self-portrait, showing him seated in the cabin of his river boat. The clean perspective lines resulting from the employment of the camera lucida are evident here. Lane was unusually adept with this instrument; he used it to excellent effect in the aerial view opposite.

No one knows how the camera lucida

was used by Lane to obtain this picture. The camera lucida was a device much favored by architectural draftsmen of the period. It is still used by beginners in art schools. In principle the instrument is extremely simple. By means of a rotatable glass prism the artist can cast a reduced image of the object upon a sheet of paper. One drawback is that the projected image is extremely dim.

Lane's remarkable "air view" shows the pyramid of Chephren from above the northeast corner of the Great Pyramid. His accuracy is evident here, but is still more emphatically shown in the next picture.

Here it has stood for four and a half millennia,

object of never ending admiration, symbol of the power and the hubris of man, subject of infinite interpretations and misinterpretations: the Great Pyramid of Gizeh, built around 2600 B.C. by Khufu, whom the Greeks called Cheops. (Lithograph from the camera-lucida drawing made by Lane in 1827.)

More than three million cubic yards of stone were piled up in the Cheops pyramid. Its height was some 480 feet, the average length of the base lines about 756 feet. According to Herodotus, 100,000 men labored twenty years to build it. Calculations indicate, however, that no more than 36,000 men could ever have worked on the pyramid at one time without hampering one another's movements. Because—in military language—the logistics of an operation requires more personnel than the combat units, Herodotus' figure may approximate the truth. This seems all the more likely as we know today that the ramps over which the stones were moved required even more material than the actual pyramid.

Herodotus also gives some figures on costs: for example, the payment to the workers in the form of radishes, onions, and garlic. It has recently been calculated that to build such a pyramid today, with the methods of the ancient builders, would cost about 100 million dollars; applying the methods of our technical age, however, the cost could be reduced to only 10 million dollars.

It was early recognized that the Great Pyramid had been built on certain astronomical principles. But the fact that it continues to be regarded, even today, as a species of oracle is due chiefly to a man whose character was a queer compound of strict science and wild mysticism.

Charles Piazzi Smyth (born the son of a British admiral in 1809 in Naples) was highly regarded as a professor of astronomy at Edinburgh—until he put forward his interpretation of the Great Pyramid. He was not the first to read the most fantastic propositions into the measurements of altitude and sides and the angles of rooms and corridors in the pyramid; but his reputation as an astronomer lent respectability to dubious conclusions, and this in part accounts for their tenacious persistency. Egyptologists pointed out that the premises on which he built his assertions were extremely shaky; mathematicians condemned his method of manipulating measurements if they did not suit his calculations. None of this could discredit his system. In the course of time the Cheops pyramid became known as a "Bible in stone" which furnished not only the most precise astronomical and mathematical data (such as the numerical value of pi or the exact distance from the earth to the sun) but also the whole of history down to the present day.

Even as late as 1949 an article appeared in a German newspaper containing the following paragraph: "In this connection we must mention the discoveries of Dr. Noetling of Stuttgart, who has found that by simple mathematical operations with the given dimensions of the Great Pyramid one can easily derive the radius, circumference, volume, and the specific gravity of the earth, the periods of the planets, the length of their orbits, the exact duration of male and female periods, the time of the climacteric in both sexes, to name only a few items."

"By simple mathematical operations with the given dimensions"—that is the bad beginning and the still more lamentable end of this method. In truth the preposterous nature of the idea can be bared only by satire. An Englishman proposed to apply the same method to London's Crystal Palace. Employing a suitable unit of measure and a moderate degree of patience, he said, he could easily show that the dimensions yielded the distance to Timbuctoo or the average weight of an adult goldfish.

Oddly enough, it was this very nonsense which sent Egyptward the man who was to be the most successful, fertile, and stimulating Egyptologist of the century: Petrie.

The bearded gentleman at the bus window

is Sir William Flinders Petrie, photographed as he was taking leave of his American hosts in Syria during his last expedition in 1935. For seven weeks this man of eighty-two and his wife (the figure in the doorway) worked, ate, and slept in the bus, while his assistant, I. C. Ellis (second from right), shared a small tent with the driver. The other persons are Petrie's youthful hosts of the Megiddo Expedition, whose comfortable, solid houses were equipped with rugs, club chairs, and phonographs.

In his old age Petrie lived and traveled exactly as he had done in his youth. His first trip to Egypt was inspired by his father, a chemist and engineer who fell under the spell of the theories of Charles Piazzi Smyth. Petrie senior saw Smyth's work as a triumphant reconciliation of enlightened science with Christianity. Desirous of finding support for Smyth's ideas, he planned a trip to Gizeh, accompanied by his sons. He was going to use superior modern instruments to measure the pyramids and obtain better results—that is to say, results closer to those required by Smyth's theories.

As it turned out, young Petrie traveled alone. He had earlier developed a passion for surveying, had worked in Stonehenge, and at the age of twenty-two published his first book, *Inductive Metrology*. During the years 1880–2 he spent nine months in Gizeh, measuring, calculating, probing, and at last publishing the best mathematical data on the Great Pyramid which had ever been ob-

tained. Only extremely minor revisions of these have since been made. However, his data also revealed the sheer silliness of Piazzi Smyth's theses. That was clear enough to Petrie, but out of respect for his father he never belabored the question.

This was his manner of life:

"Excellent accommodation was to be had in a rock-hewn tomb . . . formerly used by Mr. Wayman Dixon, C.E. His door and shutters I strengthened, and fitting up shelves and a hammock bedstead, I found the place as convenient as anything that could be wished. The tombs were sheltered . . . and preserved an admirably uniform temperature. . . . The usual course of a day's work was much as follows: . . . Lighting my petroleum stove, the kettle boiled while I had my bath; then breakfast time was a reception hour, and as I sat with the tomb door open, men and children used to look in; . . . often a friend would stop for a chat. . . . After this, starting out about nine o'clock; . . . if triangulating, it was Ali's business to hold an umbrella, so as to shade the theodolite from the sun all day—the observer took his chance; . . . I always had to get on as well as I could during Ali's dinner hour. At dusk I collected the things. . . . Then, when all was safely housed in my tomb, Ali was dismissed to his home, and about six or seven o'clock I lit my stove, and sat down to reduce observations. Dinner then began when the kettle boiled, cooking and feeding going on together. Brown ship-biscuit, tinned soups, tomatoes (excellent in Egypt), tapioca and chocolate, were found practically the most convenient and sustaining articles. . . . Then, after washing up the dishes, I sat down again to reducing observations, writing, etc. till about midnight. Ali's slave Muhammed, the negro, and his nephew, little Muhammed, used to come up about nine o'clock and settle in the next tomb, to sleep as guards, safely locked in. . . . During the excavations I turned out earlier—about sunrise; . . . when working inside the Great Pyramid, I always began in the evening, after the travellers were clean away, and went on till midnight, with Ali nodding, or even till eight o'clock in the morning; thus occasionally working twenty-four hours at a stretch. . . . The tomb I left furnished, as I inhabited it; . . . it will, I hope, be useful to anyone wishing to carry out researches there. . . ."

This excerpt from Petrie's book *The Pyramids and Temples of Gizeh* displays a modesty that has become all too rare. Petrie's accuracy and his introduction of new methods proved to be of enormous importance for Egyptology and archaeology. He provided the best descriptions of Egyptian monumental structures, but was also the first to recognize the value of small works of art, of ceramics, vases, and shards ("the true alphabet of archaeologists in every country"), for chronology. He was interested in modern as well as ancient and even prehistoric Egypt, and wrote on the science and art, the religious and social life of the country. In 1893 he was appointed to a professorship and concurrently published *Ten Years' Digging in Egypt*, which proved widely popular and brought him fame beyond the confines of specialist circles.

He died on July 28, 1942, en route to Jerusalem—aged almost ninety. The picture above shows him around 1880 in front of his quarters at Gizeh.

Pyramid of Snofru

Final true pyramid

Second stepped structure

Entrance gallery

First stepped structure

Burial vault

The graves of the kings.

These seemingly simple diagrams of the three big pyramids—of Snofru at Medum, of Chephren, and of Cheops—are actually the distillation of about a century of measurement and research. Flinders Petrie's work would, in its essentials, have been impossible without the preliminary labors of the pioneers; the proper evaluation of his and others' researches awaited the publication of a survey such as *The Pyramids of Egypt*, by I. E. S. Edwards, from which these drawings are taken.

Of the many pioneers who are listed in the chronology at the end of this book, two merit special attention. Richard Lepsius's expedition of 1842–6 for the first time yielded material scientifically arranged. Auguste Mariette, on the other hand, was something more than a successful excavator. Not only was he the founder of the Egyptian Museum, now located in Cairo, but he was also the person responsible for protecting Egypt against further plundering excavations.

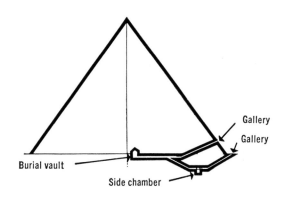

Burial vault

Gallery

Gallery

Side chamber

Pyramid of Chephren

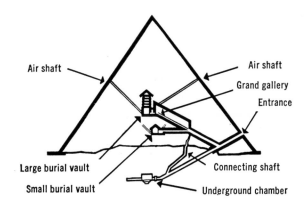

Air shaft

Air shaft

Grand gallery

Entrance

Large burial vault

Small burial vault

Connecting shaft

Underground chamber

Pyramid of Cheops

The pyramids at Abusir,
as drawn by Ludwig Borchardt,

are a fascinating object lesson to those who look to archaeology to bring buried civilizations back to life, not only back to the surface. This was reconstruction with the crayon, but it was the result of scientific labor over a span of four years.

What Borchardt saw during his preliminary investigation in 1901 was a grouping of stone piles in the desert sands, the central one about eighty feet high. There followed a series of excavations from 1902 to 1904 in which he was able to define the outline of a tremendous burial ground. He inferred the architecture and the positions of the temples in front of the pyramids, their connection with temples in the valley by vast, lofty ramps, originally roads for the transportation of building materials, and later routes for processions. He was able to date the pyramids. They were erected by kings of the Fifth Dynasty, about twenty-five centuries B.C., by Nefer-er-ke-re, Ne-user-re, and Sahu-re.

A contemporary archaeologist would consider that he had done enough in finding and mentally reconstructing so vast a complex. But around the turn of the century there was as much emphasis on finds in the form of concrete objects as in the form of knowledge. An expensive expedition had to bring home trophies. And so railroad track supplied by the Prussian Ministry of War was laid down upon the ancient soil, and soon gigantic granite pillars and colossal lions were rolling away from the temple area—on their way to Cairo and Berlin. It took two weeks to move each pillar nine miles, because the track had to be pulled up behind each rolling flatcar and laid down again piece by piece in front.

No modern archaeologist is seriously out for trophies because, as we have said, the scientist nowadays is more interested in knowledge than in booty. But even if he wanted to, he could not take anything away without breaking the law. (In rare cases he might obtain a special export license.)

Egypt is now independent, is aware of the value of her antiques, and has passed extremely strict laws to protect them. It was a matter of tradition for the Egyptian Antiquities Institute, founded by Mariette, to be administered by Frenchmen. Mariette, in fact, secured the first protective legislation. In 1952, however, the last French director of the Institute, Abbé Drioton, resigned his post. His successor was an Egyptian, Mustapha Amer.

"We spoke very little until we entered the chamber

where the sarcophagus lay, and once again I stopped to admire the beauty of the simple alabaster box, the sides of which reflected the brilliant light of the electric lamps which we had installed within the chamber. . . .

"I thought of other archaeologists who had stood on the brink of great discoveries: Carter when he opened the sealed antechamber of the Tomb of Tutankhamen; Reisner when he found the deeply hid burial *cache* of Queen Hetephras. . . .

"At last all was ready, and I gave the order to begin the operation. Two of my workmen began to haul on the rope, while others applied crowbars to the crack between the lower part of the panel and the sarcophagus.

The men heaved with all their might; there was a scraping of metal on stone. Nothing happened, the panel was wedged tightly in position. The men heaved again, but for a long time the heavy panel resisted all our efforts to move it.

"Then at last it began to move, a mere inch or so. Wedges were inserted in the aperture, and I carefully examined the panel to make sure that no damage had been done. I was right in my assumption that there were vertical ribs running down each side of the panel, sliding in grooves. I gave the order to continue. In all six men were at work on raising the panel, but such was its weight (about 500 lbs.), and the tightness with which it was sealed with a mixture of gypsum plaster and glue that nearly two hours had passed before at last it slowly began to go up. I went down on to my knees and looked inside.

"The sarcophagus was empty."

This is the account of the climax of an expedition, by the Egyptian archaeologist Zakaria Goneim. On June 27, 1954, Goneim, hitherto virtually unknown outside his country, had made his way into a newly discovered, never completed step pyramid near Sakkara. He cherished the hope, as did the whole world of archaeology after reading his

first reports, that the untouched mummy of a king of the Third Dynasty would be found inside it.

Goneim, a member of the youngest generation of Egyptian archaeologists, had studied in Cairo with Percy Newberry and Hermann Junker. In 1951 he began digging at Sakkara, near the pyramid of King Zoser. In November 1953 he found a corner of a hitherto unknown pyramid built by a hitherto unknown king, later identified from an inscription as King Sekhem-khet. The construction of this unfinished pyramid was begun during the Third Dynasty (Goneim dates it 2780–2720 B.C.). When, in 1954, a burial vault with an obviously undamaged sarcophagus was found, there was every reason for excitement to run high among archaeologists. For a royal mummy not plundered by grave-robbers is a great rarity.

Goneim's experience is similar to that of G. A. Reisner, the Harvard archaeologist who on March 3, 1927, opened the completely untouched sarcophagus of Queen Hetepheres—the mother of Cheops—and found it empty.

There are various theories about why the Queen's sarcophagus was empty, but none can be fully proved. A theory accounting for the empty sarcophagus of Sekhem-khet is that a genuine interment was never planned. Possibly a sham sarcophagus had been placed in the vault, meant not for the King but for his *Ka*; the unusual sliding-door arrangement of the sarcophagus lends support to this idea.

Reporters and photographers flocked to the scene of Goneim's excavation, just as they had to Reisner's. As far as they were concerned, the empty sarcophagus was a huge disappointment. It was not so for the Egyptologists. Reisner's excavation proved to be of great significance to scholarship, and the data Goneim obtained from the layout of the unfinished pyramid will provide specialists with material for study for a long time to come.

On his deathbed

Mariette learned of his greatest error. The theory he had so vehemently advocated, that all the pyramids are mute—that is, that inscriptions would never be found in them —was proved wrong. In 1881 the thirty-six-year-old French archaeologist Gaston Maspero (1846–1916) discovered in the pyramids of Sakkara no less than four thousand lines of text in the most ancient hieroglyphs. These inscriptions threw invaluable light on funeral rites, veneration of the dead, and Egyptian beliefs concerning the hereafter.

The photograph shows the entrance to the pyramid of Unis, the last ruler of the Fifth Dynasty. This pyramid had been reduced to ruin in ancient times. Here Maspero found the first long inscription, carved into the limestone and painted blue. The photograph was taken in 1881 by Emil Brugsch, brother of the then celebrated Egyptologist Heinrich Brugsch (1827–1894), a diplomat who worked for both the Egyptian and the Prussian foreign services. Heinrich Brugsch was the author of a seven-volume hieroglyphic-demotic dictionary. In 1891 he had returned to Europe with one of the greatest collections of papyri ever amassed: some three thousand rolls.

His younger brother Emil is credited with one of the most sensational discoveries ever to be made in Egypt. He accomplished this feat not at the head of a great expedition, but all alone with an Arab thief in a landscape of craggy wastelands.

"Mumia is that which is found in the graves of embalmed people."

This definition appeared in 1557 in an edition of the principal medical treatise of the age, *Hortus Sanitatis*. The picture at right dates from 1574; it is taken from the last page of a book whose Latin title translates as follows: "Affidavits by the most noted doctors, historians, and philosophers on the most mysterious and precious exotic curatives, and especially on the *mumia*, as well as on everything connected with it and the manner in which it was formerly used in Judea, Egypt, Arabia, and quite generally elsewhere." The Latin in the upper right-hand corner of the woodcut declares that this is the "image of a real Egyptian mummy." The German in the lower left-hand corner speaks of the mummy's "right magnificent antiquity." The book claims that this mummy was booty taken at the Battle of Lepanto, the heathens having used it as a talisman.

From the point of view of archaeological history, it is interesting to see that the artist strove for an exact representation. A curi-

ous detail must be noted; if the script on the mummy's bindings is followed from top to bottom, it can be seen how the artist gradually turned the hieroglyphs into Hebrew letters—which were undoubtedly more familiar to him.

Expressa veræ Mumiæ Aegyptiacæ effigies.

Allhie zu sehen fur augen Geber/ Ein recht hertzlich Antiquitet.

"Mumiya," an Arabic word,

actually means raw pitch, which in early times was thought to have medicinal properties. This was one of the substances used for embalming Egyptian mummies—after a good deal of trial and error. And from tombs the pitch found its way into Europe's pharmacies, where it remained down to the nineteenth century. Gradually the distinction between "mummy" and "mumiya" was lost, and potions made of pulverized bodies of Egyptian rulers were actually prescribed for rich patients as expensive medicines.

The picture is taken from the *Histoire générale des drogues,* a book published in 1694 by a Parisian merchant and apothecary named Pierre Pomet. He hoped, by his horrendous depiction of the eviscerated corpse in the foreground, to convert readers away from using pulverized mummy as a panacea. Pomet expressed his own repugnance to the practice by inserting the word "gabbaras" between the pair of mummies on the left; this word may be the ancestor of English "garbage."

Despoiling of mummies

is one of the oldest forms of Egyptian grave-robbing. Sir J. Gardner Wilkinson published this sketch in his *Manners and Customs of the Ancient Egyptians* (1837–41). He describes the picture as follows: "Interior of a mummy pit or sepulchral chamber, at Thebes, with a Fellahs woman searching for papyri and ornaments."

The dancing mummy.

The Sphinx connotes mystery, the pyramids monstrous magnificence. But for hundreds of years mummies have connoted eeriness. Cheap novels, poor plays, and bad films are forever making use of mummies to stir horror. A party given by the French amateur archaeologist Emile Etienne Guimet at the beginning of the twentieth century also drew upon this theme for theatrical effect. A genuine Egyptian sarcophagus was brought into Guimet's drawing-room. While subtle, dramatic lighting played upon the scene, a mummy rose up out of the sarcophagus. She represented Thaïs, the courtesan whom the hermit Serapion converted to Christianity. Dressed in swathings perfectly imitating those of a real mummy, she performed a macabre dance. At the end the "mummy," impersonated by a noted dancer, sank back into her sarcophagus.

This might have been only a foolish prank if the host, Monsieur Guimet, had not actually been a scholarly collector who founded the excellent museum that bears his name. Moreover, the man who supplied him with the mummies that inspired the dance was likewise a serious scientist, Gayet, a specialist in Coptic art.

Nevertheless, in their collecting these two gentlemen from the very start merged science with the most frivolous sort of romanticism. For example, the expedition that went to Egypt to work in Antinoë in 1900–4 was entirely inspired by the hugely successful novel of one of the greatest nov-

"As much as possible of the brain is extract[e]

elists of the period, namely *Thaïs* by Anatole France, which had been published in 1890 and created an extraordinary stir. In this novel France had exercised poetic license to cast the well-known story of Thais and her hermit in a new form. Gayet came home with two mummies and, in order to gratify his patron and backer Guimet, presented them as the preserved bodies of Thais and Serapion. What was more, he was able to fabricate enough reasons for this claim to have the scientific world accept it for a time.

On the reverse of this page is the dancer in the costume of Thais, performing the "mummy's dance."

and what the hook cannot reach is rinsed out with drugs; next the flank is laid open with a flint knife and the whole contents of the abdomen removed; the cavity is then thoroughly cleansed and washed out, first with palm wine and again with an infusion of pounded spices. After that it is filled with pure bruised myrrh, cassia, and every other aromatic substance with the exception of frankincense, and sewn up again, after which the body is placed in natrum, covered entirely over, for seventy days—never longer. When this period, which must not be exceeded, is over, the body is washed and then wrapped from head to foot in linen cut into strips and smeared on the under side with gum, which is commonly used by the Egyptians instead of glue. In this condition the body is given back to the family, who have a wooden case made, shaped like the human figure, into which it is put. The case is then sealed up, and stored in a sepulchral chamber, upright against a wall."

This method of mummification is de-

through the nostrils with an iron hook,

scribed as "the most perfect process" by Herodotus, who traveled through Egypt around 450 B.C. Modern study bears out his description. To supplement such written accounts, archaeologists have learned much about the process from Egyptian tomb reliefs such as the one shown above, included in the posthumous fourth volume of Champollion's *Monuments de l'Egypte et de la Nubie* in 1847. Both the technique of bandaging and the painting of the face mask can be seen here.

The religious rationale for mummification has not been fully clarified. Most likely the Egyptians believed that the soul, after escaping from the body at death, would return to it again. But how could it find a body that had fallen into dust? Thus they began their struggle against the dissolution that to almost all other peoples seemed the inexorable fate of man. If we consider time on a human scale, they won their battle, for mummies of astonishing completeness have been preserved down to our day.

Mummification certainly had begun by

the time of the pyramid-builders. The masks that later were made of precious materials —in the case of Tutankhamen, of pure gold —were in the beginning simple plaster casts. The more complicated technique described by Herodotus did not develop until the Middle Kingdom. From the Twenty-first Dynasty on, the embalmers began their remarkable imitations of life. They forestalled the shrinking of the skin; they filled the cavities of the body; they added artificial eyes.

Much has been said and written about the "riddle of mummification," by which is meant not only the grotesqueness of the whole procedure but also the apparently lost chemical technique. Recent research has shown that excessive use of chemicals frequently destroyed instead of preserving, and that the success of so much mummification was due to a peculiarity of the Egyptian soil and climate rather than to the skill of the embalmers. One of the best examples of this was found in the wild, rocky valley of Deir el-Bahri. . . .

More than sixty dead warriors, buried in a mass grave,

were found in 1926 by a New York Metropolitan Museum expedition under the direction of H. E. Winlock. The site, Deir
el-Bahri, is near the Nile, opposite Karnak
and Luxor. The men must have fallen in a
heroic battle—for Pharaoh Neb-hebet-Re,
who had led them to fight in Lower Egypt,
had their bodies transported from the battlefield all the way back to the vicinity of
the capital, in order to honor them by common burial. In fact, a start was made on
embalming them, although at this time embalming was usually the prerogative of aris-
tocrats. But interest in the heroes must
have faded swiftly, for the embalming was
begun only for some, and then very casu-
ally; not even the intestines of the corpses
were removed. Nevertheless, the bodies of
all these soldiers, who fell under a rain of
arrows around 2000 B.C., were found in a
miraculous state of preservation!

Not chemicals, but the unique dryness
and bacterial sterility of Egyptian soil, together with the constant heat, had produced mummification. Forged mummies
are further proof that this can happen. At
the end of the nineteenth century, when
mummies were in great demand, many
such frauds were offered to collectors. In
many cases it could be conclusively proved
that the bodies were recently dead, name-
less corpses mummified by the desert sands
alone. The counterfeiters had merely out-
fitted them with a few amulets and scraps
of genuine bandaging to strengthen the
claim that these were real mummies from
the days of the pharaohs.

The climactic point of the excavations near the precipitous cliff at Deir el-Bahri, however, was not the discovery of the "unknown soldiers" of the Eleventh Dynasty. Some time earlier, under exciting circum-stances, Kings had been exhumed. The shaft that housed so many kings is marked by a white arrow in the picture on page 117, taken during the excavations of 1932.

The Arab tomb-robber Abd-el-Rasul

of the village of Kurna is shown here with Gaston Maspero (lolling figure with parasol), Director of the Egyptian Museum in Cairo, and his assistant Emil Brugsch. They are looking into the shaft entrance to the cliff tomb of Deir el-Bahri, the most amazing burial vault in the world.

Thutmosis I (1545–1515 B.C.), of the Eighteenth Dynasty, made a break with tradition. Instead of erecting an impressive monument over his tomb, the Pharaoh had his tomb cut into the living rock in a secret place. The pyramid architects, despite all their skill in covering their traces, had not prevented the discovery of the entrances to pyramid tombs. Tomb-robbers had invariably broken into the sealed bastions, found the sarcophagi, got at the mummies, and robbed them of all their precious adornments. But the cliff tombs proved to be no safer. Even Thutmosis was not left in peace. The tomb-robbers, abetted by corrupt guards and high officials, ravaged so many royal graves that the priests attempted to save the mummies of their kings by moving them secretly, in the dead of night, to other burial chambers.

Thenceforth the grisly scenes of "wandering mummies" might be witnessed all over Egypt. Mummies that had been cut open, battered, and robbed by the pillag-

ers were often embalmed anew by the priests and toted from tomb to tomb— for centuries.

Not much was known about this in 1881, when one of Gaston Maspero's assistants drifted about the bazaars of Luxor in an attempt to track down the source of a swelling black-market in antiquities. The result of his detective work was the arrest of Abd-el-Rasul, who was soon exposed as the current chief of a dynasty of robbers operating from the village of Kurna which had been pursuing the business of tomb-robbery almost continuously since the thirteenth century.

On July 5, 1881, another of Maspero's assistants, Emil Brugsch, stood near the base of the cliff at Deir el-Bahri, in front of an uninviting hole in the ground, to which he had been led by the confessed criminal Abd-el-Rasul. When he had himself lowered thirty-five feet into the burial chamber, he saw scattered everywhere innumerable utensils, numerous sarcophagi half opened and only partially plundered by Abd-el-Rasul and his clan—and mummies! Some forty mummies had been hidden there, including the greatest kings of Ancient Egypt: Ramses the Great, Sethos I, Amenophis I, Thutmosis III.

The mummy of Ramses the Great.

This and the following photographs were taken by Emil Brugsch. They are from a group of photographs he personally sent to the British Museum, which had them bound and preserved in a volume along with his accompanying letter. These "incunabula" of early archaeological photography have great documentary value, for the condition of the mummies, after removal of their bandages, has greatly deteriorated since Brugsch first found them.

Ramses II (1301–1234 B.C.), pharaoh of the Nineteenth Dynasty, reigned sixty-seven years and probably reached an age of almost one hundred years. Script can be seen between the second and the third horizontal bandages. The inscription gives an account of the fate of the dead king's body. When his own tomb appeared to be endangered, he was carried to that of King Sethos I, from there removed together with Sethos to the grave of Amenophis I, and finally transferred to his last resting-place in the collective tomb where Brugsch discovered him after more than three thousand years.

The most uncanny sight

may well have been the mummy of Sethos I
(Nineteenth Dynasty, 1320–1301 B.C.), the
father of Ramses the Great. Its bandages
were unwound by Maspero in the presence
of Brugsch on June 9, 1886. "Around the
time of Amenophis III," says the Egyptologist Kurt Lange, "the art of embalming for
preserving the cadaver must have reached
the height of its development. For the
bodies . . . have preserved so much of
their original appearance that we must aver
we find many persons still living who look
more decayed!" This mummy, too, enjoyed
little repose. It was opened and ravaged;
then priests, according to inscriptions, restored it and moved it. Its first refuge was
the tomb of Princess Inhapi. Then it was
placed with Amenophis I, and finally joined
Ramses in the common grave.

Heaped with flowers—

this was how the mummy of Amenophis I (Eighteenth Dynasty, 1559–1539 B.C.) was found. These flowers were identified as skillfully as the body they wreathed. They consisted of a type of delphinium, Acacia nilotica, Sesbania aegyptiaca (a breeding-ground for caterpillars), and Carthamus

tinctorious (safflower). A wasp that had been among the flowers by chance proved to be likewise "mummified."

Although this mummy had been twice plundered in ancient times, its condition was so good that Maspero refrained from unbandaging it, in order not to destroy it.

The Queen's wig

and the box that went with it (left) were considered no less important than the lavish meal placed in her tomb to equip her for the long journey (at right on opposite page). Her *Ka* could take its choice of a leg of lamb, a leg of gazelle, two geese, and a calf's head—all almost as carefully mummified as the corpse itself.

Pretty little Queen Isimkhobiu,

wife of a king of the Twenty-first Dynasty. This mummy, found in the same tomb as the preceding ones, is just over five feet tall. It was very carefully swathed, and the interior of the third coffin was richly painted with representations of the dead queen's fine reception by the gods Osiris, Isis, and Nephtys. Left, the innermost coffin. Right, the mummy itself.

The death agony

is still imprinted upon the Pharaoh's shriveled features. He was Tau-a-quen III, a king of the Seventeenth Dynasty, of which we know little. Hence it was a boon to the scholars to encounter a mummy whose state tells us certain definite things—which may someday be verified by other means, thus filling in the blanks in the historical crossword puzzle.

Dr. Grafton Elliot Smith (1871–1937), the first physician to examine mummies with all the resources of medical knowledge, determined that the King had suffered five severe wounds from spears and battle axes. He had been struck repeatedly in the head. The variety of the weapons suggests that the attack was carried out by several persons. Moreover, he seems to have been embalmed very hastily, in a more or less temporary fashion, immediately after his death. It seems likely, therefore, that he fell on the battlefield.

Such deductions are dangerous, of course. In fact, Elliot Smith assumes, from a medical point of view, that the first or second wound may well have been fatal, and therefore speculates that the King may have been assassinated. But scholarship cannot move ahead without hypotheses. We must await the day when a new find transforms one or the other hypothesis into historical fact.

Opinions differ on the best-preserved Egyptian mummy

insofar as anatomists and archaeologists judge the matter from different points of view. Dr. Smith, the anatomist, nominated Princess Nsitanebashru (above left: photo taken during the unwrapping; right: completely unwrapped) as the best-preserved mummy he had ever examined—and he had examined many. At one time in 1903 Mas-

pero sent forty-four mummies to him. Like all pioneers, Smith was resourceful. Placing the mummy of Thutmosis III on the seat beside him in a hired carriage, he drove to a sanatorium near Cairo which owned the sole X-ray apparatus in Egypt. He was probably the first person to ever look inside a mummy without destroying it.

Under the withered, leathery skin we can still imagine the living Princess Nsitane-bashru. Her brown hair was once waved, and her manicured fingernails and toenails testify to her careful grooming. The skepticism of those full, arched eyelids and high forehead, the arrogance of that hooked nose, the extraordinary protruding lips, al-most apish in quality, suggest that this was a woman of deep licentiousness. . . . But enough of such speculations, which scientists justly abhor. These are matters for the historian and the poet. That history and poetry at their finest must be identical cannot be said too often.

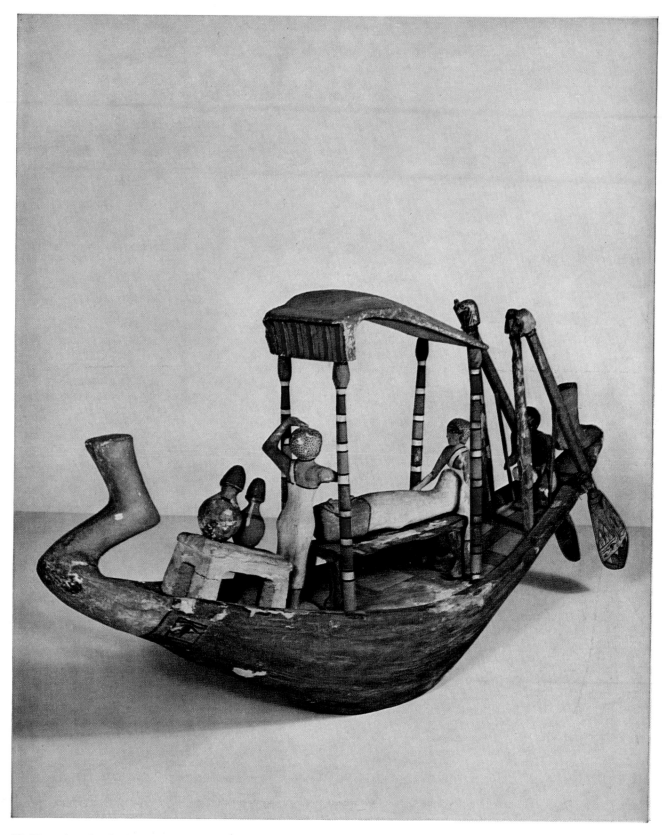

V. Egyptian death ship. Model carved in wood, probably from Thebes (Eleventh Dynasty, *c.* 2000 B.C.). At the head and foot of the bark stand the protective goddesses Isis and Nephthys (see also p. 146).

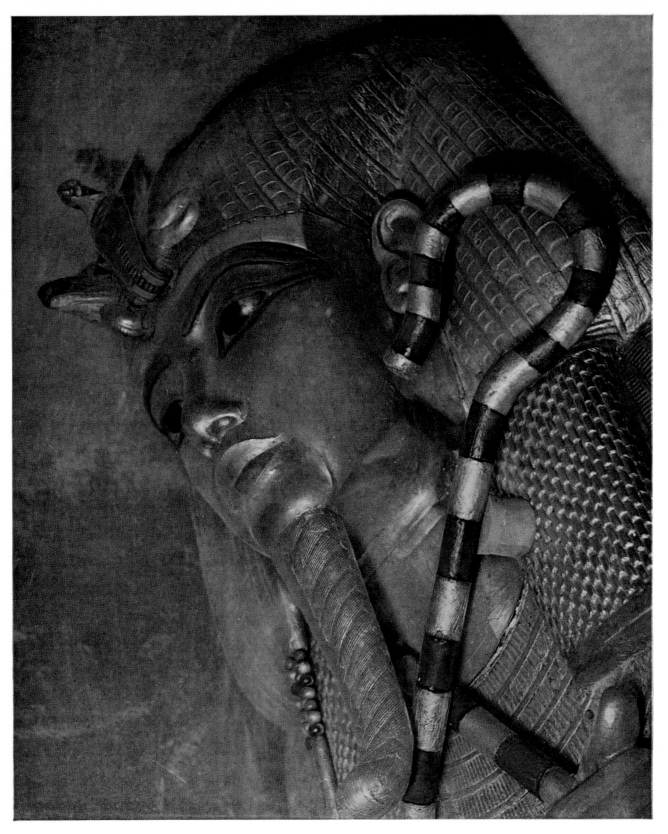

VI. Pharaoh Tutankhamen. Image on the golden lid above the mummy of Tutankhamen (Eighteenth Dynasty, *c.* 1350 B.C.). Found in the Pharaoh's tomb in the Valley of the Kings by Carnarvon and Carter.

Among the earliest portraits painted—

that is to say, the first attempts to depict individuality with the brush—were those found on the small plaques that, during Egypt's Roman period, supplanted masks as face covers for the mummies. These reproductions also show the high elaboration given to the mummy bindings at the beginning of the Christian era. The Greek boy (left) who was found at Hawara in Fayum seems to have been treated with the utmost care. We know he was Greek from his appearance. But by this time mummification had already become an empty form. Its religious content had been lost. Consequently, the aim ceased to be preservation of the body itself, but representation of that body's outer appearance during life. An even better example of this is the mummy of a boy shown at right. It is also of the Roman period. The shroud is painted; the dead boy holds a bunch of flowers in his hand. This is no longer mummification, but trickery—an illusion produced by a skillful painter. This picture has not been published before.

This is the mummy of Wah,

one of the estate stewards of Chancellor Meket-Re (Eleventh Dynasty, about 2000 B.C.). It was discovered in 1920 by H. E. Winlock, head of the New York Metropolitan Museum's Egyptian expedition, in the western part of Thebes, at the foot of the Chancellor's tomb. The position of the body and the inscription identifying Wah as a steward led the diggers to the conclusion that there would be no precious ornaments hidden with him. Thus, the mummy arrived still wrapped at the museum, where it stood for fifteen years. In 1936, however,

Elliot Smith's example was followed: the mummy of Wah was X-rayed. The first X-ray photograph yielded a sensational surprise. The photographs in sequence show:

1. Wah's mummy as it was found, wrapped in an enormous linen cerecloth that bore traces of having once been dyed red.

2. and 3. The X-rays reveal that the body of this "poor, simple steward" was bedecked with ornaments. Photograph No. 2 shows strings of beads at the level of the

(128)

ear, others between arm and chest. No. 3 indicates the presence of a heavy necklace.

4. In 1940 scholars began the unwinding process. Removal of the cerecloth revealed more fully the mummy's plaster mask.

5. After removal of many bandages and much padding, the first layer of the chemical preparations appeared: a conglomeration of resinous substances which had turned quite black.

6. Along with this layer of hardened gum, another dozen bandages were removed, exposing the first ornaments at the mummy's neck. A total of 450 square yards of linen was unwound!

7. The bandaged body itself appears. The rich ceramic necklace was only slightly dislodged in the course of some four thousand years. Further examination of this steward who had been buried at his master's feet yielded: silver and gold ornaments; four large reproductions of the sacred scarab, two made of massive silver, one of lapis lazuli, and one of blue faience; and sets of beads of various precious materials.

(129)

Mummified animals—

that is to say, mummified gods. Innumerable animals were worshipped as divinities in Egypt: bulls, falcons, cats, and crocodiles, among others. Whole cemeteries of sacred animals have been found—the most famous of these being, probably, the cemetery of the Apis bulls, which Mariette discovered. Animal cults were usually local; they took on greater importance only in the later period of Egyptian history, under the

Ptolemies. Hence they should not be considered typical of the religious life of Egypt at its peak. Even the Apis bulls, which were mummified and entombed with incredible pomp, did not reach the pinnacle of their glorification until the Eighteenth Dynasty.

Below, crocodiles, one wrapped and one unwrapped. Left, a cat mummy from Abydos, and, right, a mummified falcon, the embodiment of the god Horus.

Today women archaeologists

are honored members of the profession. (The picture shows one examining a late-period mummy.) In the last century they were still a great rarity. Young Sophia Schliemann, who helped her husband so actively at Troy, was considered a phenomenon. Lady Petrie, who also accompanied her husband, became something of a myth in the Arab countries. Today women lead expeditions of their own. The American archaeologist Hetty Goldman dug in

Anatolia. At Karatepe a young Turkish woman, Halet Çambel, was in sole command of a crew of thirty Turkish laborers for an entire season. Since 1953 Theresa Goell has been directing an American expedition that has been excavating the outdoor temple tomb of Antiochus I of Commagene (ruled about 69–34 B.C.) on the summit of Nemrud Dagh, in southeast Turkey, about 6,500 feet above sea level. A dozen other examples might be listed.

Jefferson Caffery, an inveterate visitor of Egyptian excavation sites when he was American ambassador in Cairo, has made some interesting comments on this question. Caffery had grown quite accustomed to the habit of the Egyptian workmen of welcoming every stranger with a friendly song. But one day, when he appeared on the site accompanied by two ladies, he was somewhat startled to be saluted with this (in A.D. 1955):

"You beautiful, you sweet creation. Your hair is like the golden rays of the sun. Your eyes outshine the stars, your mouth is like Solomon's ring, and your teeth are more beautiful than the best of pearls. . . . When you walked in as though angels were carrying you, your silken clothes waved in the breeze, and you looked like the daughter of the moon. Your earrings and bracelets of gold, your necklaces of precious stones, are beyond compare, and you rustle your beautiful ornaments as does the horse of a rich prince!"

Caffery observes dryly: "As I recall, the

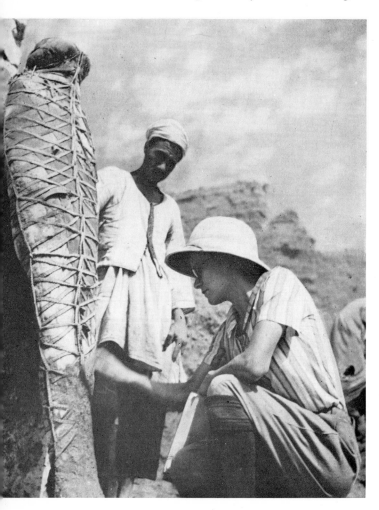

ladies wore simple clothing and little jewelry. But tradition is stronger than fact, and
they graciously accepted the compliments"
(*National Geographic*, November 1955).

We mention this incident in order to
compare these tributes with a love-song of
the time of Thutmosis IV, more than
3,350 years ago. The reader may make his
own surmises as to the relationship between
the two texts:

"With high throat and shining breast,
she has hair of genuine lapis lazuli; her
arms surpass those of the goddess of love,
her fingers are like the cups of the lotus.
With solid loins and narrow waist, she—
whose thighs dispute each other's beauty,
who walks with noble carriage when she
steps upon the earth—she steals my heart
with her greeting. She makes all men turn
their necks to look at her. . . . When she
stepped out of the house, it was as if we saw
the one and only One. . . ."

Almost a thousand years after

the last mummifications in the old religious tradition, a mummy like the one
above was embalmed—around A.D. 400–500.
The eye sockets were sealed by the age-old
technique, and the same resinous substances were employed to preserve the body.
We show the face of the so-called Thais
(see page 113) who was discovered in 1900,
placed first in the Musée Guimet, and then
transferred, as of purely anthropological interest, to the Musée de l'Homme in Paris.

No less than forty pharaohs' tombs

in the Valley of Kings were already known
to the Greeks. This valley was the original
resting-place of all those kings whom
Brugsch found in the mass grave at Deir
el-Bahri. The first modern account of the
valley was given by an English traveler
named Richard Pococke, in 1743. He, too,
spoke of bands of robbers who made the
valley a dangerous place for strangers.

Left is the vestibule to the headquar-
ters set up by the Robert Hay Expedition
(see page 78). The tomb is probably that
of Ramses II. The pencil drawing of the
interior, by E. W. Lane, shows the archaeologists relaxing in picturesque Oriental
style in the antechamber of the tomb. The
three gentlemen in fezzes are Lane, James

Burton (called Haliburton), and either
Bonomi or Catherwood.

Then came Belzoni's discoveries, and
those of many other diggers—plundering
parties, for the most part, such as accorded
with the nineteenth century's collecting
mania. Sir Austen Henry Layard (see pages
211 ff.) candidly stated that his aim was
"to obtain the largest possible number of
well-preserved objects of art at the least possible outlay of time and money."

Nowadays the Valley of Kings is a tour-
ist mecca. It harbors more than sixty
tombs. In one of these, open now to sight-
seers, a find was made which had the most
direct bearing on the foremost archaeological sensation of the twentieth century.

Pick something special to show to a VIP—

that was the word passed down to Edward Ayrton, head of the Theodore Davis Expedition digging in 1908 in the Valley of Kings. Luckily, Ayrton had just dug up a number of large storage jars. The first of these—position of find marked by arrow at lower left in photograph—had contained a charming face mask. But when Ayrton opened the other jars under the eyes of Sir Eldon Gorst, a visiting fireman, he found nothing but "trifles"—some carefully wrapped chemicals, a few cloths, simple utensils, and several wreaths of once-fresh flowers. The VIP thanked him for an excellent dinner and took no further thought of the finds he had been shown, thereby ignoring one of the most dramatic clues in the history of modern archaeology. For these "trifles" had served, about 3,250 years earlier, for the embalming of Tutankhamen, the king who for reasons not yet determined was buried in greater splendor than any ruler before or after him.

Ayrton too put the finds aside, although they bore the seal of Tutankhamen and therefore should have alerted him to the presence of a royal tomb in the vicinity. When eventually they reached the Metropolitan Museum in New York, they were again ignored. No account of them was published until 1941, fifteen years after Tutankhamen's tomb (the site of which Sir Eldon had passed unaware) had been opened, the whole world standing agog. H. E. Winlock, constrained, because of the war, to "dig" in the museum rather than in Egypt, then reported on them. Thus a connection was finally established between these "routine" finds and the greatest discovery in archaeology.

The age of discovery in the Valley of Kings was past.

That was the general opinion among professionals in 1914 when Lord Carnarvon took over the Davis expedition's excavation franchise and engaged the British archaeologist Howard Carter to conduct new excavations for him.

War conditions prevented their beginning until 1917. In 1919 and 1920 they unwittingly dug in the immediate vicinity of Tutankhamen's tomb. But they ceased work there and dug at another spot, in a lateral valley—dug for two winters without success. Pledging themselves to devote only one more winter to the Valley of Kings, they went back to where they had begun several years before. In November 1922 they plunged their spades into the ground again—and found the entrance to the tomb of Tutankhamen.

Thereafter the excavation was a tense drama of rising hopes alternating with crushing disappointments. The rubble-strewn passage lying behind the entrance led Carter to believe that here at last was the realization of the dream of all Egyptologists: an unviolated royal grave, a mummy that had never been pillaged. But then he recognized that seals of various periods had been applied to the door; hence, others had been here before him. Presently he reached a narrow tunnel that robbers had made long before. But when Carter broke through the second sealed door and flashed a lamp into the dark chamber beyond, he was so shaken by the sight before him that for a while he was unable to speak. The chamber contained whole piles of precious objects, all thrown helter-skelter. Robbers had certainly been here, but for reasons unknown they had obviously plundered very little or not at all.

Right: view of the antechamber. Carter replaced the sealed door with a strong iron grill.

The contents of this antechamber provided such extraordinarily vivid information regarding an epoch of Egyptian life that any single piece would have delighted an archaeologist who had spent a whole winter's digging to find it. But here lay hundreds of objects, from simple utensils to the most luxurious ornaments. In the left foreground we see parts of the young King's war-chariot. It later posed a difficult problem in restoration, as the harness leathers had dissolved into a slimy mass. Here stood (on right) couches such as had never been found before: gilded, inlaid with ivory, fashioned into fantastic sacred animals: the rear was an elongated, rhinoceros-headed lion, the front some form of cattle in panther skin. In addition there were chairs, tables, and storage chests. In the strange cases beneath the couch were ducks and other foods. The most resplendent, artistically surprising, and at the same time most precious piece in this motley assortment was the King's throne, with Tutankhamen and his wife depicted on the back rest, in graceful positions. It can be seen lying on its side at the right.

It is easy to understand why the discoverer of such treasures went wild with excitement when he found a sealed door in this antechamber, and a hole in the wall behind one of the couches. The hole proved to be the entrance to a small annex. When it had been widened, Carter crawled in and raised his flashlight. The cone of light played upon a new wealth of treasures, strewn indiscriminately about the room. Here the robbers had committed depredations and—this seemed the obvious explanation—had been surprised and forced to flee without their booty.

Confronting a third sealed door, which appeared untouched, the archaeologists looked at one another with a single wild surmise: was the King's mummy laid to rest behind this door?

Lord Carnarvon (left) and Howard Carter (right),

at two fifteen on the afternoon of February 17, 1923, about to open the third sealed door. George Edward Stanhope Molyneux Herbert, Fifth Earl of Carnarvon (1866–1923), sportsman, yachtsman, immensely wealthy collector of art, and Howard Carter (1873–1939), a student of Petrie's who had been excavating since 1899, formed a good team. Lord Carnarvon's controlled enthusiasm paired well with Carter's cool scientific precision. Consequently, the excavation of Tutankhamen's tomb was conducted with unprecedented care. Moreover, the party had sufficient funds at its disposal to make the best use of modern technological equipment and organization.

The stones were pried apart with an air of solemn ceremony. Some twenty persons attended. Carter, working with pedantic deliberation, made an opening in the wall large enough to permit the introduction of a flashlight. While all the onlookers sat in breathless silence, he peered through the hole. He saw something that seemed to be a wall of solid gold. It was, as it turned out, the front of a tremendous gilded shrine. This shrine contained a second gilded shrine, with an unbroken seal covering the bolts! Although the archaeologists stood before the most precious golden treasure to come down from antiquity, that small unbroken seal was of more staggering significance to them. It meant that the innermost shrine must contain an undamaged mummy!

VII. A dead man's prayer. The dead man prostrate under a palm tree. Wall painting in the tomb of Pashedu at Der el-Medineh (Eighteenth or Nineteenth Dynasty, between 1580 and 1200 B.C.).

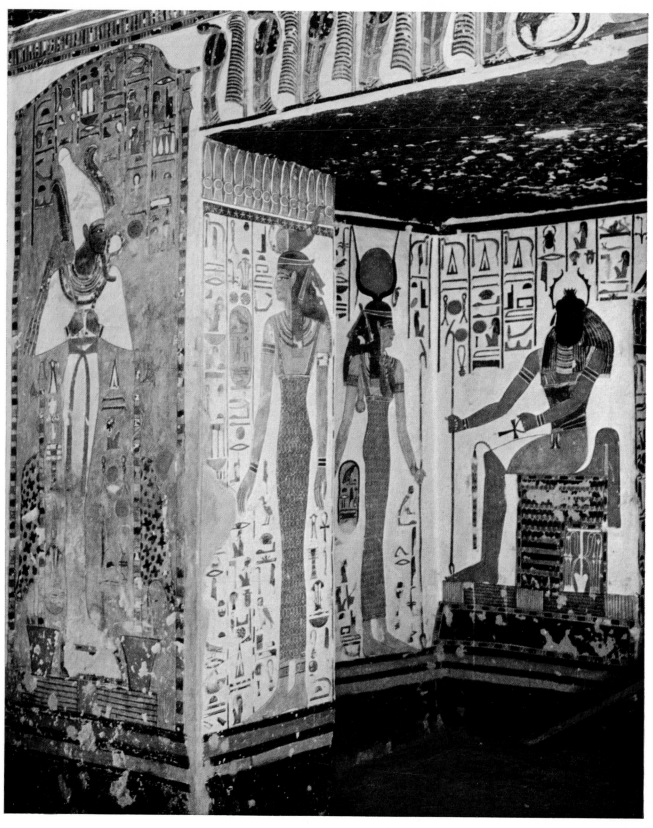

VIII. Entrance to the tomb of an Egyptian queen. The antechamber of the tomb of Queen Nephertari at Thebes. The paintings are executed in slight relief against a stucco background. (Nineteenth Dynasty, thirteenth century B.C.) The tomb was discovered in 1904 by an Italian expedition.

Inside the second shrine stood a third, inside the third a fourth—all sheathed with gold. In the fourth shrine stood a yellow quartzite sarcophagus, 8.8 feet long and 4.8 feet high. Would it contain the mummy?

Who was this king

who had literally been enshrined in gold?

This bust of Tutankhamen was found at the entrance to the tomb at the very beginning of the excavation. The head is of painted wood. In accordance with tradition, the neck rises out of a lotus blossom, like the young Sun God rising out of the waters.

It is almost incredible, but this king, who was buried with such unprecedented pomp, was remarkable solely for having died and been buried—as Carter himself commented. He reigned around 1350 B.C., was the son-in-law (and probably the son as well) of Amenophis IV, otherwise known as the "heretic king" Ikhnaton. He was married very young and died, according to anatomical evidence, at the age of eighteen. Probably we shall never learn why this particular royal youth should have received so magnificent a burial. How utterly fantastic that burial was, the archaeologists did not discover until the sarcophagus was opened. By then the project had become such a sensation that the world's newspapers carried every latest development in banner headlines.

(143)

The ropes and pulleys groaned as the granite lid

of the sarcophagus, weighing more than 1,300 pounds, rose into the air. Layers of linen cloth appeared. But when these were removed, the dazzled onlookers beheld a golden face encrusted with gems: the Pharaoh's image.

All sorts of circumstances cropped up to hamper continuous progress. It was not until 1925–6, by which time Carnarvon was dead, that Carter proceeded to open these sarcophagi. For there was not one sarcophagus; inside the first rested a second (again an image of the King as Osiris,) and inside

the second a third. This third displayed another golden face (shown here), surrounded by a collar of pearls and flowers that still retained something of their erstwhile colors and could be botanically identified.

The third coffin was of solid gold. And inside this precious coffin rested the body of the Pharaoh, untouched by the robbers, exposed to the light of day for the first time in 3,270 years. Alas, it was badly eaten by the excess of oils and resins the embalmers had used.

The comeliest goddesses

bequeathed us by the artists of the New Kingdom. Three of four golden statuettes are shown here; Neith, Isis, and Selquet. They stood in the small annex, watching over the heart and internal organs of Tutankhamen.

It was a great pity that the Pharaoh's mummy should have been in so poor a state. But this was a small disappointment when set against the amazing plenitude of other finds, whose artistic and scientific value is altogether inestimable, and whose purely material value has to this day not been fully calculated. The value in gold of the innermost coffin alone has been reckoned at around $175,000.

The principal finds, such as the chairs and the chariot, have been reproduced innumerable times. For that reason, in the following illustration we show some of the minor finds, of which hundreds upon hundreds were discovered in the tomb and on the King's mummy.

The King wore seven bracelets on his right forearm,

six on the left. Above: appearance of the bracelets at the time they were found; right: the bracelets after cleaning. They are of gold, semi-precious stones, and glass beads. Eight of the thirteen are amulets; the Eye of Horus occurs on five bracelets; the scarab, betokening the protection of Isis and Re, on three.

The photograph also conveys something of the grossly decayed condition of the mummy, which made the cleaning an extraordinarily tedious and difficult process; parts disintegrated when barely touched by a sable-hair brush. Nevertheless, the position of the arms crossed over the chest is quite plain. One must imagine that the King is lying with his head toward the bottom of the page. On the little finger of the right hand (upper left-hand corner of photo) can be seen one of the golden sheaths that protected all the fingers and toes. The round shield is the border of the heavy gold mask that covered the King's head and shoulders.

Tutankhamen's grave was a treasure trove in every sense. Archaeologists could now see and handle a multitude of objects whose existence had hitherto been only deduced from texts and paintings.

On the following pages we leave behind the ornateness of a pharaoh's life and death, and catch a glimpse of the existence of the average Egyptian.

(149)

Reliefs like this one

offer an answer to the ever recurring question of how the Egyptians could have transported enormously heavy stone objects. It records the transportation of a twenty-two-foot-high alabaster statue of Prince Thutihotep (Middle Kingdom). Extensive study has taught us that reliefs of this type are for the most part amazingly precise in their data. Thus, we are justified in assuming that the size of the crew shown in this picture was not determined arbitrarily. The artist has depicted 172 persons involved in the work, and that number must correspond approximately to the facts.

The statue is lashed with ropes to a wooden skid. Cushions protect the delicate alabaster wherever the ropes might damage it. Four other ropes serve as tow lines; a total of 88 laborers draw on these lines. The operation is directed by the overseer, who is stationed on the statue's knees, beating the rhythm of "pull and slack" with his hands. An assistant overseer amplifies the sound of the clapping hands by striking wooden mallets together. In the prow of the skid a worker stands pouring water on the roadway, to diminish friction. Three water-carriers are supplying him. Three workers stand ready to thrust a notched beam under the skid when a rough piece of ground is reached. Behind them stand three overseers, accompanied by twelve assistants. Sixty soldiers in six groups, armed with clubs and lashes, escort the party. In other words, the number of actual workmen, counting the one overseer on the knees of the statue and his assistants, is $88 + 6 + 3 = 97$. This proportion is surprisingly in accord with Petrie's estimates of the numbers employed in building the pyramids (see page 102). He estimated that eight workers would have sufficed to move one of the largest blocks in the Great Pyramid—a weight of more than 2.5 tons—into any desired position.

According to Herodotus, the cutting and setting of the blocks required about twenty years. Petrie estimated that there are 2,300-000 blocks in the pyramid, but this is an arbitrary guess because no one knows how big the rock core of the pyramid is. From these figures he concluded that during the annual spell of forced labor from late July to early November—the time of the Nile flood, when the farmers were not otherwise occupied—some 120,000 blocks were transported. From the size of the workmen's barracks, traces of which Petrie found, he estimated that from 3,600 to 4,000 men were quartered in them. If it is assumed that these were professional stonemasons, who labored the year around, then it is possible that with the means at their disposal, a team of four men could prepare ten blocks a month. Four thousand men could therefore handle, during a year's work, the 120,-000 blocks that were transported in the summer and fall.

Labor on the pyramids was organized in military fashion. The largest unit was a "company" of from 800 to 1,000 men. Each of these units immortalized itself by chiseling its name into the stone. We know, for example, that the company called "The white crown of Khufu is mighty" worked on the Great Pyramid. One of the Third Pyramid companies was named "Men-kau-Re is drunk."

Every company was divided into four "watches" whose nautical designations such as "Stern Watch" and "Bow Watch" suggest that they were derived from the Nile boatmen. Each watch consisted of from 200 to 250 men. These watches, finally, were subdivided into groups of from 10 to 50 men known by animal names such as "Antelope Group" or "Ibis Group."

If we consider, then, the vast hordes of workers employed in moving these great loads, whether pyramid blocks or statues, it becomes clear that the ancient Egyptians by no means performed superhuman feats.

Readers may be impelled to check the count of figures in the illustration. I therefore assure those who attempt to make their own reckoning that (excluding the statue) there really are 172 figures depicted: 79 face left and 93 face right.

What implements and techniques did the pyramid-builders have?

1:100 LARGEST GRANITE BEAM OF KHUFU RAISED BY ROCKING
ON ALTERNATELY RAISED SUPPORTS. IVDYN.

STONE

CRADLE

ALTERNATE
WEDGES

ROCKING UP STONE ON A CRADLE

Today we know that they were familiar with the lever, the roller, and the inclined plane. They had pickaxes and copper chisels, plumb lines and carpenters' squares. They knew the trick of driving wooden pegs into chiseled holes, then pouring water continually upon the pegs until the swelling of the wood cracked the rock away from its cliff. Whether they knew the use of block and tackle remains a moot question.

These diagrams by Petrie from his *Egyptian Architecture* show the extremely simple devices by which the Egyptians could move the greatest weights. In the upper diagram we see how even granite beams twenty feet long can be raised with comparatively little effort by supports applied close to the center of gravity. The lower diagram shows another method, better suited to upright blocks. The stone is mounted on a rocker base, and as it is swung from side to side wedge-shaped supports are slipped under it alternately from each side. Once the stone starts swinging it is easily kept in motion by its own momentum.

Stonemasons at work

with wooden mallets and copper chisels. This drawing is a copy of portions of wall paintings in the grave, at Thebes, of Rekhmara, last chancellor of Thutmosis II. The paintings were done some time after 1445 B.C. By way of explaining the sometimes staggering feats of the Egyptian builders, we should point out another factor that has been overlooked until quite recently. This is the workman's psychological relationship to the work demanded of him. Present-day sociologists have rediscovered, rather than discovered, not only that such a relationship exists, but that it can be measured and taken account of as a factor in production on a large scale. Today, in the age of social welfare, strikes, and union contracts, apparently inhuman tasks that ancient civilizations required of the laborer may well seem unfair. But the moment we see this relationship between the workman and his work in its historical context, we are forced to realize that feats which today seem prodigious were in those days accepted as a matter of course. The great monuments were not always the product of forced labor. The ancient Egyptian worker would not have thought in terms of exploitation. We are speaking here not of his hours and the conditions of his work, but solely of what he was expected to and did accomplish.

In this connection, Goneim in *The Buried Pyramid* tells a story that demonstrates how the workman's attitude, combined with those technical tricks which are mothered by necessity, can result in astonishing feats. Speaking of his Egyptian workers, Goneim writes: "They work among the monuments which their ancestors built, and it would seem that some of the ancient skills have descended to them; for instance, an extraordinary facility in moving heavy objects with little mechanical assistance. An English friend told me how he watched with some amazement and trepidation the moving of a granite colossus in the Cairo Museum, a statue weighing perhaps a hundred tons. 'A few wiry little chaps in *gallabliyehs*,' he said, 'gathered around the statue with iron levers and a few baulks of timber. There was an awful lot of shouting and heaving, the thing began to rock and catastrophe seemed imminent. I felt like shutting my eyes and stuffing my fingers in my ears, but in a short time the colossus was shifted several yards and ended up in its new position quite unharmed.' "

Very likely European or American workers would have refused to touch the statue without heavy equipment. Indeed, they probably would have asserted in good faith that such a monster could not possibly be moved without modern machinery.

Not toys but images of life itself—

so the Egyptians of the Middle Kingdom looked upon the little houses and ships, peopled with men and animals, which they deposited in their tombs along with the dead. Indeed, these clay and wood models were supposed, according to the Egyptian faith, to transform themselves ultimately into genuine workrooms and work people who would serve the dead man as he had been served in his lifetime. The Egyptians' stress on the accurate representation of the everyday surroundings of the deceased before his death has afforded archaeologists knowledge of their most intimate domestic institutions, their crafts, and their commercial life. The clay figurines in the wooden box enact work in a granary during the Eleventh Dynasty. The model is from the tomb of Meket-Re.

Almost equally informative are the little ships of the dead,

which were often found in pairs. One was to carry the dead man through the heavens, one through the underworld. The model below shows the shipment of a mummy, accompanied by a priest, protected by the goddesses Isis and Nephthys; it comes from a Middle Kingdom grave in Thebes and dates from about 2000 B.C. The vessel upper right is a rich man's yacht; it too comes from Thebes, from the tomb of Meket-Re,

a chancellor of the Eleventh Dynasty.

Excavation goes on continually in Egypt, and new finds are still being made. The soil of a country that has harbored three millennia of rich civilizations is inexhaustible. On May 26, 1954, a solar ship was discovered in the course of road work close to the Great Pyramid—that is, in a spot where not a square inch of the land had not been explored and probed countless

times. Kamal El-Malakh, director of all excavation work at Gizeh, discovered it, and
it was dug out by the archaeologist Zaki
Nour. This was no small model; it was a
beautifully formed death ship, 120 feet long,
built for a pharaoh of the Fourth Dynasty.
The wooden parts were well preserved; the
ropes, with which the pharaoh was to be
tied down for his long journey, were still
intact. Below is a drawn reconstruction.

An archaeological find is meaningless in itself.

Its significance is all in the interpretation. Modern archaeologists can take pride in knowing more about ancient Egypt—the life of the masses as well as of the elite, the thought and beliefs of the average man as well as those of the educated minority—than did the Greeks who were two thousand years closer to them in time.

In addition to paintings and narrative reliefs, scholars find a wealth of information in the innumerable papyri that have been recovered. All the great museums in the world now possess specimens of these. The reproductions at left show "pages" from the so-called "Egyptian Book of the Dead," whose original title, *Per-em-hru*, has been translated into English as *The Book of Coming Forth by Day*.

Both the script and the illustrations are executed with great neatness and care. And the sheets are so well preserved (the manuscript reached the British Museum in 1888) that it may be considered one of the finest examples of Egyptian papyri. The entire papyrus contains 190 chapters, which deal in detail with the Egyptian cult of the dead. Three chapters are shown here. In one square we see the jackal-headed god Anubis, the heavenly embalmer, performing his office. To the left of him kneels the goddess Isis, sister and wife of Osiris and mother of Horus. To the Egyptians she was the kindly goddess of love and motherhood. During the imperial age of Rome demonic powers were ascribed to her, and her cult, which had in the meanwhile acquired many strange and unsavory rites, had to be suppressed by force A.D. 560. Opposite Isis kneels Nephthys, her sister and the sister of Osiris, who bore to Osiris the god Anubis.

Egypt was opened up for archaeology in 1798 with the Napoleonic expedition. At that very time travelers were visiting a neighboring country and bringing back accounts of strange ruins. The land between the Euphrates and the Tigris was not explored by archaeologists until long after the Egyptian monuments were widely known. Yet this was the land that figured more in the Bible than any other, and where was reared an edifice that has remained a symbol to this day: the Tower of Babel.

BOOK III

Early Travelers to Babylon and Persepolis

The Decipherment of Cuneiform Script

Layard in Nineveh and Koldewey in Babylon

Methods and Results of the
Excavation at Ur

The Tower of Babel,

of which we read in Genesis xi, 4: "And they said, Go to, let us build us a city and a tower, whose top may reach unto heaven; and let us make us a name. . . ." But then "the Lord came down . . ." and he confused their tongues and "scattered them abroad from thence upon the face of all the earth. . . ." Babel, which originally meant "gateway of God," became the synonym of confusion.

Herodotus, the Greek historian, and Ktesias, the personal physician of Artaxerxes II, King of the Persians around 450 B.C., have described the building. It has exerted end-

less fascination over men's minds, has remained for poets and painters the symbol of human arrogance. As Pieter Brueghel the elder (1525–1569) renders it (right), it is a structure of sinister complexity and mystery, while in the French miniature of 1423 (from the Duke of Bedford's missal, page 165) it is an exalted pleasure pavilion. In reality what the Babylonians built was not a tower, but a pyramid-like brick structure 288 feet square, 288 feet high, with seven terraces, crowned by a temple that Marduk, the great god of Babylon, was said to favor with his presence. The Babylonian ziggurats, as these step pyramids were called, were not tombs like the Egyptian pyramids; they were temples built for the nation, and as such were not allowed to fall into neglect. Only a few fragments have been found of the "tower" mentioned in the Bible, for it was destroyed several times. Nabupolassar and Nebuchadnezzar rebuilt it around 600 B.C. and made it greater than ever, "grounding its base securely upon the breast of the underworld." Xerxes the Persian (485–464 B.C.) destroyed it once again. Alexander the Great, on his way to India, paused in admiration before the ruins; he set first 10,000 men and then his entire army to work cleaning up the rubble. Empires rose and fell; sand drifted over the Babylonian remains, until nothing remained but the legend of this building whose pinnacles had strained upward to the skies. Twenty-two centuries had to pass before someone came to dig and discover what had truly existed.

Robert Koldewey's excavation of Babylon will be discussed later in this book. For Koldewey, though the excavator of the "Tower of Babel," was not the actual rediscoverer of its site.

It was a dangerous adventure,

until well into the nineteenth century, to follow the ancient pilgrims' route through Venice, Cairo, Sinai, Palestine, and along the borders of Mesopotamia as far as the Tigris and Euphrates rivers—those waters of Babylon by which the Jews once wept when they remembered Zion. But again and again bold individuals found their way to the spot, impelled by—by what? "What is the purpose of this toiling in a distant, inhospitable, dangerous land?" asked Friedrich Delitzsch (1850–1922), the great German Assyriologist and philologist, in his famous lecture "*Babel und Bibel.*" "What is the reason for this expensive churning up of rubble that has lain undisturbed for many thousands of years, for this digging down as deep as the ground water, with no hope of gold or silver? . . . What is the basis of this ever-mounting, world-wide in-

terest in the excavations in Babylonia-Assyria?" His climax was one calculated to fire the minds of our fathers and grandfathers: "To both questions there is one answer: . . . the Bible!"

The first travelers to bring back fresh accounts from the lands that figure so gloriously and terribly in the Bible were adventurers, some rich and some poor, some learned scholars and some ignorant curiosity-seekers. The reports of these discoverers, most of them men of the seventeenth century, conjure up an exotic and forbidding scene:

"It may still be seen . . . but is so decayed and in ruin that it is of no height at all, and the ground is everywhere about for half a mile so full of vermin that no one dares go near. . . . Among these vermin are especially small beasts which in the

(164)

ur on edifia la tour de babilome et langue re fuft mue en .lr.rij. langages et les auoyt ee la circuirut.

Persian are called *Eglo*, . . . and are very poisonous; they are larger than lizards and have three heads. . . ." Such is the acount given in 1582 by Leonhard Rauwolff, a physician and botanist of Augsburg, ten years after he had visited the place.

In similar vein, George Mainwaring writes in 1598 of "the Tower that Nimrud built. . . . It standeth in a wilderness, and so many wild beasts be about it that a man cannot come near to it by two miles or more; but it may be seen plainly."

However, "I made a complete circuit of these ruins," reports the first traveler of the seventeenth century, in which men of the West began to feel an ardor for digging up their past. "I climbed to the highest point, walked all over the crags and made a detailed examination." The traveler who wrote this was Pietro della Valle (1586–1652).

The picture on page 164 was first published in 1679 by Athanasius Kircher in his learned work *Turris Babel*, and purports to be based on the observations of "Petro a valle" (see scroll at the top of the picture). The Pietro whose authority was thus appealed to was an Italian nobleman who, rejected by a lady whom he had wooed passionately for years, decided to make a pilgrimage to the Holy Land. From there he rode off into the desert and fell even more passionately in love.

Pietro had difficulty curing her of the habit of wearing a nose ring.

Her name was Sitti Maani; she was a young Nestorian Christian girl from Baghdad, by all accounts bewitching, and she turned Pietro's head completely. In 1616 he married her.

Her portrait would not belong in this book if this girl, whom Pietro first had to educate, had not become for him the same inspiration that the lovely Greek girl Sophia became for Schliemann centuries later: not only a wife, but an assistant, a brave and indefatigable companion on journeys that

(166)

soon became legendary. This ideal partnership lasted only five years; then Maani died from a fever resulting from a miscarriage. Pietro brought her body back to Rome to be buried in his family mausoleum.

All in all, Pietro della Valle spent some twelve years traveling in the East, venturing as far as India and Goa. In 1626 he returned to Europe permanently. A first volume of his account of his travels, *Viaggi di Pietro della Valle il Pellegrino*, was published in 1650; two further volumes appeared six years after his death, in 1658. They had a profound effect upon the mentality of Europe.

Pietro was the first European traveler in the East whom we may credit with a scientific point of view. He was also the first to describe the ruins of that legendary metropolis of the Persians which henceforth was repeatedly to become the starting-point of new research: Persepolis. His books are valuable for their descriptive rather than for their pictorial material; for illustration he used copies of drawings by other eyewitnesses. A period of twenty-four years intervened between the end of his travels and the publication of his first book. Meanwhile, others had followed his footsteps to Persepolis, and had not waited so long before publishing their view of one of the proudest cities of ancient history.

The first view of Persepolis.

"From this room is a stately prospect of all the Plaines thirty miles about it. The ascent to this is cut out of marble Rockes, the staires (reserving their durance and beauty to this day) are ninetie five, and so broad that a dozen Horsemen may ride up abreast together. . . . The breadth of the Gate is sixe of my paces, the height of each side or Gate (engraven with a mightie Elephant on one side, a Rhynoceros on the other) thirty foot high, very rarely cut out of the marble, fixt and durable for ever."

Instead of attempting to convey this overall grandeur, the artist employed by the

RVINES of

PERSÆPOLIS

The Valley

traveler concentrated on reproducing all the details furnished by the traveler's text—details altogether false because they were seen in classical and Biblical terms. Thus, a rearing Pegasus appears (as shown on page 167) amid the ruins of Persepolis, and elephant and rhinoceros are presented as tidy little sculptures, not as reliefs. The traveler was Thomas Herbert, who found the artist's work so unsatisfactory that for the third edition of his book he had the drawings done anew by Wenzel Hollar, the famous landscape artist (as shown above). Hollar gave a sense of the splendor and spaciousness of the ruins, but his work, too, left much to be desired.

Thomas Herbert (1606–1682) set out on his first journey to the East in 1626, a penniless boy of twenty attached to the retinue of two profit-hungry diplomats, Sir Robert Sherley and Sir Dodmore Cotton, whose sad end is described with notable brevity in the *Dictionary of National Biography*: "They then visited Mount Taurus and Casbin, where Cotton and Sherley died." Herbert coolly and simply concludes his report: "At Kazvin . . . where we left our two ambassadors in their grave, the Shah sent each of us two long mantles or coats of gold brocade, as a sign of his favour." Three years later he returned home via Ceylon, and served Charles I as chamberlain. He remained so unflinchingly loyal to the King until and beyond Charles's execution that Charles II later knighted him.

(168)

Persepolis was the capital

of one of the mightiest empires of antiquity. Cyrus (559–529 B.C.), Cambyses (529–522 B.C.), and Darius I (521–485 B.C.), starting from the existing kingdoms of the Medes, the Lydians, the Chaldeans, and the Egyptians, absorbed Iranian principates extending as far as the Indus, took over the politically chaotic coastal countries of Asia Minor, and forged all this into a Great Persian Empire that extended from Cyrenaica in Africa into Europe as far as the Danube. For two centuries that empire governed the destinies of the ancient world.

The City of the Persians (*Parsa* in Old Persian) was the metropolis of this immense empire. Darius I founded Persepolis as a fortress on an enormous artificial terrace. The site is colossal; only the latest ex-

cavations, undertaken for the Oriental Institute of the University of Chicago between 1930 and 1940 by Ernst Herzfeld (1879–1948) and Erich F. Schmidt (b. 1897), have revealed the tremendous wealth of buildings. The royal palace contained vast treasure and countless works of art—one of the early travelers speaks of more than two thousand reliefs. It was set afire by Alexander the Great after the battle of Gaugamela (331 B.C.), in which he overwhelmingly defeated Darius III. Ancient writers relate that the razing of the palace was an act conceived in drunkenness and arrogance.

The picture shows the first view of these ruins which was actually drawn on the spot —the artist being a young French merchant, André Daulier des Landes, who accompanied the explorer Jean-Baptiste Tavernier from 1664 to 1666. He drew these ruins in 1665 and published his work eight years later.

It would be wearying to list examples of the many copies of this one drawing; the seventeenth century was not scrupulous about artistic or intellectual property. But it is amusing to watch for the peregrinations of the small rider in the foreground from copy to copy. Almost every copyist included him, but each placed him in another spot.

After these last examples some reader may ask why pictures so obviously faulty by the light of present knowledge should be reproduced. There are three reasons. First, these drawings abound in quaint details that have a charm of their own. Second, matching these early views with later, scientifically inspired pictures of the same scene offers dramatic proof of the progress of scientific archaeology. We can actually see how the first tentative sketches necessarily proceeded from wholly inadequate accounts, and with what painful slowness scientific reports developed out of fabulous narratives. And the third reason is the respect due to the men themselves, who were driven to far places by an insurmountable craving for knowledge, and who almost always risked their lives to bring home these first tidings; they pioneered the path to the sources of our civilization.

Blood-soaked soil.

The simple-hearted historical maps of the past locate the Garden of Eden in Mesopotamia. (The map below is modern.) Whether or not it was here that Adam toiled and Eve span and mankind had its cradle, it was very likely the cradle of human civilization. Here emerged the earliest scripts, the earliest architecture, and the earliest sciences. Here the Sumerians and their successors, the Babylonians and Assyrians, founded the first states. Egyptians and Persians invaded them; rarely did peace prevail in these lands, which nevertheless gave birth to the religion of peace and good will. Here the road traveled by Abraham still winds across the plain, and here the teachings of Mohammed took hold and spread. Here was the world of the Arabian Nights, the world of Harun-al-Rashid. Here Greeks, Romans, and Arabs ruled; and through this gateway passed all the trade and bustling commerce between Orient and Occident. Buffer land, occupied land, border land—Mesopotamia has always been in upheaval, down to the present day.

Jean Chardin was a jeweler.

Born in Paris (1643–1713), he went to Baghdad in 1666. Thence, as Sultan Suliman III's gem expert, he was sent to India, and returned to Paris around 1670. On his first journey, perhaps, he had been nothing but a man seeking worldly success by adventurous routes. But on his second he manifested a lively interest in the history, languages, and monuments of Persia. As it happened, in 1666 *Philosophical Transactions*, the journal of the Royal Society, then the most important body of scholars in the world, had queried: "Whether, there beeing already good Descriptions in *Words* of the Excellent Pictures and Basse Relieves, that are about *Persepolis* at *Chilminar*, yet none very particular; some may not be found sufficiently skill'd in those parts, that might be engaged to make a Draught of the Place, and the Stories there pictured and carved?"

When Chardin arrived in England in 1681, after much voyaging, he was knighted, appointed court jeweler, and elected a Fellow of the Royal Society. He had provided an answer to the Royal Society's challenging question.

(172)

This was the reception given a distinguished European traveler

around 1666 by one of the lesser Persian potentates. The viceroy of Tiflis, Kanavas Khan, held this feast in honor of Jean Chardin. The scene is the princely banquet hall, 110 feet long and 40 feet wide. Chardin is seated at left foreground, accompanied by Capuchin monks. The Khan is presiding at the other end of the huge pavilion. Before the feast he had received several presents from Chardin: a watch, a rock-crystal mirror framed in silver, an enameled gold box for his opium pills ("most Persians take these pills several times a day"), as well as a handsome set of surgical instruments.

Many archaeologists' reports even today testify to the importance of Oriental hospitality and to its often disconcerting features. The field archaeologist must be not only a scholar, but also a diplomat and man of the world. He must hold his own with cabinet ministers as well as with bands of rioting workmen. Frequently the success or failure of an expedition is decided at a banquet!

One hundred and two pounds and a few shillings

posthumously bought not only this picture but also the complete manuscript left by Engelbert Kämpfer (1651–1716), a German physician who had returned from his travels in Persia with an amazingly accurate sketchbook. The purchaser was Sir Hans Sloane, avid English collector, whose bequest formed the beginning of the British Museum. The folio is still there, one of the museum's original treasures.

Of all the early visitors to Persia, Kämpfer was the first to anticipate the spirit of the coming century. He was the first to speak of the artistic value of the discoveries, and again the first to mourn the senseless destruction of antiquities. Speaking of the

portals to the throne room of Xerxes in Persepolis, he wrote: "These gates are decorated with most elegantly sculptured reliefs, and offer a most outstanding example from which to understand the excellence the arts had attained in those ancient times." And he adds: "One must deplore the criminal act of the tyrant who caused the main portions of these images to be defaced, as well as the ravages wrought by the centuries passing over them, in the course of which most of the lintels and part of the doorjambs were broken, apart from those which have been carried off from time to time for private use by those living nearby."

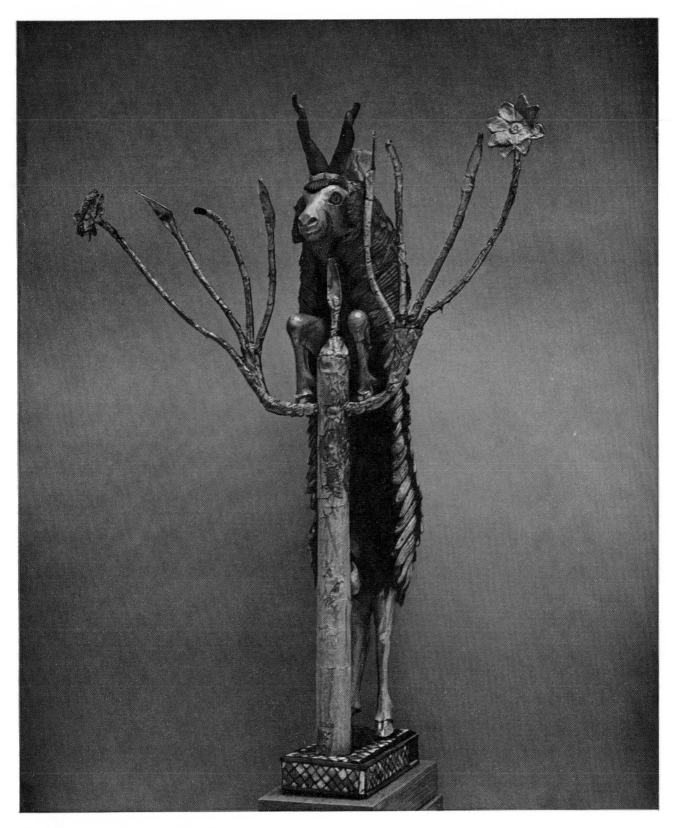

IX. Billy goat at the tree of life. Polychrome figure on wooden core (*c.* 2500 B.C.). From Ur of the Chaldees, the home of Abraham.

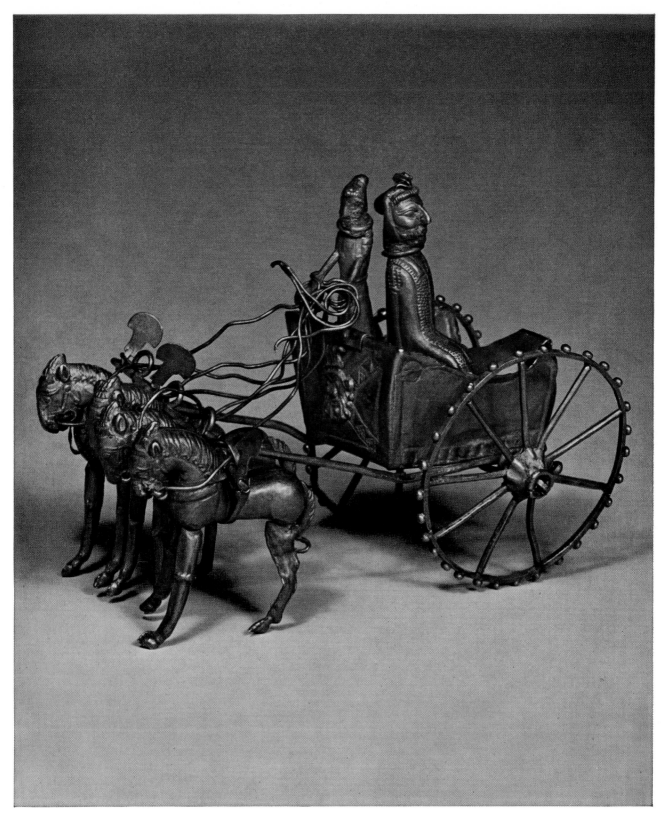

X. Model of Persian war chariot. Fifth to fourth century B.C., from the "Oxus treasure," found 1877.

The strange world of the East

was extraordinarily difficult for men with Western eyes to render. That fact emerges clearly from the reproductions on this page and the next. Above is the very first representation of the human-headed, winged bull that guarded Xerxes' gates at Persepolis. It seems almost incredible that this unfortunate and stilted engraving was made by a professional draftsman who had been at the site, but so it was. It was by Guillaume Joseph Grélot (born around 1630), who had accompanied Chardin and who worked from Chardin's sketches.

Contrast such crude work with the drawing by Cornelis de Bruin (1652–1726/7) on the next page. De Bruin, we may well say,

had the first critical mind among the early travelers. He reproduced the lineaments of the original with almost photographic faithfulness. Moreover, he left blank those portions of the sculpture which were broken, in preference to filling in with fanciful details of his own. Nowadays we take for granted such striving for exactitude; in De Bruin's time it was an eccentricity for someone to wish to depict what he actually saw.

De Bruin consciously stressed his critical approach and took issue with the copying, "restoring," and pure plagiarisms current at the time in his pamphlet: *Remarks of Cornelis de Bruin on the Plates of the Ancient*

Palace of Persepolis Published by Sir John Chardin and Mr. Kempfer, "in which their faults and lacks are clearly shown," and in his *Travels over Muscovy, through Persia and India,* where he commented: "I can affirm, too, that I have drawn with my own Hand, and immediately from the Life, all the Plates, now presented to the Public, without having recourse to any ancient Authors who have described *Persepolis* and its Antiquities, and without adding or diminishing one Particular." He continues: "I might say much the same of *Persia,* and the august Ruins of the Ancient Palace of *Persepolis,* of which several travellers have published Discriptions, without due Examination of what they saw. For which reason their accounts have more the air of Romance than of any Reality, or compleate Knowledge of those fine Antiquities, which is not to be obtained without pains."

With Cornelis de Bruin we come to a new chapter in the March of Archaeology. For not only did he bring back the first reliable descriptions of the world of the Orient; he also brought back not the first, but the first legible cuneiform texts in as accurate a transcription as could be had at the time. Studying one of these transcriptions, the German schoolteacher Grotefend hit on the solution for the decipherment of cuneiform script. His was a fantastically bold hypothesis—but was the first step in the West's penetration of the mentality of the ancient East.

From right to left or from left to right?

These are the first five signs in cuneiform script that reached Europe. They were transcribed in a letter from Pietro della Valle to his friend Schipano in Naples, and later appeared in the first printed edition of this and other letters.

The substance of Pietro's letter, dated Shiraz, October 21, 1621, is most interesting. His first question was the very one any decipherer must pose when confronted by an unknown script: in what direction are the figures to be read? A clay tablet presents many possibilities—not only right to left and up and down; a widespread mode of writing—used, for example, by the Hittites—was the fashion later called *bustrophedon*, which means: "as the ox turns in plowing," namely ⇒⇐ , so that the first line is read from right to left, the second from left to right, the third like the first, and so on.

Remarkably enough, Pietro immediately deduced correctly from the position of the wedges that the script was written "in our manner, from left to right," as he puts it on the page of his letter reproduced here.

His transcription is not accurate. And he could not guess that by chance he had selected a group of signs which, as we know today, forms part of the Achaemenidean title "king of kings"—the very inscription that some 180 years later allowed a German schoolteacher to unlock the riddle of cuneiform script.

annoch nicht begreiffen kan.

Es mögen nun dieses gleich bloſſe Buchſtaben / oder gantze Wörter geweſt ſeyn / ſo habe ich fünff derſelben/ die ich in dieſer Schrifft am öfterſten geſehen/ und gekandt/ſo gut/als mir müglich geweſt / abgeſchrieben. Weil es aber gantze Zeilen geweſt / ſo kunte ich nicht wiſſen / ob man dieſe Buchſtaben / nach der Orientaliſchen Völcker Gebrauch / von der rechten / zur Lincken / oder aber / auf unſere Weiſe / von der lincken zur rechten Hand ſchreiben müſſe. Die fünff Buchſtaben nun/ die ich auffgezeichnet / waren folgende.

Der zweyte Buchſtabe aber / welcher in vier Strichen beſtunde/ worunter drey gerad/ und unten zugeſpitzt / der vierte aber überzwerch darüber geſetzt war / gab mir ein Anzeichen / daß ſie / auf unſere Weiſe / von der lincken zur rechten Hand geſchrieben werden können; alldieweiln das Obertheil an dieſen Strichen / wie an allen andern Buchſtaben zu ſehen / breit iſt / und wann ſie gerad ſind/
M 4   allzeit

"Like bird tracks on wet sand."

This is how cuneiform script struck the first Europeans to lay eyes on it. Some called it "nail script," but a good many persons, among them serious scholars, denied that it was a script at all. Unlike the Egyptian hieroglyphics, cuneiform script had already been forgotten in classical times. Herodotus barely mentions it as *Assyria grammata.* Yet cuneiform script had been diffused far more widely than hieroglyphics. Along the whole of the eastern Mediterranean coast, in the empire of the Hittites in Anatolia, in the land of Urartu in the Armenian mountains, in southwestern Iran, and as far as the land of Elam, many languages adopted cuneiform script for their writings. It was a vital script at the time of the Persian Great Kings.

The apparently hastily done transcription reproduced here is in fact an amazing prize. This first long example of a cuneiform text comes from Engelbert Kämpfer's sketchbook. After his long journey through Russia, after crossing the Caspian Sea, and after months of vain attendance at the Shah's court in Isfahan—the Shah refused to help him, claiming that the astrological signs were unfavorable to the venture—

Kämpfer reached Persepolis in 1685. Events did not permit him to remain longer than three days amid this vast congeries of ruins. During those days he labored feverishly, forgetting to eat, drink, or sleep, making innumerable notes and sketches. Later he was fully conscious of the value of what he brought home. His pride rings out in his aside: "My uninspired engraver has not succeeded in rendering the beauty of this lettering, for he has not given it the proper spacing which makes the characters stand out distinctly. I mean by this, that my own copy of the inscription which served as model to the engraver, is far more accurate." But then he admits, still overwhelmed in memory as he recalls his toil: "In truth the copying of this single tablet made such an unthinkably lengthy job, particularly as the place is so high up which makes the sun most obnoxious, that I was forced to give up the idea of copying the others. . . ."

A man who had not only a keen eye but also an astounding organizing ability brought home the next cuneiform texts. He was a Dane whose books Napoleon always had by him during the Egyptian campaign.

and returned home alone.

Carsten Niebuhr (1733–1815) was a geographer who by no means confined his interests to his specialty. Accompanied by Herr von Haven, a philologist, Forskål, a natural-scientist, Cramer, a physician, and Baurenfeind, an artist, he set out on an expedition in January 1761. Although they sailed on a Danish ship of war, it took them almost two years to reach their destination, Yemen. In the course of the following year all the members of the expedition except Niebuhr died. His account of this in his *Reisebeschreibung von Arabien und andern umliegenden Ländern* (*Description of Travels in Arabia and Neighboring Lands*), published in Copenhagen in 1774–8, is certainly singular:

"The scholars . . . might surely have expected to bring back much important information on Arabia, if we had remained as long in this country as we intended, and if all had returned. However, we did not arrive in Yemen until the end of December 1762. Mr. von Haven died very soon, on the 25th of May, at Móchha, and Mr. Forskål on July 11th at Yeri, another town in Yemen. After the sudden loss of these two companions, the rest of us decided to go to Bombay aboard the last of the ships that were sailing this year from Móchha to India. On this voyage Mr. Baurenfeind died at sea, near the island of Socotra, on August 29th, and Mr. Cramer on February 10, 1764 at Bombay. Although death has almost entirely wiped out our company, I do not believe that this fact should deter others from undertaking journeys to Arabia. . . ."

This curt catalogue of successive deaths brings to mind the children's jingle, "Ten little Indians . . . then there was one." Niebuhr was a cold man, but he was possessed of extraordinary intelligence and a gift for observation. It may well have been his youth that brought him safely through the unspeakable hardships of this hazardous expedition, and enabled him to return with such a bag of scientific trophies.

The plate from Niebuhr's book, reproduced here, shows reliefs from Persepolis and six lines of cuneiform signs. (The legend above these signs reads: "Various letters of the oldest Persian script.") Without these, Grotefend, the Göttingen schoolteacher, would probably never have succeeded in his attempt at decipherment. For Niebuhr's transcript was not a mere sample of an inscription. With admirable keenness and instinct he had sorted individual signs out of the numerous inscriptions and drawn up a list of forty-two characters. (Assyriologists nowadays reckon with thirty-nine basic signs.) Futhermore, solely from the number of signs, he correctly deduced that the script must be based on letters—that is, it was an early form of alphabet—simply because there were too few signs for syllabic writing. On the other hand, he perceived that there were too many signs for a purely consonantal alphabet; vowels must also be included. And finally—this is the most astonverschiedene Buchstaben der ältesten persischen Schrift.

ishing feat of all—he recognized that three different systems of writing were represented by the inscriptions at Persepolis. Scholars later named these systems Old Persian I, Elamitic II, and Babylonian III. Incidentally, he also made vital observations on ancient geography. While scholars were still assuming that ancient Babylon had been located in the vicinity of present-day Baghdad, Niebuhr stated bluntly and correctly: "There can be no doubt that Babylon was situated in the neighborhood of Helle [Hilla]." He established the site of Nineveh with equal accuracy.

To explain the manner by which cuneiform script may be deciphered, we must leap somewhat ahead of the state of knowledge in Niebuhr's day.

Cuneiform script also developed out of pictures.

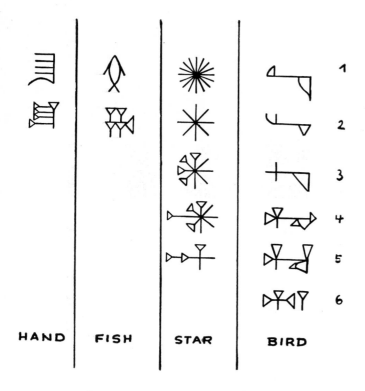

HAND	FISH	STAR	BIRD	
				1
				2
				3
				4
				5
				6

While this is fairly obvious in the case of Egyptian hieroglyphics, cuneiform writing seems at first glance quite another proposition. The examples above, however, make the evolution from picture to sign quite plain. The five fingers of the sign for "hand" are intelligible enough, as are "fish" and "star." We may not, however, recognize at once that the uppermost sign on the right represents a bird, as it is already so highly abstract. Nevertheless, it is a bird flying from right to left.

A factor making for radical stylization was the writing materials themselves. The Egyptians used ink and papyrus; Babylonians, on the other hand, impressed clay tablets with a stylus. The more laborious method necessitated a simplification of the script.

The publication of Niebuhr's *Reisebeschreibung* in the late eighteenth century sent a wave of excitement through the scientific world. More and more scholars pored over cuneiform script. In 1798 a German orientalist, Olav Gerhard Tychsen, identified an apparently insignificant but highly important sign. It was an oblique wedge, which he recognized as the word-divider. He was thus able to insert some order into the apparently endless lines. He also hazarded, quite correctly, that three different systems had been employed for writing three different languages. Friedrich Münter, a Danish scholar, ventured still further in 1802. For historical reasons he maintained that the Persepolitan inscriptions dated from the Achaemenidian period, the era of the Great Kings of Persia, between 500 and 330 B.C. He also advanced the thesis that the trilingual inscriptions contained the same text in three languages.

These were conjectures that turned out to be marvelously apt. In point of fact, these early investigators were voices crying in a wilderness; wrong theories by and large prevailed. The first real decipherer to approach the inscrutable scratchings found the way to a solution blocked by a host of wild theories. His primary task consisted in sifting the few correct hypotheses out of the many that were utterly misleading. He succeeded.

(182)

In 1802 Georg Friedrich Grotefend made a wager.

While walking with his friend Fiorillo, secretary of the Royal Library at Göttingen, Grotefend (1775–1853) wagered that he would decipher the cuneiform scripts from Persepolis if Fiorillo would supply him with the previously published literature on the subject. This daring fellow was twenty-seven and a mere nobody; he taught at the *Gymnasium* in Göttingen and knew scarcely anything about the ancient languages of the Orient. By a stroke of genius this man performed one of the most amazing feats of human intelligence. Not that he became famous thereby; he continued on through life as a schoolmaster without ever again climbing to the chilly heights of intellect which he had scaled at his first youthful attempt.

In contrast to Champollion, who had spent more than fifteen years in preliminary study of ancient languages before he tackled the actual decipherment of hieroglyphics, Grotefend's professional equipment was scanty. The specimens at his disposal were also scanty, and he had no way of ascertaining whether these were exact. Above all, he had not a single parallel inscription in a readable language, like the Greek on Champollion's Rosetta Stone.

Nevertheless, Grotefend deciphered Persepolitan cuneiform script! He set forth his conclusions in three reports. As the subject was of such high current interest, these were read almost at once before the Academy of Sciences in Göttingen on September 4, October 2, and November 13, 1802.

Grotefend himself did not read his papers —how could an obscure young schoolmaster deliver a lecture before that illustrious learned society? But he was honored by having the above-mentioned Professor Tychsen read his reports. Tychsen also published a first account of Grotefend's work in the *Göttinger Gelehrten Anzeigen* on September 18, 1802. It was not until 1815 that Grotefend was given the chance to present a complete account of his decipherment in less transitory form. His summing-up appeared in the appendix to someone else's book, Heeren's *Ideen über die Politik, den Verkehr und den Handel der vornehmsten Völker der alten Welt* (*Ideas on the Politics, Communications, and Commerce of the Principal Peoples of the Ancient World*), at Heeren's own request. Thus the incredible happened; due to a lack of publicity, Grotefend's brilliant contribution fell into oblivion. Decades later Persepolitan cuneiform script had to be deciphered anew.

Here is the same text twice,

once in De Bruin's excellent copy (right, above), and again as re-transcribed by Grotefend and cast into alphabetical equivalents. Grotefend's method can be presented here only in the most rankly simplified form. For a first step, Grotefend examined the available texts, including the one reproduced above (inscriptions taken from the folds of the clothes of Darius' and Xerxes' portraits; in the heading Grotefend writes Lebrun instead of De Bruin), and reviewed the existing hypotheses. He accepted the thesis that there were three systems of writing, that the content of all three texts was the same, that the inscription must be ascribed to the Achaemenides, the Persian Kings, and that the single oblique wedge represented a word-divider.

Second step: He decided to begin his solution with Script I, Old Persian, because this Indo-European language might be easiest to crack with the assistance of recent researches in Sanskrit. The character of the script and the site at which it had been found led him to the conclusion that he was dealing with royal inscriptions. Hence Old Persian kings ought to be mentioned by name. He knew some of the Achaemenidian kings from the writings of Herodotus (to this day we are scarcely any wiser on the subject than was Grotefend). And he set up the premise that the inscriptions began, as such did in New Persian, with a list of generations, thus:

X, Great King, King of Kings, King of A and B, Son of Y, Great King, King of Kings. . . .

Third step: In counting up the groups of signs, he found precisely the repetitions which, according to his hypothesis, must mean *king*. But he also found a new arrangement, namely:

X, King, son of Z,

Y, King, son of X, King.

Here he had worked out, in pure theory for the time being, a distinctive dynastic succession. Father and son had been kings, but the grandfather had not been a king. Now he took the names of known kings and tried to fit them into his scheme. Some were eliminated immediately because their names contained too many or too few letters. After much trial and error, only Darius and Xerxes remained. And they matched, for the father of Darius, Hystaspes, had not been a king.

Fourth step: One great difficulty still remained. Herodotus had given the kings' names only in Greek. But what were the Old Persian forms? There were a great many possibilities. But in choosing among them Grotefend demonstrated amazing intuition. For although, as we know today, he made many errors, he also found a great many correct correspondences. He interpreted rightly a large number of letters, and thus laid the basis for his decipherment of cuneiform script.

Persepolitanische Inschriften des Darius und Xerxes auf den Falten des Gewandes ihrer Bilder.
Lebrun N. 133.

1. II. ... III. ... D ā r h ā usch. R. no hu.

2. II. ... Dā r h ê u sch. R. z à z ro. We sch tà ç p. á-

3. I. ... ā ç p a h ā. p u th. a kh ā o s ō sch ō h.

4. I. ... D ā r h ō u sch. R. ê gh r ê. G ō sch t

5. VII. ... Kh sch ā th r sch. R. Dā r h ê u sch. R. á ghe r.

6. I. ... D ā r h ê a u sch. Kh sch ā h i ō h a h ā. p u th.

(185)

To anticipate: Grotefend deciphered only the Old Persian form of the Persepolitan cuneiform scripts. Decipherment of the Babylonian and Elamite inscriptions—far older forms of cuneiform writing—were matters for professional philologists, as we shall see shortly. "Decipherer and philologist," says Professor Johannes Friedrich, one of the foremost German philologists, "must not be confounded." He pays ample tribute to the genius of the decipherers, but points out that final interpretation and establishment of all the grammatical laws in the deciphered script and language are the business of the pure professional. Grotefend himself, incidentally, had made the same point.

For all that, Grotefend's inspired solution remains immortal. It is one of the incomprehensible whims of history that Champollion won an international reputation, while Grotefend was almost ignored.

"It was accidentally discovered by a director

of the East India Company that one of their young cadets was a perfect self-taught master of the Arabic, Persian, and other Oriental languages," *The Times* of London reported in 1804. The young cadet was Claudius James Rich (1787–1821), born in Dijon, France, and taken to Bristol, England, at an early age. He was an authentic child prodigy: while still a boy he acquired a command of Turkish, Persian, Arabic, Hebrew, Syrian, and a little Chinese. The East India Company was eager to employ a young man with such linguistic gifts. He was sent to Bombay in 1807, en route passing through Mesopotamia for the first time. In Bombay he won the hand of the eldest daughter of the chief magistrate, Sir James Mackintosh, for all that he had not a penny to his name. This portrait of Rich, from the British Museum, is by an unknown artist.

Baghdad, where he settled with his wife in 1808, served him as the starting-point for many scientific excursions. His first visit to Babylon in December 1811 lasted only ten days; the material and observations he brought back from this little jaunt were sufficient to keep scholars occupied for years. With a tiny crew of ten workmen, he had conducted a regular excavation and reaped a fine harvest of inscribed stones, clay tablets, and seals. In 1817 he made a second trip, accompanied by Carl Bellino, a young artist who acted as his secretary. Bellino happened to be a good friend of the schoolmaster Grotefend, who was thus supplied with new texts to study. Rich's two publications, *Memoir on the Ruins of Babylon* (Vienna, 1812) and *Second Memoir on Babylon* (London, 1818), aroused great excitement, and not only among scholars, as the following lines from Byron's *Don Juan* (V, 62) indicate:

But to resume,—should there be (what may not
Be in these days?) some infidels, who don't,
Because they can't, find out the very spot
Of that same Babel, or because they won't
(Though Claudius Rich, Esquire, some bricks has got,
And written lately two memoirs upon't,)
Believe the Jews, those unbelievers, who
Must be believed, though they believe not you.

Rich himself commented modestly that his work was but "the first fruits of imperfect research," and he added: "I had expected to find on the site of Babylon more, and less, than I actually did. . . . I announce no discovery, I advance no interesting hypothesis."

Bellino died in 1820. In the following year Rich was once more in Shiraz. A cholera epidemic broke out. Rich refused to leave the city; he took a hand in nursing the sick and dying, and organized shipments of medical supplies into the city. On October 4, 1821, he too fell victim to the plague, and was dead the following morning—at the age of thirty-four.

His collections were purchased by the British Museum for a thousand pounds. They included eight hundred Oriental man-

uscripts and thirty-two cuneiform tablets. Moreover, he left behind voluminous writings from which his widow extracted several books. Although these were published under his name, she unfortunately included a heavy admixture of her own ideas.

This plan of Babylon exemplifies

the precision of Rich's work. On his first visit to Babylon in 1811 he surveyed the area of ruins on the eastern side of the Euphrates, and had Captain Abraham Lockett, then British military commander at Baghdad, execute the map shown here. It is the frontispiece of his *Memoir on the Ruins of Babylon*, published in 1815. Amazingly enough, this plan largely coincides with one Robert Koldewey was to make nearly a century later—after he had excavated the ruins.

A painter of battles

gathered new lore of the empires of the Babylonians and the Assyrians. Robert Ker Porter (1777–1842), whose once highly admired pictures no one ever looks at nowadays, switched careers in midstream, so moved was he by the sublime monotones of the Mesopotamian landscape, and by the mute testimony of its scattered monuments. He gave up flamboyant painting for painstaking copying. It was through a friend, Alexis von Olenin of St. Petersburg, that he came to realize the need for such dispassionate recording. One day in 1817 Olenin showed Porter four drawings (shown assembled on the next page), by Niebuhr, De Bruin, Morier, and Chardin, all of the same carving. Comparing the four, Porter's practiced eye at once recognized how strongly subjective differences had influenced the artists in their treatment of the same subject.

Ker Porter must have been a cosmopolitan spirit with a great flair for society. Born in Edinburgh, he was elected a member of the Royal Academy at the age of fourteen, and at twenty-three painted his 130-foot panorama, *The Storming of Seringapatam*, which created a great sensation. As a matter of fact, this immense canvas is by no means devoid of artistic and technical skill. In 1804 he resided at the court of Czar Alexander I as the official painter of battles. There he fell in love with Maria, daughter of Prince Theodore Sherbatoff. This was not regarded favorably, and he was forced to leave the country.

Eccentric King Gustav IV of Sweden knighted him in 1806. By 1811 Porter had managed to return to Russia, and after the retreat of the Napoleonic army he married his Princess Sherbatoff. His reputation as an artist, his polished manner, and his many influential connections brought him knighthood in England in 1813. By grace of George IV he was thenceforth Sir Robert.

After 1817 he traveled through the Caucasus to Teheran, Isfahan, and Persepolis.

(189)

In October 1818 he met Rich in Baghdad. For the next two years he drew and described whatever he saw—with sterling accuracy.

On November 18, 1818, Bellino, Rich's secretary, dispatched a letter from Baghdad to his friend Grotefend in Göttingen, Germany: "On October 13 an Englishman arrived here from Persia. His name is Sir Robert Ker-Porter. . . . His drawings . . . surpass everything that anyone in the past has made of these antiquities, in the opinion of Mr. Rich, who draws well himself. . . . Although they differ from those of earlier travelers, I do not doubt that he is concerned chiefly with fidelity to his origi-nal. . . . The drawings which Sir Robert has prepared here of Babylonian cylinder seals and other objects are also uncommonly faithful."

In 1821 Porter published his book, *Travels in Georgia, Persia, Armenia and Ancient Babylonia*. Typhus robbed him of his princess in 1826, and he sought forgetfulness in the New World, assuming the post of British consul in Venezuela. There he painted what has come to be the best-known portrait of Simón Bolívar, the liberator of South America. He died of a stroke in 1842 —all in all, a remarkable personality, whose biography remains to be written.

Four artists, four different conceptions.

Here is the sample Olenin showed to his friend Ker Porter. All four artists had drawn the Naksh-i-Rustam reliefs, which had earlier been drawn by Kämpfer. It is highly instructive to see the distortions Niebuhr, De Bruin, Morier, and Chardin imposed on the selfsame subject. The juxtaposition is itself a nice example of the romantic manner; completely in keeping with the spirit of the age, it is tricked out with two Babylonian inscriptions, above; a cylinder seal; three Greek inscriptions; and finally, at the top, three different representations of Alexander the Great, from three coins.

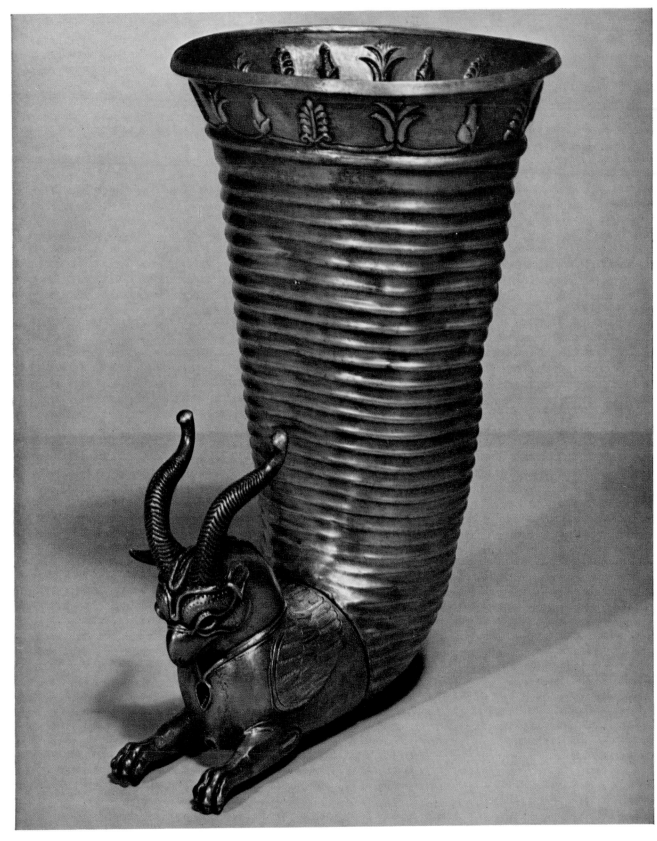

XI. Persian drinking-horn. Gold and silver (fifth century B.C.). From the "Oxus
treasure," found 1877.

XII. Headdress of a queen of Ur. Golden ornaments of Queen Shub-ad, from the royal graves at Ur (*c.* 2500 B.C.). Leaves were the favorite ornamental motif of the period. British Museum, London, from the finds of Leonard Woolley.

"The figure drawn up,

to explore the interior of the Tomb of
Darius Hystaspes, is that of Sir Robert Ker
Porter himself—a height of 60 feet," wrote
his sister Jane. It is amusing to visualize
the gentleman-painter portrayed on page
189 in such a situation—and this in 1818,
when there might have been at most a few
dozen persons in the world who could
understand a man's risking his life for the
sake of archaeological knowledge.

"The morning was at first stormy,

and threatened a severe fall of rain; but as we approached the object of our journey, the heavy clouds separating discovered the Birs frowning over the plain (and presenting the appearance of a circular hill crowned by a tower, with a high ridge extending along the foot of it). . . . Just as we were within the proper distance, it burst at once upon our sight, in the midst of rolling masses of thick black clouds, partially obscured by that kind of haze whose indistinctness is one great cause of sublimity, whilst a few strong patches of stormy light, thrown upon the desert in the back ground, serve to give some idea of the immense extent, and dreary solitude, of the wastes in which this venerable ruin stands."

The picture at left, above, by Ker Porter (the text is by Rich) shows Birs Nimrud, on the Tigris near Mosul, as seen from the west. The diagram Porter presents in the drawing below it is an inspired piece of deduction, although the height is wrong. Porter reckoned about 240 feet instead of the 140 calculated by modern archaeologists.

"I should suppose," Rich wrote, "the mass we now see to be no more than the base of some loftier superstructure, probably designed for the double use of a temple and an observatory; a style of sacred edifice common with the Chaldaeans and likely to form the principal object in every city and town devoted to the idolatry of Belus and the worship of the stars."

This intuition of the purpose and original

form of all Babylonian "towers," the zig-gurats, inevitably struck his age as revolutionary. But people were already beginning to ask for more than drawings and narratives. Museums sprang up; originally mere curio-cabinets, they now grew into scientifically classified collections. Their nucleus consisted of sculptures and casts of the Greco-Roman period, but now monuments from the Ancient East were in demand. Soon the demand was supplied. A Scottish army officer, defying innumerable difficulties and bad luck, proved the feasibility of transporting such monuments.

"Take your steamship on your back and walk . . .

from the Orontes to the Euphrates."

A Scottish officer, disgruntled because he could not participate in the fight against Napoleon, sought a different kind of adventure in the Orient.

Captain (later General) Francis Rawdon Chesney (1789–1872) brooded over the possibility of opening new routes between England and India. After a voyage to Egypt in 1829 he published a report on the possibility of piercing the Isthmus of Suez—a dream that decades later prompted Ferdinand de Lesseps, the builder of the canal, to dub him "Father of the Suez Canal."

Unable to muster support for the Suez undertaking, Chesney turned his attention to another possible route, and this by chance led him past those ruined cities whose names were soon to be on everyone's lips: Assur, Babylon, and Ur. The fantastic route he had in mind was the following: from the Mediterranean near Antioch upstream on the Orontes, then by land to the Euphrates, downstream to the Persian Gulf, and on to India.

The wildness of this plan seems obvious. How could ships be transported overland? Moreover, was the Euphrates navigable at all, especially for steam vessels?

In 1830–1 Chesney began investigating the navigability of the Euphrates. The lithograph reproduced here (upper right), from the account of the journey which he later published, shows him, disguised as a Moslem, aboard a raft in the middle of the river. As he was having difficulties with the Turkish government, he used only two simple instruments for sounding the river and determining the best channel: a pocket compass and a ten-foot pole, which he thrust through a hole in the center of the raft in order to measure the depth of water. In this way he mapped some 180 miles of river, from 'Ana to Hit.

Is this not reminiscent of those ancient Egyptian scenes

of a pharaoh's statue being hauled to its final site (see page 82)? The object being moved with so much effort is actually a steam boiler. Chesney had returned to England and spent four years convincing the government that his plan was practicable. Finally the House of Commons granted him twenty thousand pounds. At the shipyard in Laird, Scotland, Chesney built two

of the most modern river steamers designed up to that time. They were iron-framed. He then had them shipped in parts to the mouth of the Orontes at Antioch. The overland trip required almost a year. Chesney had a staff of thirteen officers and large numbers of artillery and engineering troops, but only the most primitive equipment. The picture below shows the triumphal entry of the last steam boiler into Port Williams on the Euphrates. One hundred and four oxen are harnessed to the load; fifty-two natives and Chesney's entire company are assisting.

In spite of dire predictions, Chesney and his men successfully reassembled and launched the steamers. The vessels set out on their voyage down the Euphrates. But they traveled under an evil star.

Calamity descended on May 21, 1836.

The two steamers, *Tigris* and *Euphrates*, had passed by a whole series of ruined cities without incident—in his *Narrative of the Euphrates Expedition* (1868) Chesney took careful note of each of the cities. Suddenly the sky darkened menacingly.

"The weather had been very fine and promising during the forenoon, but a change took place soon after we left Sala-hyah, and the atmosphere became thick and gloomy—but not more so than had been the case occasionally of late, especially on the preceding evening—and we proceeded on our voyage without the slightest uneasiness being felt by any of our party. At 1.35 p.m. on May 21, both steamers left the bank with the full expectation of reaching Anna that afternoon; but only twenty minutes later, just as we were rounding the bold chalk cliffs on which stand the prominent ruins of Corsote, an ominous change took place in the weather. Clouds, much more threatening than any we had yet seen, appeared and spread rapidly,

accompanied, as Mr. Ainsworth remarked, by a portentous fall of the barometer. Still we did not feel any particular alarm, believing that the storm would pass by, as it had done of late on previous occasions. But we soon found that this was not to be the case now.

"In the course of a few minutes, dense masses of black clouds, streaked with orange, red, and yellow, appeared coming up from the W S W., and approaching us with fearful velocity. To secure the steamers against what promised to be an ordinary strong gale, immediately occupied all our attention, at the very moment that we were arriving at the rocky passage of Is-Geria. Indeed we were already so close to it that there was no sufficient space to round to and bring up: consequently, it became most prudent to steam onwards, the result of which I now give in the words of Mr. Fitzjames:—

" 'A squall was observed on the right hand, which it was thought would not reach us; but just as we were going through the rocky passage of Is-Geria (which, however, we did not see, as there were three feet of water over the rocks), the squall was observed coming in our direction from the W S W. with great rapidity, and looking like a large cloud of black mud. As soon as the rocks were passed, the "Tigris" made signal to pick up our berth, and she rounded by us to the left bank. As our broadside came to the stream, we were taken with the violence of the hurricane, which made us heel considerably; but being too near the "Tigris," it became necessary to back our paddles, to avoid a fatal collision. It was blowing tremendously, and the air so thick

with sand that we could scarcely see. On our bow touching the bank, Charlewood and a number of the crew jumped ashore, and by the greatest exertions got an anchor out, which, with the full power of steam, held her till two chain-cables were got out, and secured by means of jumpers driven into the ground; but with all this she dragged, and would have gone down at her anchor had the storm continued—for the waves were then four feet above the bank of the river. When at its height, we saw the poor "Tigris" fall off from the shore and drift past us at a fearful rate, broadside to the wind, and heeling over considerably. She soon disappeared in the cloud of sand, but on looking astern, soon after, I saw her in a sinking state, with her bow already under water—in fact going down, and it is believed that, on reaching the bottom, she turned keel upward. . . .'

"Barely 25 minutes had seen the beginning, progress, and termination of this fearful hurricane."

The entire crew went down with the vessel. The *Euphrates* completed her voyage to the mouth of the river. The adventure bore fruit in two ways: the ruins, already known in a general way, were systematically listed and the Euphrates was proved navigable.

"Arise," the Lord said to Jonah,

"go to Nineveh, that great city, and cry against it; for their wickedness is come up before me." Excepting Babylon and Sodom, no city of the ancient world has so impressed itself upon the mind of the Christian West as the epitome of urban arrogance and rampant luxury, as a nest of all vice, as has Nineveh. This is, of course, the Bible's doing.

The first European to recognize the site was Carsten Niebuhr (see page 180). In March 1766 he was on the way to Mosul.

"Heading westward for Mosul, we must first ride through Nineveh. . . . I did not learn that I was at so notable a spot until I was close to the river. Here I was shown a village on a large hill, which is called Nunia, and a mosque in which the prophet Jonah lies buried. . . . Another hill in this vicinity is called Kalla Nunia or the castle of Nineveh. Upon this eminence is a village named Koinsjug [Kuyunjik]. At Mosul, where I stayed close by the Tigris, I was also shown the walls of Nineveh, the which I had not noticed in passing through, thinking them a line of hills. Afterwards I sketched a plan of all these points." (1. The mosque with the grave of Jonah. 2. The village of Nunia. 3. The walls of Nineveh. 4. Mount Ain Safra.)

At this place, in the nineteenth century, Mesopotamian archaeology was to have its birth.

One of the first Assyrian reliefs.

Its unearthing brought Europeans face to face with an advanced civilization whose existence no one had hitherto suspected. It shows the siege of a citadel. These sculptures dug up in and around ancient Nineveh by a French physician were extraordinarily beautiful, although their beauty had a rigid and alien quality. One could see at first glance that they represented the art of a highly developed, sophisticated people.

The French doctor was Paul Emile Botta (1802–1870). As a young man he had toured the world. Then, after an interlude in the consular service at Alexandria, he was appointed consular agent in Mosul in 1842. Botta could not resist the lure of the sand-drifted mounds. In December 1842 he began to dig at a mound near Kuyunjik which was later to yield astounding treasures—but not to him. He gave up there and tried anew at Khorsabad, ten miles away. And here luck was with him from the start. Like a magician's hat producing rabbits, the earth disgorged reliefs, statues, winged bulls with faces of bearded men. The outlines of a tremendous palace came to light—the palace of Sargon (c. 710 B.C.), of whom the prophet Isaiah speaks.

Botta went on digging like a madman, despite refractory conditions. His government began to send him funds, and when he asked for an assistant "capable of preparing drawings," he was fortunate in being given Eugène Napoléon Flandin (1809–1876). This brilliant draftsman not only made copies; he saved the finds for posterity. For when those wholly unique alabaster figures were brought into the sunlight for the first time after thousands of years, the delicate stone began to crumble. And Botta himself did them further violence. Paris had been begging to see some of the actual sculptures, instead of mere drawings. In order to trans-

port the gigantic blocks of stone, Botta actually had each of them sawed into six pieces! Then the worst disaster of all took place. The first large shipment, loaded onto crude rafts known as *keleks* for floating down the Tigris, was caught in raging rapids. The gods and kings of Assyria, but newly recovered, were lost once more in the depths of the river. But Botta was not a man to give up easily. A new shipment was assembled, the problems of river transport were mastered, and in May 1847 Europe saw the art of Assyria exhibited for the first time at the Louvre.

We cannot blink at the fact that Botta's hectic methods in Khorsabad made his excavations mere plundering operations like those of Belzoni in Egypt. Science, nevertheless, was to benefit indirectly from what, in spite of everything, was shabby treatment accorded to this pioneer. For instead of promoting Botta, an ungrateful French government transferred him to a less important post in Syria. Thus the way was cleared for a successor who was to work far more carefully.

In Botta's day,

and for some time afterward, the techniques of transporting mighty loads of sculpture across desert country and on unpredictable rivers were scarcely better than they had been in the first millennium B.C. Victor Place (1822–1875), who succeeded Botta at Khorsabad, handled the task far better. He did not saw the sculptures into pieces, but took the bold step of shipping the colossal statues (one winged bull weighed thirty-two tons) in one piece, on specially constructed wagons and with the aid of hundreds of natives (see picture on left). But he, too, suffered disaster on the river. Of the hundreds of pieces of sculpture ultimately excavated from the 209 large chambers and the 31 hallways and courtyards of

Sargon's palace, 235 were finally shipped off on specially constructed *keleks*, shown above. But at the mouth of the Tigris and Euphrates the *keleks* were attacked by hostile Arab tribes; only two of the rafts went unscathed, hundreds of irreplaceable art works were lost, and only twenty-six reached the Louvre at last on July 1, 1856.

In the meantime, scholars and the public alike were becoming increasingly eager to know something more about these mighty monuments. This meant a reading of the inscriptions. And in 1843, the same year that Botta began his excavation, an Englishman, unaware of Grotefend's labors, deciphered cuneiform script for the second time.

A few remarkable examples of Assyrian art.

The king hunts: reliefs from the gatehouse of the palace of Assurbanipal at Nineveh, brought to the British Museum by A. H. Layard. Below, the king, accompanied by his guard, pours sacrificial oil upon the lions he has slain.

The relief at left shows wild asses attacked by dogs, and beset by hunters' arrows. What range of style these two scenes comprise! The artist has given the figures in the sacrifice scene that hierarchic stiffness which the Assyrians considered the due of such solemn subjects. In the other plaque the artist obviously rejoices in the grace of animals leaping and running so lithely and freely. For all the realistic details, the treatment is no simple realism; one feels the vastness of the plain where the animals dwell, one hears the clamor of the hunters pursuing the frightened beasts. A supreme facility, a mastery of artistic form, is evident here. No wonder these Assyrian reliefs stirred the hearts of those men of the nineteenth century who were seeing them for the first time after twenty-five hundred years. Their beauty and power is still intact.

To copy an inscription,

a young British army officer named H. C. Rawlinson had himself lowered from this cliff in 1837. Robert Ker Porter, who drew the picture below, could detect the lettering only by means of a telescope, and could barely make out the contours of the tremendous relief, whose subject he arbitrarily and wrongly identified as "the ten tribes before Shalmanesar."

The relief is in fact a self-glorifying representation of Darius, King of the Persians (521–485 B.C.), chiseled into a two-thousand-foot cliff along the ancient cara-

van route from Hamadan to Kermanshah in Persia. To dangle from a rope more than three hundred feet above the floor of the valley and slowly work along the sixty-foot length of the relief, copying with extreme accuracy a completely strange writing—this was certainly an extraordinary athletic feat. Yet the scientific feat that resulted from this exploit was even more impressive.

The carved figures in the photograph at right (which suggests the enormous height of the Behistun relief) are completely surrounded by the massive inscriptions.

"I was in excellent health,

was in the heyday of youth, had tremendous spirits, was distinguished in all athletic amusements . . . and had the whole world before me."

So Henry Creswicke Rawlinson (1810–1895) described the period of his lieutenancy in India, when he and his comrades of the First Grenadiers spent their time in "running, jumping, quoits, racquets, billiards, pigeon-shooting, pig-sticking, steeple-chasing, chess and games of skill." But he also occupied himself with far more serious matters. On the four-month voyage to India he had made the acquaintance of Sir John Malcolm, Governor of Bombay, who was not only a soldier but also an orientalist and linguist. "It was, without doubt, an enormous advantage to the lad of seventeen to be associated with the 'Historian of Persia,' whose tales of his battles with the Mahrattas, and his experiences amongst the Persians, probably fired Rawlinson's youthful imagination, and gave that bent to his tastes which resulted in his subsequent choice of a career," comments a biographer.

When Rawlinson was transferred to Persia in 1835 on a purely military mission, he found his own true work awaiting him at the cliff of Behistun. We have no way of knowing whether, when he copied the Darius inscription, he knew anything of Grotefend's preliminary labors. Nor is the question vital. For Rawlinson immediately went far beyond Grotefend's readings. He was fortunate in having the actual texts be-

fore his eyes; Grotefend had had only transcripts, and by no means good ones. Moreover, Rawlinson was a person who could make the most of his opportunities, as is shown by his copy of the Behistun inscription, as well as by his drawing of the whole panorama, which appears below right.

Military duties interfered with his work on the inscriptions for eight years, and it was not until 1843–4, when he was appointed British consul general at Baghdad, that he could concentrate on his studies. Soon thereafter, in 1846, he published *The Persian Cuneiform Inscriptions at Behistun,* in which were presented translated inscriptions that properly won him the epithet "Father of Assyriology."

This scholar who had started as a soldier and shifted to diplomacy later occupied a high place in the Council of India. But he never lost his passion for penetrating the secrets of cuneiform script. Nor was he ever at a loss for problems, because thorny new and old ones awaited solution.

One of the smaller inscriptions at Behistun

as copied by Rawlinson for his famous book. It is the uppermost right-hand in- scription over the head of Darius. (Darius is the tall figure third from the left.)

of the same inscription, which contains a great many names of kings. We will recall that Grotefend too chose to decipher the text that held the greatest number of clues, the Old Persian text called Class I. But there were also Classes II and III. And while Rawlinson was battling indolence and corruption as reorganizer of the Persian Shah's army, and later while he was pursuing a highly dangerous life as a political agent in Afghanistan and Turkish Arabia—all this without ever neglecting his hobby, cuneiform script—other scholars were doing their utmost to crack the still undeciphered scripts. Prominent among them were Burnouf, Lassen, Hincks, Oppert, Norris, and Löwenstern.

An extremely confusing and difficult situation arose. The following quotation gives us some idea of the dilemma of the cryptologists. In 1850 Rawlinson wrote resignedly:

"I will frankly confess, indeed, that after having mastered every Babylonian letter, and every Babylonian word, to which any clue existed in the trilingual tablets, either by direct evidence or by induction, I have been tempted, on more occasions than one, in striving to apply the key thus obtained to the interpretation of the Assyrian Inscriptions, to abandon the study altogether in utter despair of arriving at any satisfactory result."

Similarly, in the same year the Irish scholar Edward Hincks asserted that in Babylonian cuneiform script there is no sign which stands for a consonant alone; rather, each sign stands for a consonant plus a preceding vowel, or a consonant followed by one. Rawlinson once again un-

derscored the confusion in 1851, writing: "It can be shown beyond all possibility of dispute, that a very large proportion of the Assyrian signs are Polyphones—that is, they represent more than one sound." "Polyphonic" signifies that the same sign in cuneiform script might be read in several different ways and given the most various meanings, depending on its context in a word or sentence.

When Rawlinson first advanced this theory of polyphony, there was a loud outcry from the professionals. Soon, however, the Royal Asiatic Society of London settled the disputes in a singular manner.

DETACHED INSCRIPTIONS.

MARKED *A*.

. **Adam** . **Dár(a)yawush** . **k'hsháyathiya** . **wazarka** . **k'hsháya**
Ego   Darius,   rex,   magnus;   rex

thiya . **k'hsháyathiyánám** . **k'hsháyathiya** . **Pársiya** . **k'hsh**
.   regum;   rex   Persidis;   rex

áyathiya . **dahyunám** . **Vishtáspahyá** . **putřa** .
.   provinciarum;   Hystaspis   filius;

Arshámahyá . **napá** . **Hak'hámanishya** . **Thátiya** . **Dár(a)**
Arsamis   nepos;   Achæmenensis.   Dicit   Da-

yawush . **k'hsháyathiya** . **maná** . **pitá** . **Vishtáspa** . **V**
rius   rex;   mihi   pater   Hystaspes;

ishtáspahyá . **pitá** . **Arsháma** . **Arshámahyá** . **pi**
Hystaspis   pater   Arsames;   Arsamis   pa-

tá . **Ariyáram(a)na** . **Ariyáram(a)nahyá** . **pitá**
ter   Ariaramnes;   Ariaramnis   pater

. **Chishpish** . **Chishpishahyá** . **pitá** . **Hak'hámanish**
Teispes;   Teispis   pater   Achæmenes.

. **Thátiya** . **Dár(a)yawush** . **k'hsháyathiya** . **awahya**
Dicit   Darius   rex: eâ

rát'iya . **wayam** . **Hak'hámanishyá** . **thahyá**
ratione   nos   Achæmenenses   ap-

mahya . **hachá** . **par'uviyat** . **amátá** .
pellamur;   ab   antiquo   invicti(?)
                   [oriundi(?)]

amahya . **hachá** . **par'uviyat** . **hyá** . **amá**
sumus;   ab   antiquo   quæ   nos-

k'ham . **tumá** . **k'hsháyathiyá** . **áha** . **Tha**
trum   stirps (erat,)   reges   fuere.   Di-

tiya . **Dár(a)yawush** . **k'hsháyathiya** . 𒐋 . **ma**
cit   Darius   rex: 8   mei

ná . **tu'máyá** (sunt) **tyiya** . **par'uwa**
.   generis   qui   prius

m . **k'hsháyathiyá** . **áha** . **adam** . **na**
.   reges   fuere;   ego   no-

wam . 𒐙 . **dhuvitátaranam** . **wayam** . **k'h**
nus (sum)   9;   diutissime   nos   re-

sháyathiyá . **amahya**
ges   sumus.

2

In 1857 a sealed envelope

was laid upon the desk of the Royal Asiatic Society: the translation of an inscription of Tiglath-Pileser, King of Assyria, by W. H. Fox Talbot. In the accompanying letter Fox Talbot made the unusual proposal that the text be submitted also to Rawlinson and Hincks (later the Franco-German scholar Julius Oppert was added) for translation, and that the separate translations should be delivered sealed to the society, to be opened in the presence of a commission. Rawlinson agreed to this at once. Six weeks later

(209)

the four contestants had delivered their versions, and the commission drew up its report.

The report was sensational. Although two of the entries were of shorter length, Hincks and Oppert having had only a brief time at their disposal for the decipherment, the parallel passages showed an astonishing agreement. Wherever there were significant deviations, the translators had in nearly every case indicated that they were dubious about their versions. In regard to

---

XLIII. (vii. 49).

Rawlinson.

The glorious offspring of Ashur-dapur-Il, who held the sceptre of dominion, and ruled over the the people of Bel; who in all the works of his hand and the deeds of his life placed his reliance on the great Gods, and thus obtained a prosperous and long life (?).

Talbot.

Great grandson of Ashur-dabalan ...... of the glorious sceptre .... who rested upon the favor of the great gods, the works of his hands and the gifts of his ....

XLIII. (vii. 49).

Hincks.

Oppert.

Son of grandson of Asar-dayan, who bore the sceptre of the rising of the star Taspir (?), who asked from (or, owed to) the great gods, the mankind of Bel-Dagon, that is the work of his hands, and the formation of his fingers, and who walked (in the right line) afterwards and formerly:

XLIV. (vii. 55).

The beloved child (literally heart of hearts) of Barzan-pala-kura, the king who first organized the country of Assyria, who purged his territories of the wicked as if they had been ...., and established the troops of Assyria in authority.

Fourth descendant of Ninev-bal-ushat, who ....

XLIV. (vii. 55).

Fifth descendant of Ninip-pal-lu-kin, the king of the commencement, the pupil of Asur, whose power grew over his land like a pine (?); who founded the first, the army of Assyria.

XLV. (vii. 60).

At this time the temple of Anu and Vul, the great Gods, my lords, which, in former times, Shansi-Vul, high-priest of Ashur, son of Ismi Dagan, high-priest of Ashur, had founded, having lasted for 641 years, it fell into ruin. Ashur-dapur-Il, king of Assyria, son of Barzan-pala-kura, king of Assyria, took down this temple and did not rebuild it. For 60 years the foundations of it were not laid.

The temple of Anu and Yem, the great gods, my lords, which in former days Shemsi-Yem, supreme lord of Assyria, son of Ishmi-Dagon, supreme lord of Assyria likewise, 641 years ago had constructed, that temple had fallen to decay. And Ashur-dabalan, king of Assyria, son of Ninev-bal-ushat, king of Assyria likewise, destroyed that temple and rebuilt it not. During sixty years its foundations were not ....

XLV. (vii. 60).

At that time the house of Anu and Iv, the great gods, my lords, which in former days Samsi-Iv, *champion* of Assur, son of Ismi-Dagan, *champion* of Assur, and so forth, built; for 641 years it went on decaying. Assur-dayan, king of Assyria, son of *Ninip-pal-içr*, king of Assyria, and so forth, threw down that house and did not rebuild it. For a period of 60 years its foundations were not laid.

Then the house of Anu and Ao, the great gods, my lords, formerly Shamshi-Ao, sovereign of Assyria, son of Ismi-dagan, sovereign of Assyria, built it; 641 years elapsed in the cycles of time, then Assur-dayan, king of Assyria, son of Ninip-pallu-kin, destroyed this same temple: he did not fear to deface the names (?); but its foundations were not attacked.

numerals, there was complete agreement.

As a result, the society put out a two-shilling pamphlet entitled: *Inscription of Tiglath Pileser I., King of Assyria*, B.C. *1150, as translated by Sir Henry Rawlinson, Fox Talbot Esq., Dr. Hincks, and Dr. Oppert.* This publication was a milestone in the history of philology.

Two pages of this pamphlet are reproduced on the preceding page.

A photograph of the original cuneiform inscription

on an eight-sided clay prism, now in the British Museum, which Rawlinson, Talbot, Hincks, and Oppert translated.

A modern translation of the third passage (compare p. 209, XLV. [vii. 60]) reads:

In those days [this happened]: the temple of Anu and Raman
the great gods, my lords,
which formerly Samsiramanu, the Isakku of Assur,
had built, and which in the course of 641 years
had more and more decayed:
Assurdân, the King of Assyria,
the son of Ninebpalekur, King of Assyria,
had torn down this temple, but not destroyed it;
throughout sixty years its foundation stone had not again been laid.

(210)

At twenty-four a romantic adventurer

with scarcely a penny in his pocket, at sixty a respected diplomat, wealthy collector of Venetian art, Knight Grand Cross of the Order of the Bath: such was Sir Austen Henry Layard, excavator of the palaces of Nineveh. His was a thoroughly English career, and one that again exemplified the tendency of the adventurer to turn to diplomacy and politics.

Layard was born in Paris in 1817, was reared in Italy, England, and Switzerland, and was fluent in several languages while still a child. Cosmopolitan in temperament, he fretted for six dull years in a London solicitor's office. Meanwhile he nursed his dream of undertaking a journey by land through Asia Minor and the Near East to India and Ceylon. By 1840 he could wait no longer; he set out, and was captivated by Turkey and Persia. The picture here, taken from his memoirs, *Early Adventures in Persia* . . . (1887), shows him (standing) and his servant Salah in the costume of the Lurians, a nomadic tribe of Asia Minor; Layard lived in their ill-smelling tents and shared their goat cheeses.

In 1842, at the age of twenty-five, Layard was back in Constantinople, full of tales about the mysterious mounds by the Tigris beneath which ancient Nineveh was said to slumber. In 1845 the British Ambassador, Sir Stratford Canning, gave him sixty pounds for a first excavation. With unprecedented luck, Layard attacked the Hill of Nimrod (see page 193) and promptly discovered the palace of Assurnasirpal II,

King of Assyria in 884–859 B.C. It was full of fabulous art treasures, far surpassing in beauty the things that Botta had found shortly before. Layard took a few months' leave from the Middle East and repaired to London to see to the publication of his book, *Nineveh and Its Remains,* which appeared in two volumes in 1848–9 and was followed by a volume of illustrations. Unlike Botta, who had received such shabby treatment from his government, Layard returned to Constantinople as an attaché. And in 1849 he chose to do something that seemed utterly mad. After reconnoitering Babylon, he went to Kuyunjik, and, with numerous other potential sites in plain view, started upon the very mound where Botta had dug for so long without result. There Layard found the tremendous palace of Sennacherib (704–681 B.C.), one of the most powerful despots of the ancient world. Moreover, he conquered the problem of transportation down the Tigris. Precious reliefs and sculptures were shipped in quantity to London.

In 1852 Layard won a seat in parliament, then twice became Undersecretary of Foreign Affairs, ambassador without portfolio, political observer in the Crimean War and in India—and finally retired to Italy, where he collected Venetian painting. He died in 1894.

Layard at the age of sixty.

His energetic and forceful character is revealed in his reports, which over and beyond their importance for Assyriology constitute first-rate travel literature. Entering Turkey all afire to begin his excavation, he found the place in uproar—the wild tribes around Mosul had just revolted against a despotic governor. Layard won the friendship of a tribal sheik, set to work on the desert sands, and struck treasure. Besides conducting his own project, he found time to examine the recent discoveries of other archaeologists.

The Great Bas-relief at Baviân,

then the newest and most exciting find. Layard, who appears in the drawing as the tiny figure suspended by a rope before the rock face, comments:

"These figures, which are about 25 ft. high, represent Sennacherib worshipping before a god. They are carved upon the rock in a valley East of Nineveh. The excavated chambers are probably tombs of a later date than the sculptures. On tablets adjoining this bas-relief are inscriptions, by which it appears that these monuments were sculptured to record the opening of some great canal by Sennacherib, and to celebrate his conquest of Babylonia."

(213)

Layard had scarcely begun probing the palace of Assurnasirpal

when the most sensational event of the entire excavation took place. He was riding early one morning to the camp of his friend Sheik Abd-er-Rahman when he was overtaken by two Arabs galloping toward him as fast as their steeds would go. " 'Hasten, O Bey,' exclaimed one of them —'hasten to the diggers, for they have found Nimrod himself. Wallah, it is wonderful, but it is true! We have seen him with our own eyes. There is no God but God.'" And Layard continues: "And both joining in this pious exclamation, they galloped off, in the direction of their tents. . . ." He turned around and spurred after them.

"The Arabs withdrew the screen they had hastily constructed, and disclosed an enormous human head sculptured in full out of the alabaster of the country. They had uncovered the upper part of a figure, the remainder of which was still buried in the earth. I saw at once that the head must belong to a winged lion or bull, similar to those of Khorsabad and Persepolis."

This find created a furor among the natives. News of it reached Mosul, and provoked a governmental investigation that paralyzed the work for days. The picture below, from Layard's *Nineveh and Its Remains*, is more descriptive of the drama of the discovery than words can be.

Some had the bodies of bulls, others of lions.

These monsters, which represented virtues, were called *lamassi* by the Assyrians. They played a role similar to that of the cherubim of the Jews.

Here is one guardian from the palace of Assurnasirpal II, taken from under the mound of Nimrod. The inscription between the legs (there are five legs—an idiosyncrasy of Assyrian style, which apparently held it necessary to show four legs even in profile) gives the name of the King, lists his titles, and recounts his victories.

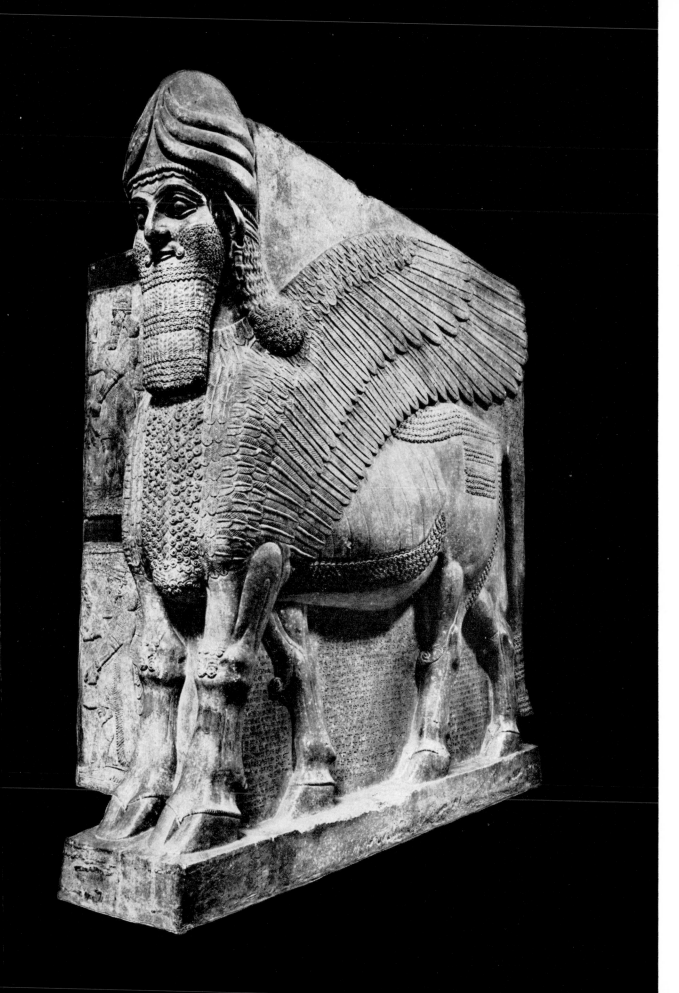

One of Layard's most interesting finds,

from the scientific point of view, is undoubtedly the black obelisk of Salmanassar III (859–824 B.C.). This obelisk, about six and one half feet high and covered on all four faces with script and reliefs, not only tells us of the King's military expeditions, but also gives us vignettes of the clothing and customs of the peoples whom Salmanassar boasts of conquering.

The sketch at right is taken from Layard's *Monuments of Nineveh*. The photograph below singles out the second row of carvings. Kinsmen of Jehu, son of a man named Khumri, are shown bringing tribute consisting of bars of metal and vessels of silver and gold. Oddly, *Khumri* was the Assyrian designation of the Jews, but they are not mentioned in the chronicle engraved on the obelisk.

A relief

that Layard found during his last excavation at the mound of Kuyunjik, the spot Botta had abandoned too soon. The recumbent lioness is outstretched in a magnificent union of power and grace beneath a cypress tree entwined by a grapevine. On the next page, a lion hunt, also from the palace of Assurbanipal. The lion is attacking the King, springing directly upon the bodyguards' deadly spears.

These reliefs created an enormous sensation when they were first put on exhibit in the Assyrian Saloon of the British Museum. The mound of Kuyunjik was to yield still another find, one that roused not only excitement and admiration but also a prolonged discussion. This find, however, was not made by Layard himself, but by one of his most talented disciples.

Hormuzd Rassam, a Chaldaean Christian

(1826–1910), Layard's pupil, had been educated at Oxford. In the midst of a brilliant diplomatic career he was so unfortunate as to incur the disfavor of the ruler of Abyssinia, who had him cast into prison in 1866. Freed two years later, he felt the lure of his early interests and went to Nineveh to dig where he had dug with Layard many years before. He laid bare a new temple, 165 feet long and 100 feet wide. At Balavat, southeast of Nineveh, he found the remains of a gate that had once been the entrance to the palace of Salmanassar III (859–824 B.C.). The bronze fittings were chased with crude reliefs picturing the King's heroic deeds. These remains not only provided the first proof that the Assyrians were acquainted with gates and doors, but also showed just how they had made to function a gate 20 feet high by 15 feet wide.

The illustration shows one of the bronze strips covering the door-jamb. In the lower left-hand corner a citadel is depicted. The clearly delineated crenelations were one of the chief clues for reconstruction of such citadels as, for example, the Late Hittite citadel at Carchemish. A citadel occurs again in the upper right-hand corner, and the disposition of the defenders makes the reason for the crenelations perfectly patent. The principles of fortification and of the battering-ram set on a cart remained essentially the same well into Europe's Middle Ages.

Fragments of baked clay,

which had held the knowledge and literature of Babylonia and Assyria, lay cracked, shattered, and half burned, in wild confusion. They made a pile a foot and a half high. These thousands of clay tablets, representing King Assurbanipal's library at Nineveh, were among the last triumphal finds made by Layard and his assistant Hormuzd Rassam in the spring of 1850. One fragment, containing part of the Gilgamesh Epic, is shown here.

None of the excavators recognized the value of this find. Consequently, they packed the tablets higgledy-piggledy into baskets, did not bother to wrap them, and sent them by rafts down to Basra, whence they were taken aboard a British naval vessel bound for England. This careless handling caused more damage to the tablets than did the pillaging of the Medes who long ago had burned Assurbanipal's palace.

The tablets were then "dug up" a second time—in the British Museum. The man who performed this feat was another of those self-taught geniuses who appear so frequently in the history of archaeology. Among thousands of tablets he succeeded in piecing together some eighty fragments containing a text that, as he deciphered it, proved more and more momentous.

The man was George Smith (1840–1876), a former bank-note engraver who by sheer erudition won himself an assistantship in the Egyptian-Assyrian section of the British Museum. What he deciphered was the literary work now called the Gilgamesh Epic—probably the first great written epic in the history of the world, composed long before Homer, long before the Bible. Gilgamesh, two-thirds god and one-third man, was the legendary hero of prehistoric times who overcame Khumbabam, the terrible ruler of the cedar forest. With supreme daring he called Ishtar, the goddess of love, a harlot when she offered herself to him. He killed the heavenly bull. But tragedy struck when his friend Enkidu, with whom he had performed all these exploits, died of an inexplicable disease. Gilgamesh set out in search of eternal life. In this hunt for immortality he encountered Ut-napishtim, "who had found life" —and it became evident to George Smith that Ut-napishtim was none other than the Biblical Noah. His heart beat faster: here in cuneiform script was the story of the Flood. But when he came to the crucial chapter, several tablets were missing. What followed was as dramatic as the content of the tablets. Smith issued an appeal to the British public, a public noted for its enthusiasm for Biblical studies. A newspaper, the *Daily Telegraph*, provided him with a grant to go and seek the rest of the tablets. Still more fantastically, Smith found what he was looking for, found the very clay tablets that were missing amid the enormous heap of rubble at Nineveh. He translated them—and established clearly that the Bible's story of the Deluge

derived from a Babylonian source. The Bible could no longer be regarded only as pure revelation; it was also a history into which age-old tales had been woven.

Another archaeologist was to discover the historical basis of the Flood—but not until the twentieth century. Excavations at Nippur later in the nineteenth century might have contributed a good deal of information bearing on this theme. Unfortunately, a number of the most significant results of these excavations were not published until very recently.

The Gilgamesh Epic remained, therefore, the single document confirming the Biblical account. Here is a passage of startling congruences:

What I had loaded thereon, the whole harvest of life,
I caused to embark within the vessel; all my family and my relations.
The beasts of the field, the cattle of the field. . . .
I entered the vessel and closed the door. . . .
When the young dawn gleamed forth,
From the foundations of heaven a black cloud arose. . . .
All that is bright is turned into darkness,
The brother seeth his brother no more. . . .
The gods feared the flood. . . .
For six days and nights,
Wind and flood marched on, the hurricane subdued the land.
When the seventh day dawned, the hurricane was abated. . . .
The flood ceased.
I beheld the sea, its voice was silent,
And all mankind was turned into mud! . . .
Unto Mount Nitsir came the vessel,
Mount Nitsir held the vessel, and let it not budge. . . .
When the seventh day came,
I sent forth a dove. . . .

Rioting, fire, and death

marked the end of the first American excavation in Mesopotamia. In 1884 the American Oriental Society decided that the United States should also delve into the ancient Land of the Two Rivers, which had hitherto been the preserve of England and France. The University of Pennsylvania undertook to sponsor the expedition and chose a minister named Peters, a specialist in Biblical history, as director. After a year of careful reconnaissance, Nippur was selected for the site of the excavation. A sizable fund (for those days) was collected, amounting in fact to $70,000 to be expended in the next ten years. Thus, the expedition started in favorable circumstances—save for one factor. The Reverend Dr. Peters was unfortunately the complete opposite of such cosmopolitan, politic persons as Botta, Rawlinson, and Layard. He was a stern, puritanical man with rigid principles who held Orientals in contempt and would not dream of making concessions to their mentality. He proved inept even in the matter of obtaining a *firman*, or permit for digging, from the Turkish government. (Nippur is about one hundred miles southeast of Baghdad; until 1918 the entire region was under Turkish rule.) Two years passed in fruitless negotiations, and the expedition, although prepared by 1887, did not arrive in Nippur until January 1889. Disputes began at once. The upright minister came with his contingent of Turkish guards. Supported thus by the central authorities,

he saw no need to present the sheiks of the surrounding tribes with the customary gifts. He next made a decision totally absurd from the point of view of excavational technique: he placed the expedition's camp on top of the hill he intended to dig, proudly calling it *kal'at America*— "American citadel." No sooner had the Arab workmen committed their first small thefts—standard practice in the country— than this professional exemplar of Christian charity issued an order without precedent in archaeological work. He instructed his watchmen to fire at suspicious nocturnal prowlers.

On April 15, 1889, after two months of excavation, a Turkish soldier shot an Arab who attempted to steal a horse. At once the tense situation passed out of control. The Arabs screamed for bloody revenge. Peters was loath to turn over to them the soldier who had obeyed his order, and instead concluded that his party had better go elsewhere. On the morning of April 18, only three days after the fateful shot, when packing was almost complete, the cry of "Fire!" rang through the camp. Sure enough, the huts were all ablaze. The Turkish troops, instead of helping, snatched whatever they could lay hands on. Arabs poured into the camp and looted left and right. Three horses, including the minister's, were burned alive. With a measure of dry insight, the Reverend Dr. Peters later observed: "Our first year at Nippur had ended in failure and disaster."

The drawing on the left is modern. Ulrica Lloyd, wife of the archaeologist Seton Lloyd, made it for her husband's book *Foundations in the Dust*. The spectacle of flaming huts and wildly dashing horsemen is based on written accounts, while the ruins are modeled after older drawings.

Peters learned a lesson from his failure. Returning the following year, he took care to placate the Arab sheiks as well as the Turkish government. By the middle of February he had struck one of the richest stores of cuneiform tablets ever to be found. Almost fifty years passed, however, before these finds were turned to scientific profit. In 1937 and then again in 1943 and 1946 the American Sumerologist Samuel N. Kramer studied them. And he learned that far back in the third millennium B.C. Sumeria had abounded in tales of Gilgamesh and of the man who escaped the Flood on a ship with all sorts of creatures aboard. He also found the conclusion, which hitherto had been missing from the epic. Gilgamesh, the passionate seeker after immortality, does not find eternal life in spite of all the advice of Ut-napishtim (Noah). He must die. But Enlil, the father of the gods, appoints him lord of the underworld. In ruling over what he had feared, he loses his fear—a remarkable conclusion indeed for the oldest epic in world history. But then it springs from an age when priests and poets were in charge of the human psyche, and there were no psychiatrists to call in.

(224)

"Koldewey took on the most gigantic task

that any excavator ever assumed—to dig up
Babylon. No comparable task remains for
any one else," writes Oscar Reuther, the
German art historian, in his obituary of
the man who had excavated Babylon.

Robert Koldewey (1855–1925) was no
beginner when he first conceived his plan.
After having studied architecture, art history, and archaeology at the universities
of Berlin, Munich, and Vienna, he acquired experience in excavation on the
Greek islands and in Italy and Syria. At
this time Dörpfeld, with his excavation at
Olympia and his highly systematic work
at the city of Priene, had already begun
to point out new paths to archaeologists,
to teach them not only to search for interesting objects, but, much more, to
discover contexts, the total picture of a
city.

Koldewey set his own goal. A man of
lively mind, he seasoned his undertakings
with humor and imagination. Anything
but professorial, he could charm people
into believing that apparently impossible
tasks were easy—though he himself never
lost his keen sense of what was really possible. "If," Reuther comments, "he had
actually communicated the plans he had
been nursing for years, his patrons, the
Administrators of the Berlin Museums
and the German Oriental Society, would
scarcely have taken him seriously."

By dint of personal magnetism he succeeded in keeping alive the interest of his
patrons for almost twenty years. Although

he frankly admitted that his excavations would harvest no material treasures, they endowed him, over a period of years, to the tune of almost two million marks ($400,000 at that time). Nor does this include the support he received from the German Kaiser, Wilhelm II, who was fond of dabbling in all the arts and sponsored other archaeological projects besides this one.

Reuther continues: "Koldewey undertook an exploratory trip, accompanied by Eduard Sachau, to the Land of the Two Rivers. Then, early in 1899, he set out with Walter Andrae as his assistant and with Bruno Meissner as the Assyriologist of the expedition. . . . In March 1899 digging started at Babylon. Eighteen years later Koldewey left the site of his life-work, having remained there until the road to Baghdad, his only exit-route, was being pounded by British heavy artillery. In those two decades, during which he took only the briefest of home leaves, and then only to recuperate from the effects of the climate, Koldewey had wrung from the ages the secrets of ancient Babylon and dispelled the darkness which covered the greatest metropolis of antiquity. Gradually the buildings rose out of the rubble and assumed form: Nebuchadnezzar's gigantic palaces . . . the city walls . . . the Gate of Ishtar . . . the Street of Processions . . . the Euphrates bridge . . . and the lengendary Tower of Babel, whose form Koldewey deduced from the ruins and the descriptions of Greeks and Babylonians with keenest logic and persuasive artistic imagination."

Walter Andrae, his assistant, and himself later to become a famous archaeologist, adds: "For nineteen years in Babylon and for the last eight years of his life in Germany—Koldewey lived for Babylon and thought of Babylon, I might almost say, day and night."

This painting gives us some impression of the magnitude of Koldewey's work.

It was done by Elisabeth Andrae, his assistant's sister, and probes the innards of the past. It shows the Gate of Ishtar, chief goddess of the Babylonian pantheon, the earth mother, goddess of love and of the reproductive forces of nature. What a city this must have been almost two and one half millennia ago, when the towers of the mighty gates still thrust into the sky and Nebuchadnezzar was king, indulging his passion for building, erecting more and more walls, palaces, and bridges, and marking them with his seal for all eternity!

Koldewey worked under fortunate conditions. Cuneiform script had been deciphered. Assurbanipal's library at Nineveh had provided an abundance of information. Items from the Bible, from Herodotus and Ctesias, from Babylonian tablets and the latest excavations, could be collated and interpreted. He was able to prove that neither the Bible nor the Greek authors had distorted the picture in essential points. Age-old Babylon, so often destroyed and rebuilt, had become under Nebuchadnezzar II the greatest city of antiquity. Was she "the great mother-city of all harlots?" In any case, she was complex and cosmopolitan—a true metropolis.

(228)

Nebuchadnezzar's Babel rises out of the earth.

A tower of the Ishtar Gate is brought to light. Koldewey spent years exposing this structure. At the start he had no idea of the tremendous proportions of the gate—which in fact consisted of two connected gatehouses—or of how deep he would have to dig. Ultimately he went down eighty feet. As the cross-sectional drawing shows, the original gates had several times been destroyed or had decayed (the long horizontal lines indicate the different levels). Time and again the streets had to be raised, additional layers built upon the towers. The original reliefs were buried under rubble, and new ones were erected on top of them. What finally came to light was the splendid street whose every stone was marked with Nebuchadnezzar's seal.

The Ishtar Gate

in Koldewey's reconstruction. It opened upon the splendid avenue meant for the processions of the great god Marduk. But the street was also a sunken road overlooked by battlements from which death could be hurled upon any invading enemy. The beetling walls were adorned by more than one hundred lions in colored glazed reliefs. Similar reliefs were on the gate itself, though here there were bulls rather than lions. There were representations also of that strange fabulous beast which may be the animal Daniel tamed in order to prove the power of his God.

The dragon of Babylon

(above, right), which was sacred to Marduk. This is the *sirrush*, or *sîr-ruššu* in our present reading of the texts. It was a fabulous monster that can scarcely be identified with any living animal, although many persons have speculated about it. The body is scaly, the neck serpentlike but with a hairy mane; from the horned head a forked tongue darts forth. The forefeet are like those of a great feline, the hind feet griffon's claws. This drawing was the first to reach Europe.

The walls of the Ishtar Gate and of the Street of Processions were studded with more than five hundred reliefs of animals. Below, right, one of the bulls. The panel of the relief is composed of unglazed bricks; the wall above it is of glazed bricks set in geometric designs.

We must visualize all this in color, mostly in blues and yellows, agleam in the perpetual sunlight, as color-drenched as the reliefs and winged beasts on the palaces at Nineveh, as vivid as the pillars of Egyptian temples—as marvelously gaudy, indeed, as the entire world of antiquity, which we still imagine as impeccably white because we know only the blanched sculptures or plaster casts of our museums. A classical Greek would shudder at the pallor of our plaster casts, our miniature replicas. How much more repelled would be the Sumerians, the Babylonians, and the Assyrians, who lived in a world blazing with color.

The actual remains of the "Tower of Babel."

These are not remains of Nebuchadnezzar's ziggurat, but of the very oldest tower, probably the one of which the Bible tells.

Koldewey dug up the greatest city of antiquity, a city surrounded by the mightiest citadel wall ever found, guarded by more than three hundred watchtowers and moats that could be flooded when the need arose. He discovered a park that had probably been the one known to later ages as the "Hanging Gardens of Semiramis." He found thousands of fragments of reliefs and cuneiform tablets. But his excavation of the remains of the Tower of Babel, and his subsequent reconstruction, count as his crowning achievement. This statement calls for some explanation. The discovery of the stele containing Hammurabi's table of laws is incomparably more important to ancient history than the whole Tower of Babel. But to those of us who are not specialists in ancient history, Babylonian law is something fairly abstract, whereas the Tower of Babel is a living concept, an image that has haunted our imaginations from childhood. Reuther says in his obituary on Koldewey: "His Babylonian tower is no structure of fantasy. . . . How close he came to reality has long since been demonstrated by the ziggurat at Ur, excavated by Leonard Woolley." Reuther is not quite accurate here. The remains and the written accounts are somewhat too scanty to allow us to say with absolute certainty that the Tower looked thus and thus.

But Reuther's comment leads us to an archaeologist who was destined to demonstrate the historical accuracy of other testimony in the Bible.

"One has to look out for all such little things. . . ."

Thus Sir Leonard Woolley (b. 1880) begins an explanation of his working methods at the excavation of Ur, the city where Abraham once dwelt. ". . . For the thin powdery white streak which represents the matting that once lined the pit, for the holes in the soil where once were the upright wooden ribs of a wicker coffin, for the rim of a tall clay vase standing in the grave and not crushed flat by the earth's weight; on encountering any such thing the well-trained Arab pick-man will stop his work and report to the foreman the likelihood of a grave; then the pick will give place to the knife for careful work, and the excavator will get out his notebooks and his measures."

Many experts consider Leonard Woolley the most important excavator of the twentieth century. Educated at Oxford, by the time he was twenty-seven he was digging in Nubia. He worked there from 1907 to 1911. Between 1912 and 1914 he collaborated with T. E. Lawrence (later to become world-famous as "Lawrence of Arabia") in Carchemish, the Hittite citadel. During the First World War he did intelligence staff work in Egypt, and spent two years as a prisoner of war in Turkey. In 1924 he began the excavations at Ur which continued until 1934, and made a name for himself by discovering the oldest royal graves in the world, and the oldest known civilized people, the Sumerians. In 1935, acting on intuition supported by admirable reasoning, he struck point-blank into a city buried for thousands of years, the former capital of Yarim Lim, "to whom twenty kings were subject," near Alalakh, present-day Atchana in the Turkish Hatay.

The photograph on the left shows him in Ur (right foreground, seated) taking notes on the precise condition of a newly discovered vase. His wife (left foreground), his faithful companion amid the agitations and excitements of camp life, is at work on one of the delicate jobs of the archaeologist: scraping away earth with a knife.

Payment of "baksheesh"

is the best procedure for preventing carelessness and theft, according to Woolley. Some excavators still refuse to adopt this procedure, although all experience bears out its wisdom. Here, in the photograph on the right, at the end of a day's work, the foremen line up with the finds their small parties have made. Woolley notes each find and values it at the price a black-market dealer might pay for a stolen object. "On an average season the 'baksheesh' bill may amount to 15 percent of the wages," Woolley writes. The gain to science is altogether out of proportion to the sum. In the first place, there is no purloining of the finds, which would then be lost to science. In the second place, the system trains the workmen to exercise extreme care during excavation, for baksheesh is paid only for objects that are not broken or damaged by clumsiness during exhumation. The system, says Woolley, "does create an astonishing amount of good will."

Salvaging cuneiform tablets

was a troublesome problem. Tablets are among the most precious of finds, for they can speak directly to us. Most of those found in Ur were unbaked clay tablets that had become soft as cheese from lying for thousands of years in damp soil. They have often become shapeless lumps impregnated with salt, which only the practiced eye would recognize as inscribed tablets. Any attempt at mechanical cleaning, even with the finest brushes, would obliterate the inscriptions. "At Ur," Woolley relates, "any lumps of clay looking like tablets are lifted from the ground still encased in their covering of earth, and are packed in metal boxes filled with clean sand; after they have been left for a few days to give the clay a chance to dry, the boxes are put into a rough-and-ready kiln heated by vaporized crude oil and are baked until the tins are red-hot and the clay is turned into terra cotta. Then the tablets are taken out; their colour may have altered, which matters little, but they are hard and strong; broken bits can be stuck together, the faces can be cleaned by brushing without any risk to the legibility of the characters; no inscription, however fragmentary, can be overlooked, and its preservation is assured."

Woolley and his wife are shown on the opposite page engaged in this delicate work. The photograph at the upper right shows his "rough-and-ready kiln," and, to the right, actual fragments of tablets before and after Woolley cleaned them.

The Royal Graves of Ur,

from which Woolley extracted extraordinary treasures in gold, and the secret of a frightful funeral ritual. The terraces and steps in the excavation site are due to the differing levels of the approximately 1,800 graves that were investigated: hence this irregular pit nearly 80 yards long and 60 wide.

Woolley discovered this royal cemetery in the autumn of 1922. And he took the amazingly strong-minded step of putting off work on it, not surrendering to curiosity, opposing the powerful urge to follow up a discovery so obviously important. In fact, he waited four years, while pursuing other work. He justified this decision as follows: In the first place the diggers were raw and clumsy, and for the clearing of a cemetery skilled labor is essential; again, Woolley was new to the country and had not time to secure proper influence over the men, for whom the temptation of small gold objects was irresistible. But the decisive argument for postponing work on the graves was this: very little indeed was

known of Mesopotamian archaeology, so little that the objects from these graves were vaguely dated by such authorities as Woolley could consult to the Neo-Babylonian, or, as more probable, to the Persian period, and though he could form no alternative theory, he felt that this was doubtful in the extreme. The more rich the cemetery promised to be, the more necessary it was to leave it alone until external evidence had given a more or less definite chronology.

This decision was certainly wise. There are, alas, all too many examples in the history of archaeology of excavators who took another attitude. Woolley deserves the greatest respect for his restraint.

During the season of 1926-7 he dug away at the vast cemetery with a crew of a hundred workmen for two months. During the third season, 1928-9, with his wife as his sole scientific assistant, he employed 140 workmen and uncovered some 450 graves, including the graves of the kings of Ur and the "death-pit."

The "death-pit of Ur,"

as Woolley called this royal grave, told a horrible story. Evidence from it and from the other graves enabled the archaeologist to reconstruct the funeral ceremonies that had taken place some 4,500 years before.

The death-pit contained seventy-four skeletons of females, presumably ladies of the court, in front of the king's grave. In addition, there were golden and silver harps, which had probably been used to play music for the uncanny *danse macabre*, and golden statuettes of rams. All the skeletons wore jewelry. Typical of the finery were gold and silver hair ribbons, the latter of which however were barely recognizable as streaks of purplish powder among the broken remnants of skulls. Beside one of the ladies an entire silver ribbon was found, rolled up; it had probably been kept in a pocket—just as today, if we wished to carry a ribbon with us, we would roll it up and tuck the end around the roll to prevent unwinding.

Plainly, something had taken place here which was unique, so far as our knowledge went, in Mesopotamia: a mass human sacrifice. But how? The skeletons lay close together, sometimes on top of one another. Most of the skeletons had their arms bent toward the mouths, and beside each lay a cup. Woolley, after painstaking examination of all the details, ventured the following interpretation of the ritual:

"When the door had been blocked with stone and brick and smoothly plastered over, the first phase of the burial ceremony was complete. . . . Down into the open pit, with its mat-covered floor and mat-lined walls, empty and unfurnished, there comes a procession of people, the members of the dead ruler's court, soldiers, menservants and women, the latter in all their finery of brightly-coloured garments and head-dresses of carnelian and lapis lazuli, silver and gold, officers with the insignia of their rank, musicians bearing harps or lyres, and then, driven or backed down the slope, the chariots drawn by oxen or by asses, the drivers in the cars, the grooms holding the heads of the draught animals, and all take up their allotted places at the bottom of the shaft and finally a guard of soldiers forms up at the entrance. Each man and woman brought a little cup of clay or stone or metal, the only equipment needed for the rite that was to follow. . . . The musicians played up to the last; then each of them drank from their cups a potion which they had brought with them or found prepared for them on the spot—in one case we found in the middle of the pit a great copper pot into which they could have dipped—and then lay down and composed themselves for death."

This was not an isolated case, for Woolley describes other such finds. "The ritual of burial included human sacrifice; the number of victims might vary from a mere half dozen to seventy or eighty. . . ." "Against the end wall of the stone chamber lay the bodies of nine women wearing the gala head-dress of lapis and carnelian

beads from which hung golden pend-
ants. . . ." "A little way inside the entrance to the pit stood a wooden sledge
chariot. . . . In front of the chariot lay
the crushed skeletons of two asses with the
bodies of grooms by their heads. . . ."
"We came to another group of bodies,
those of ten women, carefully arranged in
two rows. . . . At the end of the row lay
the remains of a wonderful harp . . . ;
across the ruins of the harp lay the bones
of the gold-crowned harpist. . . ." "The
bodies of two women attendants were
crouched against the bier [of Queen
Shub-ad], one at its head and one at its
foot."

"Few people, looking at such an object in the glass case of a museum,"

comments Leonard Woolley, "realize what it cost to get it there." In freeing these harps from the surrounding soil and restoring them, Woolley performed a signal feat, for, unlike Carter at the tomb of Tutankhamen, he did not have a whole staff of specialists at his disposal. Nor was he equipped like a contemporary American expedition, which moved into the desert with a first-class photographic laboratory and even a captive balloon, in order to be able to photograph the terrain from the air. Right, below, Woolley with his wife working on the still-embedded harps; they are scraping around the relics with a knife and blowing the soil away with a small bellows. The position of the 4,500-year-old instruments (made of wood covered with gold and silver, and ornamented with mosaic) is difficult to make out; behind Woolley's right foot is a silver-covered harp, which can also be distinguished at the top of the photograph on this page. Below are others. At first the state of preservation appeared to be good; at any rate, precise measurements could be taken. But moving the silver-covered harp proved to be extraordinarily difficult. The metal sections were nothing but layers of silver chloride; the sheathing on the rods of the frame had been crushed. Only with the aid of a great deal of wax and wax-soaked linen cloths could the instrument be patched together for shipment. Even so, it could never be placed on exhibition. The condition of the harp covered with gold leaf (illustration on opposite page, foreground) was quite different. The wood of the frame had vanished completely, but the wide mosaic trimming could be lifted with a wax-soaked cloth in one piece and almost undamaged. As for the bull-headed harp (also dimly seen above left), whose animal-head detail is shown at right, there was enough left of it for Woolley to venture a reconstruction.

The art works Woolley found in the graves were richly made and plentiful. Some pieces stunned the discoverer and his colleagues in archaeology, for no one had suspected that more than 4,500 years ago any people had been so versatile in their creativity. We reproduce only one example here, not only for its decorative value, but for its testimony on the life and times of the Sumerians.

The "mosaic standard of Ur,"

found in one of the royal graves, is a living picture-book of Sumerian life before 3000 B.C. Its purpose has not been definitively established. The figures are fashioned of mother-of-pearl and lapis lazuli embedded in asphalt on a wood base. The scenes on the standard are fairly clearly divided into a military and a civilian side, showing the life of a king among his people and among his soldiers.

The civilian side is on the left. Above, we see a banquet scene; the second complete figure from the left is probably the king; on the extreme right is the harpist, followed by a singer; below, two long lines of servants and farmers bringing gifts. Scholars find it useful to know that goats, sheep, and cattle were already domestic animals at this time, as well as donkeys. The donkey appears on the military side of the standard, at right, as a draft animal hitched to wagons. The horse was not employed in this manner until around 2000 B.C. Such carts with soldiers standing on a board at the rear at first led historians to conclude that the ingenious Sumerians had also invented the war-chariot, which later, under the Hittites, developed into a speedy two-wheeled weapon that, drawn by trained horses, revolutionized warfare in antiquity. But these carts with their four spokeless wheels are heavy transport vehicles; pulled as they were by donkeys, they probably could not even keep pace with rapidly advancing infantry.

A ruler of the mysterious Sumerians,

perhaps Gudea, perhaps his son Ur-Nin-gursu. The statue cannot be easily identified because it was not scientifically excavated by an archaeological expedition; it fell into an art dealer's hands via the black market in antiquities, and was purchased in the late nineteenth century by the British Museum for £7,500. The perfection of carving, the artistic coherence in form are astonishing. The material is green-spotted diorite; the fingernails were once gilded, and the pupils of the eyes were painted.

To this day we do not know with certainty whence the Sumerians came. Perhaps their original homeland was the Iranian plateau, possibly the valley of the Indus. They were not Semites, but what they were we do not know. They brought with them a manner of writing and a number of basic architectural forms, such as the pillar and the dome. Moreover, they were acquainted with all the techniques on which the peoples who succeeded them based their own advanced cultures. Their intellectual influence survived long after their city-states had fallen to ruin; their fundamental conceptions of social structure, law, and morality outlasted them by thousands of years. They foreshadowed the Mosaic laws before 3000 B.C., and the tale of the Flood, a late retelling of which was found in Nineveh, is Sumerian in origin.

The mighty scale
of Sumerian work

is shown by the remnants of their temple tower, the ziggurat of Ur, which Woolley also excavated; he reconstructed it as it probably looked under the Third Dynasty. The photograph to the right shows the ruins as they now look. The tiny human figures on the stairway to the left convey something of the enormous size of the building. The structure was begun by Urnammu and his son Dungi, kings of the

Third Dynasty of Ur (around 2100 B.C.). We know the Sumerian kings from king lists that have been unearthed. The first dynasty is recorded under the title "List of Larsa No. 1." To this a brief explanation was appended. It read as follows: "Now came the Flood. And after the Flood the kings of the mountain peoples assumed dominion."

It fell to Woolley to prove the historical reality of such a flood in the Land of the Two Rivers. The evidence lay at such a depth that the flood must demonstrably have taken place shortly after the Sumerians settled the country. What Woolley found under many layers of cultural remains was a thick layer of clay, which every geologist could recognize as an alluvial deposit resulting from a tremendous inundation. Comparison of the king lists, the Gilgamesh Epic, and the testimony of the Bible led inexorably to the conclusion that this deposit had been left by *the* Flood. It is not unreasonable to suppose that this particular flood, which was obviously of such gigantic proportions, so impressed the survivors that they immortalized it in myth, which was passed on and passed on to become that magnificent symbolic story related in the Bible. On the other hand, we know today that the delta of the Tigris and Euphrates was much smaller five thousand years ago than it is today. Ur, therefore, was situated close to the Persian Gulf, and there must have been fairly regular floods, which unquestionably swelled to great disasters more than once. Finally, the layer of mud found by Woolley does not explain the existence of stories of the Flood among the peoples of other continents. But, however that may be, there can be no doubt that this Sumerian flood supplied the historical background for the Biblical Deluge.

Most of the great nations of the world have sent specialists to launch excavations at Kish, Fara, El-Obeid, Tello, Warka, Nippur, Assur, Mari, and Ugarit. Thanks to the labors of archaeologists of many lands, we are able today to write the history—at least in outline—of the oldest known human culture, the culture whose influences were so far-reaching that they still affect our lives and our thoughts.

* * *

We turn our attention now to a geographical entity on the other side of the world, and to a group of civilizations whose spirit is alien to our own heritage. Although they perished not millennia but only a few centuries ago, they left behind them deeper riddles than any we have hitherto encountered.

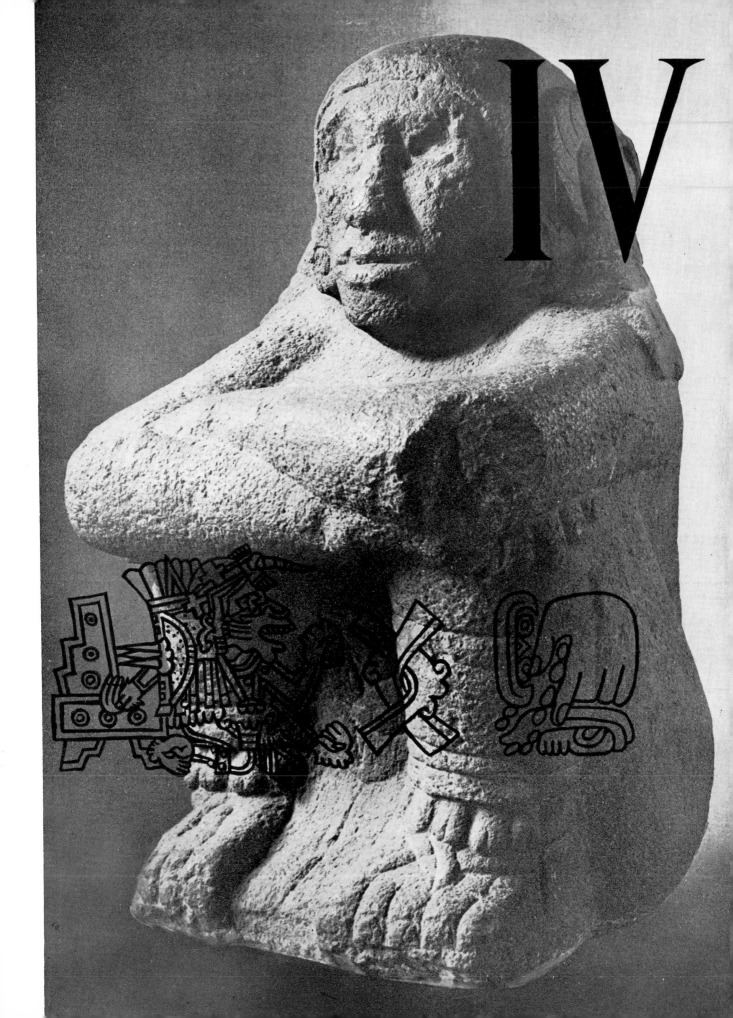

IV

BOOK IV

*First Accounts of
the Conquest of Mexico
In the Service of a New Science
Conquest of the Jungle Cities
New Problems in Mexico*

Archaeology in Middle America * began amid war—

and very nearly ended there. For no "scientific commission" like Napoleon's in Egypt accompanied Hernán Cortés to Mexico. Four hundred men in armor destroyed the highly civilized empire of the Aztecs and erected, at the instruction of their priests, the Christian cross upon the *teocalli*, the heathen temple towers. The Spaniards then methodically extirpated the culture of the Indians. Only a few among them saw anything worth saving in the folkways and artifacts, the buildings and

* This term as used by archaeologists includes Central America and Mexico.

the accumulated lore of the vanquished.

The drawing at right shows Cortés on November 8, 1519, at his first meeting with Moctezuma, the emperor of the Aztecs, in the "floating" capital of Mexico—for the city was at the time a kind of Venice. The woman with Cortés is his mistress and interpreter, Marina (Malinche); standing on a balcony is one of his personal guards; below are tributary gifts: maize, birds, game; seated is the Emperor, attended by three Aztec generals.

Marina was a slave girl, as cruelly used by her stepmother as a heroine in a Grimm fairy tale. Her father, a rich cacique of the south, had no sooner died than her stepmother sold her to a chieftain in Tabasco and seized the inheritance for herself. This had one advantage for Marina: she learned the Mayan language in addition to her Aztec mother tongue, so that after the landing of the Spaniards she was able to help Aguilar, the official interpreter, who knew only Mayan. She translated the Aztec into Mayan, and Aguilar then put the Mayan into Castilian. She must have been both attractive and highly intelligent, for she advanced rapidly, becoming first Cortés's secretary, then his mistress. Later she bore him a child. Marina was a real intermediary; wherever she could, she deftly furthered the interests of her own people, as well as those of her lover.

The Mexicans themselves left a moving record of their downfall. The picture is taken from the *Lienzo de Tlaxcala*, an im-pressive hanging painted on cotton cloth, probably made around 1560, which depicted in eighty-six separate scenes the part played by the Tlaxcalans in the conquest. The Tlaxcalans, a people with democratic and republican traditions, were the only firm allies of the Spaniards. The textile painting was preserved in the town hall of Tlaxcala. The Emperor Maximilian, the unfortunate Hapsburg whom Napoleon III placed upon the Mexican throne, had the painting brought to Mexico City so that a good copy of it might be prepared. In the confusion following the uprisings and Maximilian's execution by Benito Juárez, the painting disappeared. Fortunately, there were earlier copies, including one in color made by the Mexican archaeologist Alfredo Chavero. The Mexican government published a facsimile of this copy for the Columbus anniversary celebration of 1892.

Contemporary portraits of Cortés are extremely rare.

"Pitilessly, almost sardonically, he looks out at the world with cruel fire in his eyes; fully to appreciate this image, we must study it for a while," comments A. Suhle in his book on Renaissance medallions. The medallion at top right, although unsigned, has been ascribed to Christoph Weiditz (c. 1500–1559) and was probably made in Italy or Spain in 1529.

The tinted pen drawing at lower right is the only full-length portrait of Cortés which has been preserved. It is taken from Weiditz's travel album. The inscription reads: "Don Ferdinando Cordes year 1529 of his age the 42nd. Which same has won all India for Emperer Charles the Fifth"— a statement that errs in two respects; it was Central America that Cortés won, not India, and he was forty-four, his birth in 1485 having been established beyond doubt.

Hernán Cortés was something of a phenomenon in the history of the Western world. There is no parallel for the bloodbath in which he drowned a flourishing civilization. The story is told superbly in William Prescott's *Conquest of Mexico*, a book that has lost none of its power in the hundred-odd years that have passed since its appearance in 1843.

(252)

The first specimens of Mexican art

to arrive in Europe created a sensation by reason of their curiosity and the richness of their materials. Yet these objects made no impact on humanistic scholars, who were entirely under the spell of the artifacts of the Greco-Roman period, which they were just beginning to investigate.

Moctezuma sent a number of presents to Cortés aboard his ship. The gifts that struck the Spaniards as especially precious and desirable were considered bagatelles by the Aztecs. Cortés's men, for example, were dumfounded by gold and silver discs the size of cartwheels, whereas the Aztecs placed far more value on their articles made of birds' plumage. They had good reason for this judgment.

Below, a feather headdress measuring

five feet nine inches at its greatest width, originally among Moctezuma's gifts to Cortés in 1519. One of the earliest descriptions of it reads: "A Moorish hat, of long, fine, glistening, greenish, and golden feathers, set on top with white, red, and azure feathers with golden roses and spangles, with a solid golden beak in front, fitting over the brow." Almost all the long feathers were taken from a bird that sports only two, or at most four, tail feathers. When we consider that there are some five hundred of these quetzal feathers in the headdress, the rarity and preciousness of this singular crown is evident.

There is a story connected with this headdress. It passed through the hands of Emperor Charles V to his brother Ferdinand, in whose collection of art and curiosa at Castle Ambras, near Innsbruck, Austria, it remained until it was transferred to Vienna. In 1878 it was taken, badly moth-eaten, from a museum cupboard where it had hung *folded* for dec-

ades. It was then restored, but scarcely accurately, the restorer being under the delusion that the headdress had been a standard. So little attention was paid to authenticity that whole skins of the East Indian halcyon, *halcyon fusca Gray*, were used in place of the blue down feathers of *cotinga maynanna Linné*—the latter being difficult to obtain.

Ultimately, however, the headdress came under the scrutiny of scholars in the field of American archaeology. In 1887 a book on this "magnificent example of Old Mexican feather work" was published. Then, in 1908, for the sixteenth International Congress of Americanists, a special study committee was formed, and Franz Heger made the drawing at the bottom of this page. It shows a reconstruction of the framework of the headdress. The committee had the headdress housed in a revolving showcase so that it could be studied from all sides without being handled.

Staggering strangeness—

such was the impression people had of the cultural artifacts of Middle America which found their way to Europe. Certainly this skull encrusted with bits of turquoise embodies an utterly alien quality. The skull probably symbolized Tezcatlipoca ("Smoking Mirror"), the lord of heaven and earth, inflicter and healer of frightful diseases, among them cancer and syphilis. Such

skulls as this probably derive rather from Mixtec than from Aztec culture. In any case, they represent one of the oldest and most heavily traditional ornamental techniques of Old Mexico. (See also color plate XIII.)

The first important artist in Europe to appreciate these alien products of Mexican civilization was Albrecht Dürer.

Moctezuma's gifts were sent from Seville to Valladolid,

and then to the Spanish Netherlands. There Dürer saw them. He made a journal entry under the date August 27, 1520: "I too have seen the thing which was brought to the King from the new golden land, a sun all of gold . . . likewise a moon all of silver . . . likewise two chambers full of all sorts of their weapons, armor, cannon, wondrous arms. . . . These things are all precious, so that they are held to be worth a hundred thousand gulden. And I must say that all my days I have not seen anything that has so rejoiced my heart as these things . . . and I have been astonished at the subtle *ingenia* of the men in foreign lands. . . ." This observation of Dürer's must be understood in its context. Here an artist of the Renaissance was confronted for the first time with exotic art— and was moved by it. The things Dürer saw may have been examples of gold work similar to those later excavated at Monte Albán in Oaxaca—such as the golden breastplate and mask shown on the opposite page, probably the image of a Mixtec god of death.

The very earliest European depiction of an Indian

in existence. These tinted pen drawings are not upside down (see the inscriptions). Rather, the Indian is lying on his back, juggling with his feet a log as heavy as a man. He was a native whom Cortés brought back to Europe in 1528, when he returned to justify himself before Emperor Charles V against the accusations of his enemies. He won not only mercy, but also honor, and was granted the privilege of accompanying the Emperor on his subsequent journeys. On one such occasion Weiditz executed the portrait of him shown on page 252 and also made these drawings of his captive Indian. Weiditz's superscribed remarks, in language and spelling quainter and even more scrambled than the run of sixteenth-century German, are as follows:

"This is an Indian who lieth on his back tossing a log on his heels. It is long as a man and as heavy so that he keepeth beneath him a mat as big as a calf's skin."

"In such wise the Indians play

with a blown up ball, hitting it with the nether parts and the hands. For moving on the ground they wear a hard leather over the nether parts so that it may receive the impact of the ball, also such leather gloves."

This, too, is a tinted pen drawing from Christoph Weiditz's album. In all probability what we are seeing here is the first rubber ball to be used in a game in Europe. Enormous ball fields were adjuncts of the temple grounds of the Aztecs, and of the Maya before them. In many cultures, games and religion were closely connected.

Weiditz's legend on the next picture is quite terse: "In such wise Indian women go. No more than one came out."

At first glance the Indian woman's dress looks as primitive as the proverbial grass skirt of a South Sea islander. In fact the costume is feather work of a high order of artistry, tied by bands exemplifying beautiful dye work and complicated weaving techniques.

These so-called savages had a civilization and a social order in some respects scarcely less advanced than that of the Spaniards. But this could be apprehended only by a man without prejudice—that is to say, a man with true Christian charity and understanding, who collected and collated the things the Spaniards were destroying.

No portrait of Bernardino de Sahagún

has come down to us. This amazing priest of the time of the conquest was born in Sahagún around 1500 and died in Mexico in 1590. Aside from his long and adventurous life, he was remarkable for having developed a method of study for bygone civilizations which was applied to the history of Greece and Rome much after his time, but was not utilized in its own proper sphere, Middle America, until 250 years had passed.

In lieu of a portrait, we reproduce a sample of his handwriting: the last page of the Spanish version of his great work on the religion, culture, and history of Mexico.

In 1529 Bernardino de Sahagún came from Spain to Mexico in company with nineteen other Franciscans—and there he stayed. For some sixty years he was a teacher—that is to say, a missionary; but at the same time he was an attentive listener to the recollections of the upper-class Indians—as a researching scholar. Immediately after his arrival he began studying the language of the country, the predominant Náhuatl. Under highly unfavorable conditions he then systematically recorded everything he could learn about the religion, art, ethics, social order, and military organization of the Aztecs. His book may truly be called an encyclopedia of Aztec civilization.

His work was all the more remarkable because even as he was writing it his superior, the Franciscan bishop Zumárraga (1486–1548), was carrying on a ruthless campaign of consigning to flames every heathen document he could lay hands on. That is the reason for the rarity of pre-Conquest manuscripts, and the reason for their extreme value.

The great work was largely completed by 1569. It was written in the Aztec language, for it consisted mostly of verbatim records of narratives by Aztec informants. Then came the grotesque sequel: Sahagún's superiors strongly opposed its publication. They went so far as to seize the manuscript and scatter parts of it among various religious institutions in Spain. At last the president of the Council of India, Juan de Ovando, intervened in Sahagún's favor; he commanded the return of the manuscript to the author, and requested a Spanish translation. Sahagún prepared a translation, and added a lexicon and many illustrations. In order to have his work published at last, he gave his consent to numerous alterations that his superiors deemed desirable. Once more the manuscript was sent to Madrid. Nothing happened. Finally one day he was told that it had disappeared. Sahagún died, alone and forgotten, in the monastery of Santa Cruz in Mexico.

Today, both versions have been rediscovered. The Mexican original has been found in Madrid; the fair copy of the illustrated bilingual manuscript is in Florence. The Spanish version was published in Mexico in 1829, then in London in 1830.

To this day, however, the far more valuable Aztec version, with its uncensored original accounts, has not been completely published. Parts of it were translated into German by the German scholar Eduard Seler. These parts were published in 1927, almost three and a half centuries after Sahagún's death. Very recently indeed, in 1950 and 1952, another German scholar, Leonhardt Schultze-Jena, has translated additional large sections of the text.

On the following two pages we reproduce some illustrations from the bilingual manuscript, together with condensed samples of the Aztec original text as rendered by Seler. These come from the voluminous chapter on the fabrication of feather ornaments.

"The feather workers who make feather mosaics, whose joy it is to do feather works, begin their labors in the following manner: First they consider how they shall design the pattern. There are first the painters who draw it."

"The feathers are put together with flour-paste; then they are pasted firmly to the agave leaf; the layer is flattened with a bone scraper. What are called shrunken feathers are only ordinary feathers. For they serve as the commencement for the perfection of the feather work. They form the first layer, acting as the bed for the various precious feathers."

"Mixing of the paste is the children's, the apprentices' task; they mix it for the master."

"The feathers are turned hither and thither, examined on all sides; that is, if feathers appear to the eye as too thin in one spot, as too thick in another, as irregular or crushed in any portion, they are thrown away."

"There is another procedure. . . . This is the way fans are made, quetzal fans, arm-bangles, insignia for the back, yellow tunics. . . . First the frame is tied together. . . ."

"When the brown and white feathers of the long-tailed cuckoo or the yellow feathers of the çaquan follow the quetzal feathers, they are all first provided with threads, the threads knotted, and then they are sewed to the frame and the ends threaded through and tied. . . ."

"What are called yellow feathers are dyed, are dyed yellow. A pigment something like flax dodder is boiled in water, with which alum and saltpeter are mixed."

"And if a very small creature is to be made, say a small lizard . . . or a butterfly, the skeleton of the creature is formed of maize stalks or of bits of paper; these are covered with the powder of the dry maize stalk, mixed with paste. Then the figure is scraped . . . and polished. And then it is covered with a layer of cotton, and the pattern laid on in mosaic of feathers. The creature that is to be imitated is used as a model, as this painting shows."

Mexico was Hispanicized and Christianized.

Sahagún died defeated, and no one attempted to carry on his work. Then, in 1615, a book appeared whose illustrations marked a new departure into regions where only the intrepid could tread. It was a new edition of a then widely known handbook of Greco-Roman mythology, by a man named Cartari. The revision was carried out by Lorenzo Pignoria, and contained a revolutionary innovation. For the first time Egyptian and Japanese gods were pictured along with the divinities of classical antiquity—and a few of the misshapen Mexican gods as well.

This book, we may say, ushered in comparative religion in an age utterly unripe for such a study. Moreover, Pignoria strove toward an ideal unrecognized by antiquarians until two centuries after him: exactitude, replicas that would retain the true character of the original. He had much to say in his preface concerning the carelessness of engravers and woodcut-makers. He himself carefully checked the work of his assistants. For his Mexican material he had copies made of drawings in the *Codex Ríos*, a Mexican manuscript also known as *Codex Vaticanus A*, which friends had obtained for him from the Vatican.

We show on the preceding page an original drawing of the god Omeyocan from the codex, and (left) the woodcut prepared after it. We who live in an age of photography are at once aware of a host of errors of detail;

but for 1615 this woodcut represents an unusually faithful replica. Pignoria's picture is supplemented by the two smaller cuts in ovals of Egyptian divinities. For Pignoria felt that there was a connection between the Egyptian and Middle American civilizations—a theory of which we shall have more to say.

In describing his pictures he adhered closely to the original text. Of this one he said: "Homoyoca, the Mexican god, who was the Jupiter of these wretched people."

"These wretched people"

figure elsewhere in his book, as, for instance, in the woodcut at far right, which is Pignoria's version of the water color from the *Codex Ríos* to the left. Here are a number of distortions on the part of the artist for which we must not blame Pignoria, who obviously had a scientific mind. We must recollect that to point out even the faintest analogy between Christianity and the pagan religions was an act of incredible boldness in an age that burned men at the stake for utterly imaginary heresies. Pignoria was risking his skin when he retailed the prophecy made to the virgin Chimalmam in Tula—namely, that she would conceive without loss of her virginity and give birth to the god Quetzalcoatl. Consequently, his explanation of this picture must be regarded only as a bit of double-

talk designed to fend off suspicion: "Thus this emissary was the Gabriel (if we may use the term) of this wretched female; that is, Satan disguised as the angel of light."

This, then, is why the messenger of the god Citlallatonac is shown in this position, rather than directly in downward flight. In order to present this messenger as a diabolic imitation of Gabriel, Pignoria shows him hovering and facing right, consistent with Christian iconography, which represents the angels of the Annunciation always moving from left to right. He also omitted the roses that gave the original its name, Sochiquetzal: "the elevation of the roses into heaven."

We must pass on beyond these attempts to reconcile Christian sensibility with scientific observation of this world of bizarre, alien gods. The Christian world also had to come to terms with another aspect of life among the Aztecs: their frightful human sacrifices, which had no parallel anywhere on earth. Cortés's method of dealing with that aspect was blunt: he closed the sacrificial towers or planted the cross upon their bloody stones. But the first person who attempted to come to terms intellectually with this extraordinary phenomenon was a woman.

Human sacrifices.

Keeping human beings in cages and then slaughtering them for sacrifice was one of the shocking customs of the heathen Aztecs which, the Christian knights claimed, made any harshness against them justified.

The charge was true. The Aztecs did not wage wars primarily to win lands or to extend their power and influence; they waged wars chiefly in order to capture prisoners whom they could sacrifice. These they put to death at the top of their teocalli (step pyramids) by tearing the heart out of the living body and then throwing the bleeding corpse down the steps, as shown in the picture at right.

Ríos, commenting on the picture at left, says: "In this manner they offer their human sacrifices; those whom we see fallen on the ground are the sacrifices, but the dancers are the same persons who are represented as dead, for they danced and sang before they were sacrificed."

A Christian woman, a nun who was later called "the tenth Muse of Mexico," daringly endeavored for the first time to draw up a searching confrontation of Christian and pagan thinking.

(266)

was a poet whose intelligence and literary gift matched her courage.

Born in 1651, she took the veil at the age of sixteen. She first entered an austere Carmelite order; then, because of poor health, she transferred to the Sisters of St. Jerome. She was one of the most cultivated persons of her age—an extraordinary thing, indeed, for a woman. In spite of all that was repellent in Aztec civilization, she felt, and expressed repeatedly in verse, that the Indians were only erring human beings, and that love, not the sword, was needed to lead them back to the right way. Thus, she preached what Sahagún had already practiced. Unlike Sahagún, she was honored, famous, a radiant example to others. But her death was scarcely less poignant than his. On June 8, 1692, the buildings of the cathedral chapter and the government archives went up in flames. Once again human sacrifices were exacted from the natives: Juana saw with her own eyes the bloody repression of the uprising; she witnessed the daily scourgings and executions. Thereupon she gave her bishop all the gifts that the court had lavished upon her—jewelry, gems of all sorts, astronomical and musical instruments, even her library of four thousand volumes. She asked him to sell everything and distribute the proceeds among the poor. Then she began to practice such terrible mortifications that her confessor had to intercede. Shortly thereafter the plague broke out in the convent. She devoted herself to tending the sick, and was herself carried off by the plague on April 17, 1695.

Here is a selection from the prelude to a religious drama by the "tenth Muse of Mexico." A personification of Indian idolatry, in open form, defends his old religion against Fides (Faith). To speak out for paganism was, for the time, scandalous audacity, even though the debate was, ultimately, no more than a literary device.

Idolatry:

Not, while my life rages hot,
Shall you, Fides, win success.
Everywhere you preach Christ's tidings,
Opening the ways for Him
By your cunning and your weapons;
Yet though nearly all the nations
Who were once my leal subjects
Have succumbed to your persuasions,
Have received you in their hearts—
Still I say to you again:
Such vast powers are not yours,
That with but a single tug
You can rip up all the roots
Of my deep and ancient customs.
Though I lie half stricken now,

Still I can protect the places
Which you threaten to o'erwhelm,
Where by right of ancient practice
Sacrifices still are taken,
Where men still are being slaughtered.

Fides:

Do you dare resist our plan,
Shameless, execrated creature?
Whence comes this effrontery?

Idolatry:

Vilify me as you please.
Still my task is to protect
Ancient rights, and still I can.
Here I stand for all the manners,
Speak for all the ancient ways
Of these lands and of these peoples,
With the voice and on behalf of,
On behest of all the Indios;
Here I stand and speak this warning:
Though you feel that strength is yours
Since you have converted them
To the banner of your Faith,
Do not seek to use your power
To transform the ancient manner
Of their human sacrifices. . . ."

"He is off on a singularly beautiful voyage,

and is a lucky and enviable man," the brother of Alexander von Humboldt wrote to Goethe. On June 5, 1799, Alexander left Europe to travel for five years in the Americas. This German baron (1769–1859) was one of the last universal men, adventurer as well as intellectual, friend of all the great people of his times. The amount of raw material for scholarship he brought back from his first voyage to North and

South America was fantastic. For decades afterward specialists were kept busy publishing the geographical, botanical, zoological, geological, physical, meteorological, and sociological results of his travels. The tremendous *Voyage aux régions équinoxiales du Nouveau Continent* began appearing in Paris in 1807; it comprised twenty folio and ten quarto volumes with 1,425 copper plates, and cost untold sums to print. Several publishers had to unite on the project; the King of Prussia provided subsidies; and Humboldt himself spent almost his entire fortune on it—more than forty thousand talers.

For our purposes it is sufficient to note that Humboldt was the first European to study old Mexican architecture scientifically. He published the first drawings of it, differentiated the styles of various periods, and finally—though with extreme tentativeness—explored the question that is still being discussed today: whether there is any connection between Mexican architecture and the buildings of the Old World in Egypt and Mesopotamia. Are the similarities more than sheer chance?

Humboldt found the parallels most striking in the case of the pyramid of Cholula.

LE BARON DE HUMBOLDT,

The gods disapproved of this structure,

which was meant to reach into the clouds, Humboldt reports. He drew his information from native Indians and from the traditions recorded in the *Codex Ríos*. Measur-

ing the height, he found the structure to be 180 feet tall. The sides ran a distance of between 1,450 and 1,500 feet; the ground area was twice that of the pyramid of

Cheops. The engraving is after Humboldt's own drawing.

Cholula is one of those places where certain features of the pre-Aztec, pre-Mayan civilization, perhaps the oldest civilization of all in Middle America, have survived. It is called the Toltec culture—but beyond its name, little is known of it.

Humboldt relates the tale of a great flood that devastated the land. Seven giants saved themselves from the all-engulfing waters. Xelhua, the architect, then built the pyramid. Bricks were baked far away in the province of Tlamanalco. In order to move them to Cholula, Xelhua set up a chain of men who passed them along, from hand to hand, the entire distance. The gods were wroth at this plan. They cast fire at the peak of the pyramid, and many work-ers were killed. Cortés himself was shown a meteorite which, he was told, had fallen upon the top of the pyramid; it was shaped like a toad. The Cholulans had a custom of dancing around the pyramid and sing-ing a song about its building—a song whose first lines were in a language unknown to the singers! . . . Who could overlook the analogies with the Biblical Flood and the building of the Tower of Babel?

Ever since 1810, incidentally, scholarly literature has always quoted these crucial passages of the Ríos text from Humboldt. Actually, part of Humboldt's narrative is not to be found in Ríos at all. Thus, Humboldt must have come across fresh native traditions on his own; his work has a value as source-history which specialists have hith-erto failed to recognize.

"The symbolism of the new religion has not entirely dispelled

memory of the old," says Humboldt, writing of the small pilgrimage chapel on the apex of the teocalli of Cholula. "The people hasten in great crowds from all directions to celebrate the Feast of Mary on top of this pyramid. An unspoken terror, a pious shudder, overcomes the natives at the sight of this monstrous mass of brickwork, covered by eternally fresh grass and shrubbery."

The pyramid of these ancient Mexican Indians has here been made into a Mount Calvary. The picture is a hand-painted lithograph from a drawing by Luciano Castañeda, a member of Captain Dupaix's first expedition in 1805. Dupaix's role in the history of archaeological discoveries may very well be compared with that of Robert Hay (see page 78).

But before we come to Dupaix we must mention a man who gave his whole life and his entire fortune to archaeology, and whose reward was a miserable death in an English debtors' prison.

An odd obituary appeared in the Gentleman's Magazine for May 1837:

"*Feb. 27.* In the Sheriff's prison at Dublin, of typhus fever, aged 42, the Right Hon. Edward King, Viscount Kingsborough. He was the eldest son of George third and present Earl of Kingston, by Lady Helena Moore. . . ."

Webb's *Companion of Irish Biography* is somewhat more detailed: "His life was devoted to the study of Mexican antiquities. This passion was acquired when a student at Oxford, when the Mexican manuscripts in the Bodleian fired his imagination. His magnificent work, replete with illustrations, was given to the world in 1831, in seven volumes, imperial folio, price £210. Two additional volumes appeared after his death at a price of £25.4.0. The book cost him upwards of £32,000 and his life; for, oppressed with debt, he was arrested at the suit of a paper manufacturer, and lodged in the debtors' prison, Dublin, where he died of typhus fever. . . . Had he lived, he would within a year have become Earl of Kingston, with a fortune of £40,000 a year. . . ."

Kingsborough collected with a passion which almost equaled that of Sir Hans Sloane (see page 174). But he collected not for collecting's sake; he was bent on proving a specific thesis that was in the air at the time. This was that the civilized American Indians had been descendants of the "ten lost tribes of Israel." Part of his huge work was a reprinting of a *History of the North American Indians* by James Adair, every page of which had for a heading: "On the Descent of the American Indians from the Jews."

He had four luxury sets with their 1,050 plates printed on parchment, and presented one to the British Museum. But not only did he die ignominiously as a debtor; his name, too, seemed condemned to oblivion. If we look up "Kingsborough, Lord" in the British Museum catalogue, we find only a reference to "King, Edward." From this we are straightway referred to "Aglio, Agostino," the artist. Not only the luxury edition, then, but the ordinary edition as well

is catalogued under the name of the artist who made the pictures. However, William Prescott, the historian of the conquest of the Aztec Empire, has paid due tribute to Kingsborough:

"The drift of Lord Kingsborough's speculation is to establish the colonization of Mexico by the Israelites. To this the whole battery of his logic and learning is directed. For this hieroglyphics are unriddled, manuscripts compared and monuments delineated. . . . By this munificent undertaking, which no government, probably, would have, and few individuals could have executed, he has entitled himself to the lasting gratitude of every friend of science."

Today his nine volumes of *Antiquities of Mexico* are recognized as vital source material for students of American archaeology and history. Even modern works depend on them for illustrations.

The preceding page shows one example: a facsimile from the *Codex Mendoza*. At the top are young messengers, the last of them accompanied by his wife. In the middle section we have the Mexican emperor, seated. He has bestowed on some of his messengers the dignity of a *taquilua*—that is, ambassador. In the lower section we have officials and judges on the left, on the right petitioners for justice. We even know the names of the judges; Number 22 is named Tequixquiuahuacatl.

The feathered serpent,

one of the incarnations of the god Quetzalcoatl. This relief adorns the pre-Aztec pyramid at Xochicalco ("city of flowers").

Close comparison between the drawing and a recent photograph (below) shows that the carving has sustained some damage since the day it was discovered. The two men who came across it along with many other valuable source materials were Captain Guillaume Dupaix and his draftsman Luciano Castañeda.

Oblivion has overtaken

Captain Guillaume Dupaix and Luciano Castañeda, so much so that they are not even mentioned in standard reference works on Middle American archaeology. This is quite inexplicable. For they conducted three expeditions, in 1805, 1806, and 1807, at the behest of Charles IV, King of Spain. Charles even provided them with a military escort. But amid the turmoil of the Napoleonic era, the fruits of their labors were not appreciated. It remained for Kingsborough to unearth Castañeda's drawings and the detailed journal Dupaix kept during the expeditions. Kingsborough's reprint appeared in 1831. Oddly enough, three years later an otherwise unknown Monsieur Baradère published in Paris an edition containing essentially the same plates and text, but in Spanish and French rather than English. He claimed to be the rightful owner of the original material, maintaining that the Mexican Senate had given it to him in 1828 in exchange for services, but that shipment had inexplicably been delayed for five or six years. The tale sounds most improbable. The edition certainly conveys the impression that Baradère put it together out of Kingsborough's compilations, adding some material of his own and of other writers and artists.

The drawing by Castañeda at upper right and the photograph below are of Zapotec urns found by the Dupaix expedition in the cities of Zaachila and Quilapa. Dupaix comments in his journal: "It was found some time ago, together with four others of similar size, shape and substance, in ploughing a piece of ground near the rector's house. For what purpose could it have been designed? . . . Perhaps the box was used to hold jewels or incense. . . . I should in vain attempt to explain the various designs *in relievo* with which the figure is embellished, since they are too complicated and too fanciful for my comprehension."

Relief from a pillar of the "palacio" in Palenque.

This spacious palace is situated in what is probably the most magnificent ruined city of Mexico. Again it is clear that Dupaix and Castañeda saw more than survives today. No wonder, for the early investigators had no way to remove the rampant jungle vegetation except to burn over the site. The fires damaged even the hard building-stone —how much more harm must it have done to the fragile stucco reliefs and terra-cotta ornaments. After Dupaix's last visit in 1807, the ruins of Palenque were burned over at least four times.

Dupaix comments on the drawing: "Like the structures which contained them, these reliefs are fast hastening to decay. . . . All that I could do was to cause those which were still perfect to be copied with utmost fidelity, the greater part having merely left an impression on the wall. . . . These statues were painted with vermilion, minute particles of which, as well as occasional patches, are still visible in the narrow folds of the drapery."

"I was carried in a litter by several Indians,

and escorted by a dragoon who had been assigned to me for my journey to Uxmal." The dragoon, wrote Jean-Frédéric-Maximilien Comte de Waldeck (1766–1875), proved extremely useful; his presence struck terror in the Indians, and when he appeared they labored all the harder at clearing the jungle growth away from the ruins.

After Dupaix and Kingsborough, Waldeck was the third European who threw himself heart and soul into the exploration of Middle America's past—at a period when the world cared nothing for it. Yet he became a legendary figure in his lifetime, if only because he attained the improbable age of one hundred and nine years. He had grown up in pre-Revolutionary France—the era that Talleyrand later called the only one worth living in; he survived the Terror, outlived Napoleon, saw the Restoration and the Second Empire, and at the age of one hundred and five witnessed the Franco-Prussian War.

Waldeck was the descendant of a noble family that had emigrated from Germany to France. He began as a painter and pupil of Jacques-Louis David, and took part in the Napoleonic invasion of Egypt. With the routing of the French, all the other members of the Scientific Commission pulled out, but Waldeck undertook a private adventure up the Nile as far as Aswan. All turned out well on this trip. Shortly afterward, however, he tried unsuccessfully to cross the Sahara and reach Portuguese East Africa with a number of others. On this venture—as with Niebuhr's ill-fated party (see page 180)—all his companions perished.

In 1821 Waldeck visited Guatemala for the first time. The following year he went to London, where he prepared the illustrations for Antonio del Ríos's book describing the ruins of Palenque. In London he met Kingsborough, and the two men engaged in such fierce discussions that they became fast friends. Waldeck maintained that the Mexicans were descended from the Egyptians; Kingsborough, as we have mentioned, was convinced of their Israelite origin. Nevertheless, Kingsborough financed Waldeck's subsequent expeditions from 1832 to 1836, and the Count tendered his acknowledgment by naming a Mexican pyramid after him.

Palenque, the temple city in the jungle,

was Mayan, not Aztec. Mayan civilization is the only advanced one in the world which subsisted without the plow, the wagon, and domestication of animals. This civilization, regulated by the rigid patterns of a highly developed calendar that had a singular importance for the Maya, was peculiar in a number of respects. There was no middle class; the caste of nobles and priests lived in strict isolation above the ignorant, characterless masses of peasantry, who vegetated like the Egyptian fellahin.

If the present correlation between Mayan and Christian chronology—on which scientists are at last more or less in agreement—is correct, Palenque was founded around A.D. 100—later than Uaxactún, Tikál, Copán, Piedras Négras, and Naranjo. The age of the Mayan state has not yet been determined. Before it, and sometimes contemporaneously with it, there were other states, the most widespread of which has been called "Toltec," for lack of a more definite name. At present the origins of the Maya are lost in obscurity. Some people used to call the Toltecs "the Sumerians of Middle American culture," on the theory that they introduced writing, knowledge of the stars, and the first laws.

The panorama shown on the preceding page is of relatively recent date (1896–9). Right foreground is the *Palacio*; behind it, from left to right: the Crucifix Temple, the Temple with the Altar, the Temple of Trophies or the Sun Temple, the Temple with the Bas-reliefs, the Temple of Inscriptions. Although the drawing is highly schematic, it conveys the sense of enchantment felt by all who came upon these ornate places of worship in the heart of primeval jungle. Count Waldeck spent three years here, and made some hundred drawings.

With Kingsborough dead, Waldeck was unable to raise the money to publish the results of his explorations. Finally, aged nearly ninety-five, he appealed to the poet Prosper Mérimée and other interested members of the French Academy. Assistance was finally granted. In 1866, when he was one hundred years old, his account of Palenque was published.

"If I had come to Uxmal only a year later,"

writes Waldeck in regard to this reconstruction, "I should not have been able to reproduce this monument so completely, for the middle had sunk, several stones necessary for the stability of the center having meanwhile been removed. In order to prevent the entire structure from collapsing, I attempted to replace the missing stones, and even intended to take one or two masons along on my second expedition in order to repair the damaged place properly and thus preserve the ruin in the interests of future travelers. . . . I have named this pyramid 'Lord Kingsborough' because it seemed to me, of all the buildings in Yucatan, the worthiest of immortalizing the memory of that noblest of all great gentlemen, to whom the world of scholarship owes that redoubtable book on Mexico."

(278)

unaware. The jungle had grown so thickly over them that even the natives in the immediate vicinity knew nothing about them. The incendiary methods of the early expeditions fought back the jungle, but at the same time furthered the destruction of the buildings. In 1787, when Antonio del Río examined the ruins, he proudly reported that "we left not a window nor a door walled up; we did not fail to tear down every partition wall; we did not fail to undertake excavations of two to three ells depth into every room, corridor, courtyard, entrance, or underground corridor."

Here is the Sun Temple, also called the Temple of Trophies, a wholly unique piece of architecture. Our illustration shows a model now in the American Museum of Natural History in New York.

Middle American archaeology was really born in 1842.

In that year the investigations that had hitherto been carried forward quietly and privately suddenly began to stir the public imagination. Waldeck's *Romantische Reise . . . (Romantic Travels . . .)* had appeared in Paris in 1838 without making any great impression. But in 1842 John Lloyd Stephens's book *Incidents of Travel in Central America, Chiapas and Yucatan,* illustrated by Frederick Catherwood, was published in New York and aroused intense interest. The bizarre, magnificent, and monstrous relics of the Middle American civilizations suddenly burst on the consciousness of all literate persons.

Stephens (1805–1852) practiced law in New York for eight years before he took up archaeology. He traveled in Egypt, the Near East, and Greece. In Egypt he struck up a friendship with Catherwood, the artist who had been a member of the unfortunate Robert Hay expedition (see page 80). In 1839 he took Catherwood with him into the jungles of Central America and began his explorations near the city of Copán in Honduras. One day, after undergoing terrible hardships, when the two men had already begun to lose faith in the native tales that had led them on, they found themselves confronting a statue in the heart of the jungle. It was a pillar in human form, ornamented with such barbaric magnificence, carved in such alien forms, that it took their breath away.

The illustration shows a drawing by Catherwood of one of the many sculptured pillars they found in Copán. Stephens's accompanying text reads:

"Monument 'T,' a buried image. It was one of the most beautiful in Copán and in workmanship is equal to the finest Egyptian sculpture. . . . It stands at the foot of a wall of steps, with only the head and part of the breast rising above the earth. . . . When we first discovered it, it was up to the eyes. Arrested by the beauty of the sculpture and by its solemn and mournful position, we commenced excavating. As the ground was level up to that mark, the excavation was made by loosening the earth with the machete, and scooping it out with the hands. As we proceeded, the earth formed a wall around and increased the labor. The Indians struck so carelessly with their machetes, that, afraid to let them work near the stone, we cleared it with our own hands. It was impossible, however, to continue; the earth was matted together by roots which entwined and bound the monument. It required a complete throwing out of the earth for 10 or 12 feet around; and without any proper instrument and afraid of injuring the sculpture, we preferred to let it remain, to be excavated by ourselves at some future time, or by some future traveller. Whoever he may be, I almost envy him the satisfaction of doing it."

F. Catherwood

Today the Mayan stelae
stand behind barbed wire.

On the opposite page is a photograph of a
stele from Quirigua, near Copán. At the
right is Catherwood's drawing of another
stele, of which Stephens says: "This statue
had suffered so much from the action of
time and weather, that it was not always
easy to make out the characters, the light
being in all cases very bad and coming
through irregular openings in the branches
of trees."

The drawing is a masterpiece of exact
representation. The fourteen hieroglyphs
are copied with surpassing accuracy—a task
all the more difficult because at the time
designs such as these were utterly novel to
the European eye.

Moonlight in Izamal.

A drawing by Catherwood which shows his highly romantic treatment of jungle ruins. For archaeologists, it is important as the only reproduction of a vanished work of art: a colossal mask on the outer wall of the wrecked step pyramid at Izamal, Yucatán. In the foreground Dr. Cabot, the young physician of the expedition, is drawing a bead on a puma, while a native looks on.

Stephens supervises the moving of a sculptured stone door-jamb

from Kabah in Yucatán. The pillar is now in the American Museum of Natural History in New York.

After having smashed valuable stones in several earlier attempts, Stephens thought of another way to preserve these extraordinary monuments for science. He obtained permission to have plaster casts made. A specialist then worked for several years, in Copán and Quiriguá especially, constantly fighting the terrible climate, the trackless jungle, and the wildly luxuriant vegetation.

Today these casts stand in New York and London—blackened by a century's metropolitan soot but as impressive as ever.

Banished to a dark corridor of the Louvre,

noticed by few, stood a sprinkling of ancient American art and documents which had come into the possession of the French state. Monsieur de Longpérier, the curator of the collection, kept another hoard of vessels and sculptures in his own office because the directors of the museum refused to allow him any more room for exhibition.

We learn of this lamentable circumstance from Abbé Charles-Etienne Brasseur de Bourbourg (1814–1874), who sacrificed his career in order to dedicate himself to study of the antiquities of Middle America. A scholar as well as an adventurous soul, he made several vital discoveries among dusty books. Two of the documents he found must be reckoned among the most important sources on ancient American civilizations.

Brasseur studied philosophy and theology. In 1845 he was ordained a priest and went to live in Canada. In 1852 he published a history of that country. But he felt an unconquerable urge to study the cultures of Middle America, for he saw that no real scholar had engaged on the task that must precede all proper historical writing: the digging up, accumulation, and interpretation of all available documents. He had held a teaching position in Canada, and at the age of thirty-two was promoted to vicar-general of Boston. Renouncing that high office as well as the certain prospect of further advancement in the hierarchy, he accepted a post as priest in the Indian village of Rabinal in Guatemala.

First of all, he learned Quiché, the Mayan tongue that was still spoken in his village. Then he took leave of his priestly duties entirely and began traveling, visiting numerous ruins, but constantly returning to the libraries of America and Europe to search for written documents. To pay for all this, he first sold his property, then began writing historical novels under various pseudonyms. These were vastly successful, and he was enabled to undertake new journeys and researches. In the course of these he discovered what is probably the most important surviving text on Mayan religion.

The so-called *Popul Vuh* is the sacred book of the Quiché Indians, written down in the middle of the sixteenth century by an unknown Quiché loyal to the traditions of his tribe. The original has been lost, but the contents were preserved in a copy made by the priest Francisco Ximénez (b. 1666) between 1701 and 1703. He, too, wrote in the Quiché language, rendered in the Roman alphabet.

Brasseur discovered this copy at San Carlos University in Guatemala, and published a fascimile edition along with a French translation. Thus, he put at the disposal of scholars incomparably valuable information on Mayan religious customs, as well as material on the textile arts of the Maya. Without his efforts, all this would have been entirely lost.

The photograph on page 287 shows a Mayan ruler at prayer; it is a detail from a relief stele from Yaxchilán (Chiapas), probably carved in the seventh or eighth century of our era. The embroidery-like designs on the ruler's garment are composed of parts of various hieroglyphs which mean *union*, *fire*, and *heaven*. This "magic armor" is strongly reminiscent of the magical bee and wasp patterns spoken of in the section of the *Popul Vuh* quoted on page 288.

XIII. Aztec skull overlaid with mosaic. The typical mosaic consists of bits of turquoise and obsidian; the eyes are of iron pyrites. (Between A.D. 1324 and 1521.) (See also p. 255).

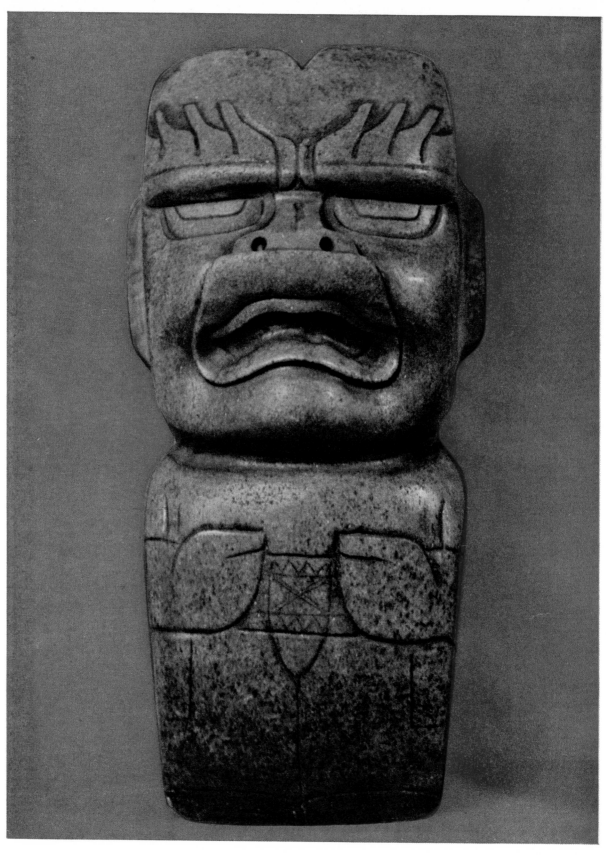

XIV. Ritual ax from Central America. Olmec ax, human face and cat face merged —highly typical of the Olmec style.

The two damsels

who played the chief part in the following story from the *Popul Vuh* may have looked like this. At any rate, they were probably dressed like these two, who are pictured in the *Codex Ríos*.

The legend goes that the Quiché Indians felt they could no longer endure the high exactions of their gods. The wizard priests Balam-Quitzé, Balam-Acab, Mahacutah, and Iqui-Balam were making innumerable human sacrifices to the gods Tohil, Avilix, and Hacavitz. The tribes held a council and discussed what they might do to protect themselves.

" 'How shall we overcome the gods?' they asked.

" 'This shall be our way of overcoming them. Since they have the appearance of youths when they let themselves be seen in the water, then let two maidens who are really beautiful, and very lovely, go and provoke in them the desire to possess them,' they said.

" 'Very well, let us go then; let us find two beautiful maidens,' they exclaimed, and then they went to find their daughters. And truly beautiful were the maidens. Then they instructed the maidens: 'Go, our daughters, go to wash clothes at the river, and if you see the three youths, undress before them, and if their hearts desire you call to them . . . then you shall say: "Give us a token of yours." And if after they have given you something, they want to kiss your faces, really give yourself to them. And if you do not give yourself to them, we shall kill you. . . . When you have the token, bring it here, and this shall be proof, in our judgment, that they were joined with you.' . . . And the two maidens, Xtah and Xpuch, were sent to the river, to the bathing place of Tohil, Avilix, and Hacavitz. This is what was decided by all the tribes. . . . And the girls became embarrassed at the moment when Tohil came, and did not speak to him. Thereupon he asked them: 'Where did you come from?' . . . And they answered: 'The lords have sent us to come here. "Go look at the faces of Tohil and speak with them," the lords told us; and "then bring proof that you have seen their faces," they told us.' Thus the two girls spoke, making known [that is, giving away] the purpose of their coming. Well, what the tribes wanted was that the two maidens would be violated by the incarnation of Tohil. But Tohil, Avilix, and Hacavitz, speaking again to Xtah and Xpuch, as the two maidens were called: 'Very well, with you shall go proof of our conversation. Wait a little and then you shall give it to the lords,' they said. Then they held council with the priests and sacrificers, and they said to Balam-Quitzé, Balam-Acab, Mahacutah, and Iqui-Balam: 'Paint three capes, paint on them the symbol of your being, in order that it may be recognized by the tribes when the maidens who are washing carry them back. . . .'

"At once the three began to paint. First, Balam-Quitzé painted a jaguar; the figure was made and painted on the surface of a cape; and then Mahacutah painted bumblebees and wasps all over, figures and drawings of which he painted on the cloth. And the three finished their paintings, three pieces they painted. Then they went to give the capes to Xtah and Xpuch, as they were called, and Balam-Quitzé, Balam-Acab, and Mahacutah said to them: 'Here is proof of your conversation; take these before the lords. Say to them, "In truth,

Tohil has talked to us; here we bring the proof." Tell them, and have them dress themselves in the clothes which you will give them.'

". . . When they [the maidens] arrived, the lords were filled with joy to see their faces and their hands, from which hung the things the maidens had gone for. 'Did you see the face of Tohil?' they asked them. 'Yes, we saw it,' answered Xtah and Xpuch. 'Very well, and you bring the token, do you not?' the lords asked, thinking that this was proof of their sin. Then the maidens held out the painted capes, all covered with jaguars and eagles, and covered with bumblebees and wasps, painted on the surface of the cloth and which shone before them. At once the lords felt a desire to put the capes on.

"The jaguar did nothing when the lord threw the first painting on his back. Then the lord put on the second painting, with the figure of an eagle. The lord felt very well wrapped within it. And he turned about before all of them. Then he undressed before all and put on the third painted cape. And now he had on himself the bumblebees and wasps which were on it. Instantly the bumblebees and wasps stung his flesh. And not being able to suffer the stings of these insects, he began to scream, because of the insects whose figures were painted on the cloth, the painting of Mahacutah, which was the third one that had been painted. Thus they were overcome. . . ."

The secrets of the sacred well.

One fine day the Mayan people left their cities behind them, abandoned their homeland, set up a new empire for themselves in the northernmost corner of what is now Yucatán—and built new cities and new temples. Surely this is one of the most mysterious events in the history of nations. The reason for this unique, apparently arbitrary mass migration has not yet been determined.

Chichén-Itzá became the center of the Mayan "New Empire." It was a gigantic city, a complex of bizarre temples, step pyramids, an observatory, a vast ballground, and a palace. That indefatigable searcher of libraries, Brasseur de Bourbourg, dug up in Madrid an account of this city by a sixteenth-century ecclesiastic, and published it in 1864. Immediately a storm broke; the ecclesiastic was suspected of having been a teller of tall tales, if not a deliberate liar. He was a Franciscan, Diego de Landa (1524–1579), one of the great zealots of the age. His zeal in burning "heathen" documents had won him the rank of Bishop of Mérida, the capital of Yucatán. It is no longer possible to say what caused this fanatic to undergo a sudden change of heart and work for the preservation of surviving Indian documents, or what impelled him to study seriously the mores and customs of the Mayan people, or what finally made him devote his attention to the altogether un-Christian Mayan calendar.

Thus, when his *Relación de las cosas de Yucatán*, edited by Brasseur, was reissued, people put little credence in its stories and interpretations. But there was one man who as soon as he became acquainted with the bishop's writings took them at their word, believed them quite literally, as Schliemann had the *Iliad*. And his instinct proved to be as right as Schliemann's. This was the American explorer and archaeologist Edward Herbert Thompson. The picture shows the Sacred Well of Chichén-Itzá, from whose muddy depths Thompson fetched the treasures that Diego de Landa, the "teller of tall tales," had said were there.

The Bishop related that the "well" of Chichén-Itzá had been a place of sacrifice. Every year in the dry season the people threw young girls, prisoners, and gems into the well to appease the rain god. Accepting this story, Thompson took lessons in diving, and descended into the dark waters.

The "well" is in reality a big basin of water, approximately circular in form. The depth is considerable, and has not yet been exactly measured. At its widest point the hole is 187 feet across. Steep limestone walls, some 50 feet in height, frame the entire basin.

Thompson began to dredge. No luck. Then he hired some sponge-divers from the Bahamas, himself donned a diver's suit, and went down into the well. The things he brought to the surface were a tremendous vindication of the Bishop. There were skeletal remains and gold work of the finest craftsmanship—the offerings to the rain god of which Diego de Landa had spoken. The golden ornaments Thompson salvaged—some of these are reproduced overleaf—are precious for their rarity as well as their metal. Gold was what the Spanish conquistadors were seeking in El Dorado; that was what had led them to the country, and for gold they conquered, pillaged, and killed. To them, the value lay in the metal, and therefore they melted jewelry, finely wrought utensils, and beautiful vessels into gold bars—these being easier to ship. Thus, almost all the Mayan works of art in gold vanished in the melting-pot—but at the mud-level of the well which Thompson reached, 80 feet underwater, such treasures lay intact.

We would never have had them but for Thompson's courageous action. Yet we must say that we cannot regard him as a really serious interpreter of his finds. He was by nature a visionary. Moreover, his diving had injured his health; he was later afflicted with lameness and partial deafness. These physical handicaps may sometimes have affected the tone of his reports, which are not always organized with precision and clarity. Nevertheless, he deserves the respect due to every pioneer.

The gold objects he found were not only interesting but also full of surprises for scholars. Most were not pure gold, but alloys—evidence of advanced metallurgical techniques on the part of the makers. Furthermore, most of them were imports; this was proved by chemical and technological studies. This in turn indicated a continent-wide commerce whose existence had not been remotely suspected.

Unfortunately, this adventure put an abrupt end to Thompson's delvings in Mexico. He had fetched gold out of a muddy hole. *Gold*—the word ran from mouth to mouth. The Mexican government accused him of theft of national property, demanded a fantastic sum in compensation, and confiscated the property he had bought in Yucatán. . . . Feeling, with some justification, that sinister forces were closing in upon him and that he was in real danger, this adventurous archaeologist took swift action. He chartered a half-finished schooner. His party consisted of twenty-six persons, and he had food aboard for only eleven: moreover, he had no nautical instruments. After a perilous thirteen-day voyage he reached Cuba. He never again set foot in Mexico.

The picture shows parts of a gold mask found in the well.

Upon the death of Eduard Seler in 1922,

the museum at Mexico City closed its doors for three days as a sign of mourning. When Seler (1859–1922) was a young man of twenty he came down with a dangerous gastric disease. It left him so ravaged that he had to abandon his plans for a career as a teacher; the authorities considered him physically unfit and refused to rehire him. Forced to find some other way to earn his living, he translated a book on American prehistory, and thus found his way into the field in which he was to be a leader and pathfinder for forty years.

Seler went to work as an assistant in the Berlin Ethnological Museum; later he became director of the Americanist Department. With his wife (daughter of the physician who had saved his life), he set out in 1887 on his series of great explorations. Seler's contributions to knowledge of the religions, the languages, and the arts of Central America are inestimable. A piece of good fortune came his way in his meeting with the Duc de Loubat, who owed his title to conquests in the realm of the intellect; it had been given him by the Pope for important research in Vatican archives. Loubat, an immensely rich man, established the first substantially endowed chairs for Americanist studies in Paris, New York, and Berlin—where, in 1899, Seler became the first occupant. Loubat also stood sponsor for those great International Congresses of Americanists at which Seler took the leading role for many years.

In his time Seler was also the foremost

student of Middle American languages. The smallest scraps of his translations serve as bases for further research today. He was the first to make something of the mysterious Mayan texts; he also grasped the system of the Aztec calendar. As a scholar, he never departed from the actual evidence. Speculation, even somewhat too audacious hypotheses were things he held in abhorrence. Consequently, with all his vast knowledge, this man never gave thought to the question of possible cultural links between Asia and America.

(293)

the strongest proof of a connection with Near Eastern and Egyptian cultures? Not only the pyramids but also certain linguistic forms, certain divinities, and a large number of other peculiarities of the Middle American civilizations virtually drove scholars to assume cultural transfusion or imitation. We have already mentioned in connection with Lord Kingsborough the theory that the Indians were descendants of the ten lost tribes of Israel who were expelled from Assyria by Sargon in 721 B.C. That thought cropped up early in post-Columbian history, and was enunciated by a Jewish traveler, Aaron Levi de Montezinos, when he returned to Amsterdam in 1644. Eleven years later the idea was developed with messianic overtones by Rabbi Menasseh ben Israel in his book *Piedra gloriosa* (*The Glorious Stone*), published in 1655 with illustrations by Rembrandt.

There were other views: that the Indians were Hindus, whom St. Thomas had once set out to convert. Or they were descendants of one of the sons of Noah. To a man of strict scientific mind like Seler, all such notions seemed dilettante nonsense. And yet as Seler and like-minded scholars went about their tasks of collecting material and arranging it, new facts bearing on the old problem emerged.

Grafton Elliot Smith, the anatomist and investigator of mummies (see page 124),

revived the question in 1924 with a flourish. The title of his essay gives us a hint of his approach: *Elephants and Ethnologists*. At the right is one of the drawings he released for publication in the *Illustrated London News*—unmistakably an elephant with raised trunk, from a stone relief from the palace at Palenque. Any keen-eyed observer could see such elephants among the reliefs of the pyramids at Copán and Palenque, as well as in Mayan manuscripts. Because there were certainly no elephants in Middle America in historical times, someone must have brought to America at least a mental image of an elephant. That, for Smith, was the only logical explanation. Some cautious scholars, it was true, circumambulated the elephant by suggesting that the animal pictured might be a rendition of the tapir, that small relative of the rhinoceros native to Mexico and South America. But Smith simply laughed at them.

The foremost champion of the most recent theory of "diffusionism"—which now holds the view that Indian cultures originated as a result of influences via China and Indo-China—is the Austrian scholar Robert von Heine-Geldern (b. 1885). It must be stressed that the problem is far from solved. But in 1949 a discovery was made which demolished one of the favorite arguments of the opponents of diffusionism.

Advocates of the independence of the American cultures had always maintained that the similarities between Mexican and Egyptian pyramids were purely superficial. (Below, a model of the pyramid of Tenayuca which reveals the growth, layer by layer, of the vast structure.) One had only to compare their purposes for the fundamental difference to be instantly apparent. The Egyptian pyramids were tombs, mighty structures raised around the burial chambers of the pharaohs. The Mexican pyramids, on the other hand, were terraced structures serving the sole end of raising a temple above the jungle and lending it commanding size and height.

This argument from function was persuasive. In fact, none of the known Mexican pyramids gave any indication of having been used as a tomb. Occasionally small chambers were discovered inside them, but as these were empty, they were disregarded. Then, in 1949, a Mexican archaeologist discovered inside a pyramid a vault that was not empty.

When Alberto Ruz began excavating

the Temple of the Inscriptions at Palenque (above, a cross-sectional drawing made after the excavation was completed), he attacked a shapeless hill covered by green jungle growth. After laborious digging, archaeologists identified what had been an eight-stepped pyramid.

Inside the temple, which stood upon the top platform, the entrance to a staircase was found. It was carefully constructed and in a good state of preservation. Descending the forty-five steps, the scientists came to a landing from which two shafts opened out; these must once have admitted light and air. After a further twenty-one steps, the excavators came across a horizontal passage that had been closed by a wall. They broke through this obstacle and found, scattered over the floor, pots, objects of jade, and a pearl. These finds, so reminiscent of the funeral furnishings of Egyptian tombs, stirred the scientists to feverish excitement, which reached its height when, close by, they found skeletons —the bones of several young men and one woman. Behind this corridor a chamber opened out. A burial vault? It lay 80 feet below the floor of the temple, 6 feet under

the base of the pyramid, and was 30 feet
in length by 13 in width. Stucco reliefs
adorned the walls. In the center of the
chamber stood a low stone structure that
was thought to be an altar. Its top was a
slab of stone 12 feet long by 6.5 feet wide
by 10 inches thick, covered with reliefs
and bordered by an indecipherable inscription.

When Alberto Ruz had this stone slab
raised, he encountered something that
shook the firm opinions of two generations
of Mayan scholars. What had looked like
an altar was a sarcophagus. The hollow
base contained the skeleton of a man between the ages of forty and fifty. Jade
ornaments lay untouched in their original
position. There were large earrings inscribed with Mayan hieroglyphics, a dia-
dem, a mosaic mask, a necklace of beads
in the form of fruits and flowers, rings for
all ten fingers, and many other objects.
Two enormous pearls were found, one on
each side of the skull. There could be no
doubt about it: Ruz stood before the mor-
tal remains of a Mayan ruler. And was it
not highly probable that the skeletons at
the entrance were those of sacrifices offered to the ruler?

A complete scientific interpretation of
this find is not yet possible. But opponents
of the diffusion theory can no longer say
that Mexican pyramids never served as
burial chambers, as the Egyptian pyramids
always did. In at least one case a Mayan
pyramid was also a mausoleum.

The territory of the Lacandón Indians,

a dying branch of the Mayan people in southeastern Mexico, is a godforsaken region visited by white men only when they are seeking mahogany trees or chicle, the raw material for chewing-gum. Here, in 1946, came a group of American moviemakers commissioned by the United Fruit Company to produce a documentary film, *The Maya Through the Ages.*

The natives are extremely primitive; they are the one Mayan tribe that has never been Christianized. The film people did their best to establish friendly relations with them, and Giles G. Healey won their confidence to such an extent that they showed him their most sacred mystery: the "Colored Walls." Thus Healey became the first white man to see a sight of priceless value to archaeologists.

A considerable number of "colored walls"—that is, frescoes—were already known. But those previously examined had pictured only religious subjects, gods and symbols. Here in Bonampak, however, on the walls of three rooms inside an ancient building overgrown by vegetation, were found representations of the daily life of the old Maya—pictures of unparalleled beauty and richness.

After Healey published an account and photographs of these paintings, a Mexican, and two years later an American, expedition went to Bonampak. But although complete lighting equipment was transported on muleback through the jungle, and although the best photographic ap-

(299)

paratus was employed, all the photographs proved to be but feeble reproductions of the paintings. It is curious that in this age of the camera the scientists had to return to the methods of the nineteenth century.

Two artists were engaged to copy the paintings as exactly as possible. They were aided and advised by professional archaeologists, and their series of paintings, now on exhibit in the National Museum of Mexico and in the Peabody Museum at Harvard University, are the most faithful of renditions. They shocked archaeologists into awareness of all they did not know about the Maya. The meaning of the various figures, who are obviously presented in a certain order of rank; the costumes, which were undoubtedly determined by ritual; the still undecipherable Mayan hieroglyphs—all these things presented riddles. Moreover—but we must put this tentatively—the style of the paintings is amazingly reminiscent of Egypt. The figures are arranged in rows, and the heads and feet of most of the persons represented are shown in strict profile.

In the jungles of Middle America lurk many mysteries whose very existence we do not yet suspect. But one by one they will yield to man's endeavors. The day will come when we shall be able to write the history of Middle American civilizations with as much specific knowledge as we have long possessed in regard to Mediterranean cultures. And if the most recent attempt at deciphering the Mayan hieroglyphs, offered by the Russian scholar Y. V. Knorosov in 1955, should prove valid, we have not long to wait before we know the truth of how those civilizations arose.

BOOK V

Retrospect and Perspective
Appendix

In 322 illustrations this book has shown Western man's awakening to awareness of his own past, his extension of awareness into detailed knowledge, and his distillation of knowledge into historical insight. Thus we have learned—or shall we say, are still learning—to understand our place in history. "The historian is a prophet turned backward," Friedrich Schlegel said.

Western man's journey into the past was inspired by the spirit of humanism. Naturally enough, then, he first sought out the near-by world of Greco-Roman antiquity. Then he traveled further, into those civilizations with which we are connected by the Bible, and finally struck back to those primeval times in which civilization was first taking shape.

Since then the journey into the past has assumed wider, global meanings. It is not only our own beginnings we are seeking; we search out alien roads as well. The historian finds that he must look to archaeology to understand the development of the world, of humanity in general. That is, archaeology has joined hands with prehistory, anthropology, and half a dozen other sciences. It is impossible to present even a bird's-eye view of the archaeological work that is going on today, as these lines are written, in China and South America, in Cimmerian Russia and in the former Holy Land. To mention a few names would be to arbitrarily omit far too many others. That revolutionary discoveries are still possible today (indeed, that we must hold ourselves in readiness for them) is illustrated by the chance finding of the Dead Sea scrolls—those Old Testament texts that must lead to a revision of many passages in the Bible. Then, too, there are the latest excavations in Jericho, which have revealed foundations of cities that are probably older than any we have hitherto known. Or, again, as in the case of the Hittites, we are suddenly in a position to write the history of old empires of whose existence we knew but dimly until

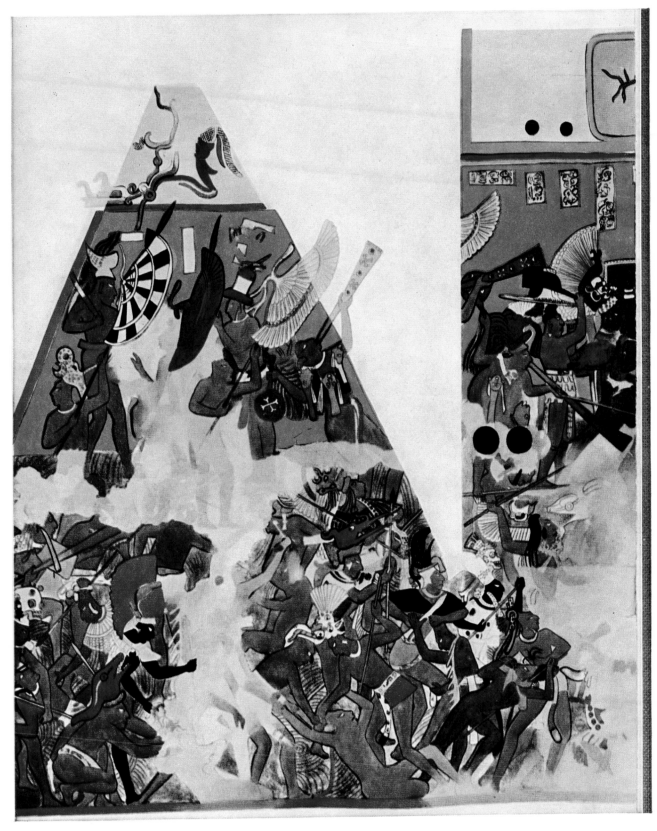

XV. Maya attack their neighbors. Copy of a wall painting from the Mayan city of Bonampak in Central America (between A.D. 317 and 987.) Discovered by an American cinema expedition.

XVI. **Aztec shield with mosaic of feathers.** Representation is a prairie wolf. (Between A.D. 1324 and 1521.) Gift from Moctezuma to Emperor Charles V (through Cortés).

recently. Perhaps a similar revelation will be forthcoming before long in regard to the still mysterious Indus culture.

The pioneering age of archaeology is past. But it would be wrong to assume that archaeology's tasks have been diminished by a wealth of accomplishment. New developments in science have enriched the apparatus and methods of the archaeologists. The spade may remain the symbol of the excavator; but modern archaeology has also made good use of airplanes, diving-gear, and atomic physics.

Underwater photograph of a diver

bringing the neck of an antique amphora to the surface.

In 1900 the Greek sponge-diver Elias Stadiatis, while returning from the Tunisian coast, was driven by a storm to the nearly uninhabited island of Antikythera off Crete. Descending into its waters after sponges, he came upon the wreck of a ship filled with quantities of bronze and marble statues. He brought to the surface a more than life-size bronze arm, because he justifiably feared that his story would not be believed without evidence.

That find by a sponge-diver probably marks the birth of underwater archaeology.

Sponge-divers again, in 1907, called the

attention of Maurice Merlin, director of monuments in Tunis, to a wrecked ship that they had found outside Mahdia, a small town on the eastern coast of Tunis. The ship had for cargo some sixty marble columns, as well as capitals, great marble torsos and busts, fauns, nymphs, statuettes of bronze. With the help of the French navy, Merlin worked from 1907 to 1913 to raise these treasures.

Ancient shipping in the Mediterranean was chiefly coastline sailing. It is not surprising, therefore, that wrecks took place close to the land, so that the sunken ships usually settled to their final rest in moderate depths. Since 1925 fishermen of Albenga on the Italian Riviera had known the position of an ancient wreck. Not until 1952 were serious diving attempts undertaken; in twelve days some five hundred perfectly preserved ancient amphorae were brought to light.

There was one trouble with all of these diving enterprises: they required too much

equipment and were too costly for an always impoverished science. Archaeologists could not lavish private or public funds like Mussolini, who had half of Lake Nemi pumped out in order to salvage the legendary galleys of Caligula.

During the 1930's an Austrian and a Frenchman pioneered entirely new methods of diving. Using no complicated apparatus, Hans Hass, the Viennese naturalist, began his undersea adventures with sharks. The French naval officer Jacques-Yves Cousteau further developed "skin" diving, invented the Aqua Lung, and achieved dives of as long as two hours to depths of three hundred feet. Archaeology seized on this technique as a means for recovering treasures buried in the sea.

Today underwater maps of the French and Italian coasts have been drawn up marking the exact positions of numerous ancient wrecks whose holds may yield wondrous things.

This Roman road, easily recognizable by the airman,

is invisible to anyone on the ground. Père Antoine Poidebard (d. 1954) of the Université St. Joseph, Beirut, was the first person to assess fully the value of aerial observation and photography for archaeology. "We had reason to believe that the Romans had built a fortified network of

roads on their frontier, consisting on the one hand of radial highways, on the other of roads which followed the border along the edge of the desert. There was scarcely any sense in searching for unknown roads on ground level, since the borders had often shifted during the Parthian wars and the struggles with the Sassanides. I realized that we would be able to see the roads we sought only from the air." (The picture shows the road to the East across the Gebel Seys, in Syria; it was taken on October 17, 1930. The dimly seen track on the far left is the modern automobile highway.)

Aerial archaeology was a war baby. During the First World War the British, French, and Germans began photographing the terrain of the Near East for purposes of military observation, and discovered that the camera saw what the terrestrial observer could not. In the past two decades the English landscape in particular has been thus surveyed; countless traces of old roads and fortifications, the outlines of vanished Roman buildings, have suddenly been made visible. Osbert Guy Stanhope Crawford, who until his death in 1957 was supreme in the field of aerial archaeology, called the surface of every ancient civilized land "a palimpsest, a document that has been written on and erased over and over again."

Archaeology has meanwhile also profited by the discoveries of modern physics. The method of "radiocarbon dating," based on the disintegration of the isotope Carbon 14, enables the scientist to make extremely accurate estimates of age wherever organic substances are available for analysis. Thus, independent of archaeological finds, philological connections, and historical points of reference, there is an almost exact criterion for the age of a charred bone, of a piece of wood from a bier, a flower found in a king's grave. We have already said that the pioneering age of archaeology is over. But only one who feels reality to be incompatible with romance and adventure could say that archaeology has therefore ceased to be a romantic adventure. History is always romantic, in the sense that we can only apprehend it through sensitivity and imagination. Flinders Petrie's noble words are still valid: "Imagination is the fire of discovery." Or, as the thought was put by that great historian Theodor Mommsen:

"Imagination, mother of all poetry, is likewise mother of all history."

CHRONOLOGICAL TABLE
of the History of Archaeology

In the selection of dates no strict method has been followed. A lecture was often more of a milestone in the development of archaeology than the several tomes on the subject which might be published ten years later; and as a rule the actual excavation usually proved more important than the first traveler's report, the first scouting expedition, or the first sampling, even though this sampling led to the discovery. The decision on the most significant dates is a highly subjective matter. I have attempted here, by my short legends, to bring the dates to life—but one cannot carry this too far. A chronology must be a précis, not a full-scale review. I have also deemed it best to deal more exhaustively with earlier developments in the field at the risk perhaps of scanting contemporary ones. Here assessments are still tentative, and such vast quantities of new material are being amassed so rapidly that their proper evaluation must remain the task of professional journals. May I hope, therefore, that the many first-rate scholars who are currently at work in the field, making discoveries of vital importance, will forgive me for being unable to mention their names here?

1119 and 1162 Decrees are published in Rome to protect from damage the columns of Trajan and Marcus Aurelius.

circa 1150 Henry, Bishop of Winchester, acquires classical statues in the course of a journey to Rome, and sends them to England.

1337 Petrarch visits Rome for the first time. He studies classical Latin, collects antique coins, and writes lives of classic figures. He is perhaps the first person to read classical writers critically.

circa 1400 The architect Filippo Brunelleschi organizes the first excavations in Rome. As was often the case with excavators up to the nineteenth century (and not always without reason), he is suspected of treasure-hunting.

1420–1427 The philologist and poet Francesco Filelfo learns Greek in Constantinople. Back home in Italy, he becomes one of the most prominent teachers of Latin and Greek, and a rallying-point for the first humanists.

1435–1436 and again in 1443–7 the merchant Cyriacus of Ancona travels about, methodically collecting antiquities.

circa **1450** Poggio Bracciolini laments that less than a dozen of the sculptures of ancient Rome are left. According to an old inventory, fourth-century Rome had 3,785 bronze statues, 22 equestrian statues, 73 gold and ivory images of gods, and 80 gilded images.

1471 Pope Sixtus IV begins collecting ancient statuary in Rome. The collections of this period were only first steps toward future museums. They were amassed planlessly, at random, and were not accessible to the public.

1485 Twenty thousand persons in Rome flock to see the well-preserved mummy of a Roman girl discovered by chance in a tomb on the Appian Way.

1506 The Laocoön group is discovered; for more than two centuries the aesthetic interpretation of this sculpture influences Europe's conception of the nature of classical art, and of art in general.

1520 Albrecht Dürer is in Brussels at the time the first Aztec art works are put on exhibition. He sets down his reaction to them in his diary.

1565 Johannes Helffrich visits the pyramids and the Sphinx in Egypt. In 1579 he publishes his journal.

circa **1566** Bishop Diego de Landa writes his *Relación de las cosas de Yucatán*.

1568–1648 The lifetime of Ixtlilxochitl (baptized Fernando Pimental, called Fernando de Alva), Chichimecan prince, whose chronicles of the Toltecs and Maya, based upon old texts and oral traditions, were given little credence until quite recently.

circa **1569** Bernardino de Sahagún, a missionary in Mexico, completes the first version of his book on the Aztecs, the most important source for the cultural history of Old Mexico.

1574 What is probably the first drawing of an Egyptian mummy to be published in Europe appears in an herbal by Joachim Strüppe.

1580–1765 The span of the lives of three travelers of the French nobility, N. C. Fabri de Peiresc, Bernard de Montfaucon, and the Comte de Caylus. In numerous books and pamphlets and thousands of letters they contribute such hoards of material on classical antiquity that sifting and interpretation become inevitable.

1605 The Aldobrandine Wedding is found, a Roman mural based on a Hellenistic prototype. Today it is considered a representation of the sacred wedding of Dionysus.

1614 Pietro della Valle sets out on his travels through the Orient. In 1621 he sends from Persepolis the first five cuneiform signs to reach Europe.

1615 Lorenzo Pignoria compares Mexican representations of gods to those of Euro-Asiatic antiquity, thus founding the science of comparative religion.

1617 García de Silva Figueroa is the first to recognize the ruins of Persepolis for what they are. His results are not published until 1661.

1622–1623 Cardinal Ludovico Ludovisi assembles, within a single year, a collection of more than three hundred antiques, including many Greek originals.

circa **1635** The Jesuit Athanasius Kircher begins the first systematic collection of antiques at the Collegium Romanum in Rome.

1640 Lord Arundel begins a similar collection in England.

1666 The Royal Society in London urges investigation of the ruins of Persepolis. The jeweler Chardin brings back the first detailed reports.

1674 Jacob Spon, a physician, travels through Asia Minor and Greece. He returns with descriptions of what he actually saw, critically set against ancient accounts. He is also the probable father of the term "archaeology."

1685 The physician Engelbert Kämpfer visits the site of Persepolis. He brings back numerous drawings and the first cuneiform text of any length to reach Europe.

1701–1703 Father Ximénez compiles the *Popul Vuh*, the sacred traditions of the Quiché Indians.

1714 Publication of a pamphlet by Cornelis de Bruin, in which he takes issue with his predecessors in regard to Persepolis.

1733 Foundation of the Society of Dilettanti in London, who actively support collecting and excavations.

1734 The Capitoline Museum in Rome, by acquisition of the Albani Collection, becomes one of the earliest museums of antiquities.

1735 The Antinous relief is found; as with the Laocoön, aesthetic interpretation of this statue establishes an idealized conception of antiquity in the public mind.

1737–1742 R. Pococke travels through Egypt, Arabia, and Greece. His works are published from 1743 on.

1748 Excavations begin in Pompeii under the direction of Alcubierre.

1749 R. Dalton makes the first reliable drawings of the Parthenon sculptures.

1751 J. Stuart ("Athenian Stuart") and N. Revett visit Athens. They publish in 1762 *The Antiquities of Athens Measured and Delineated*.

1753 Uncovering of the Villa dei Papiri in Herculaneum. Scrolls are found, and Piaggio succeeds in unrolling a number of these.

1753–1759 Foundation and opening of the British Museum.

1761 G. B. Piranesi's evocations of Roman architecture are published. His romantic conception stirs general interest in antiquity.

1762 Carsten Niebuhr reaches Arabia. As the only survivor of his expedition, he publishes a travel book that Napoleon is to find useful during his Egyptian expeditions.

1764 J. J. Winckelmann publishes his *History of the Art of Antiquity*, commonly considered to mark the beginning of modern archaeology.

1771 William Jones discovers relationships among the Indo-European group of languages. His discovery is the foundation of modern linguistic science and, for archaeology, of many future decipherments.

1772 Sir William Hamilton sells his famous collection of vases to the British Museum.

1787 Antonio del Ríos undertakes first investigations of the ruins in Mexico. His work is published in 1822.

1788 Publication of Abbé Barthélémy's *Voyage du jeune Anarchasis en Grèce*, a much-translated book that popularizes an idealized picture of Greece.

1793 The Louvre is opened as a French museum, with 117 antiques. In 1815 it contains 384 pieces. An innovation: the public is admitted free of charge.

1796 In the armistice of Bologna, Napoleon includes a special article that requires the delivery of numerous ancient monuments and documents to France. "Legitimate" pillage of art by such treaties remained the rule up to and including very recent times.

1797 Georg Zoëga, after innumerable bungling attempts by others, for the first time undertakes a serious study of Egyptian hieroglyphs. He recognizes the significance of cartouches.

1797–1799 Friedrich Hölderlin's *Hyperion* is published, presenting an idealized Hellenism as the goal of romantic longings.

1798 Bonaparte embarks at Toulon for Egypt. The researches and collections of his Scientific Commission form the foundation of modern Egyptology.

1799 In the Nile city of Rosetta the trilingual Rosetta Stone is found—the basis for decipherment of the Egyptian hieroglyphs.

1800–1803 Lord Elgin succeeds in transporting the most important parts of the Parthenon frieze to England.

1802 G. F. Grotefend deciphers the Persepolitan cuneiform script. His discovery is scarcely noticed by scholars.

1803 The first book on Ancient Egyptian architecture is published by A. C. Quatremère de Quincy. (It had been written as far back as 1785.)

1804 Lord Elgin requests the sculptor A. Canova to assume the task of restoring his Greek sculptures. Canova refuses; he argues that works of such quality should not be touched. Restorations have hitherto been customary; this is the first clear proclamation of respect for the originals.

1805– Captain G. Dupaix and L. Castañeda travel in
1807 Mexico. Their extensive collections of material on Old Mexico are not noticed until 1831.

1807 Claudius J. Rich travels through Mesopotamia. In 1811, employing ten workmen, he undertakes the first excavations in Babylon.

1809 Disguised as "Sheik Ibrahim," Johann Ludwig Burckhardt begins his travels through the Near East.

1809– Publication of the *Description de l'Egypte*, the
1822 scientific harvest of Napoleon's expedition.

1814 The British Museum buys the great frieze of Bassae. This, added to earlier acquisitions, makes the museum the greatest storehouse of antiquities in the world.

1815 By this time numerous travelers have combed the entire area once dominated by Greco-Roman civilization: the Englishmen E. D. Clarke, E. Dodwell, W. Gell, J. P. Gandy, F. Bedford, G. R. Cockerell, and J. Foster; the Danes O. Bröndsted and G. Koes; the Germans Baron von Stackelberg, Haller von Hallerstein, and J. Linckh. These men have visited and brought to the attention of the public the ruins of Tiryns, Mycenae, Bassae, and many other places.

1818 Ker Porter meets Claudius Rich in Baghdad. Porter's drawings, which he brings back from his adventurous journeys, are far superior to those of any predecessor in reliability.

circa A farmer in Melos finds fragments of a statue
1820 of Aphrodite of Parian marble. As the Venus de Milo it becomes the most popular of all the sculpture of classical antiquity.

1820 G. B. Belzoni's account of his Egyptian excavations is published.

1820– The R. Hay expedition explores Egypt. Its vast
1839 gleanings remain to this day in manuscript in the collection of the British Museum.

1821 Publication of W. M. Leakes's *Topography of Athens*—the first purely topographical description of an ancient city, divorced from a description of travel.

1821– In the course of the Greek revolt the Acropolis
1826 of Athens is twice bombarded. The west front of the Parthenon and the Erechtheion are damaged.

1822 J. F. Champollion, utilizing the Rosetta Stone, deciphers the Egyptian hieroglyphs.

1825 William Lane, with the aid of the camera lucida, begins his meticulous drawings of Egyptian monuments.

1825 Eduard Gerhard begins collecting Etruscan figurines.

1826– Publication of J. I. Hittorf's *Architecture an-*
1830 *tique de la Sicile*. Hittorf is the first to assert that classical sculpture and architecture were painted all over.

1827 In Corneto (Tarquini) the first colored Etruscan murals are discovered in tombs. Soon afterward similar discoveries are made in Chiusi, Veii, Cervateri, and Orvieto.

1828 The Duke de Luynes examines the ruined temples of Metapont on the Bay of Tarento.

1828 Tombs are discovered in Vulci containing incredible quantities of painted vases. The owner of the property, Prince Canino, employs one hundred workmen daily for the excavations. In 1831 Gerhard publishes the first account of these finds.

1829 J. J. Dubois and Abel Blouet dig at the Temple of Zeus in Olympia. They send the Louvre several reliefs that show distinct traces of painting.

1829 First session of the *Instituto di correspondenza archeologica* in Rome, under the direction of Gerhard and attended by the sculptor Thorwaldsen.

1830 Paul Dubrux discovers near Kerch in the Crimea rich hoards of the gold of Scythian rulers.

1830 Publication of Karl Otfried Müller's *Handbuch der Archäologie*, a bold summary of the work accomplished up to this time. For years this Handbook of Archaeology remains a standard work on the subject.

1831 The first volumes of the *Antiquities of Mexico*, Lord Kingsborough's vast collection of material, are published.

1832 In this and succeeding years Charles Fellows travels through Asia Minor and becomes one of the first to describe the ruins of Lycia. After 1842 he directs excavations.

1832– Count Waldeck travels in Mexico. He names 1836 the Mayan pyramid of Uxmal after his patron, Lord Kingsborough.

1833– Charles Texier explores Asia Minor. He is the 1837 first to describe the Hittite capital of Hattusas (Boghazköy), although without suspecting what it is.

1834 Gottfried Semper's *Preliminary Remarks on Painted Architecture and Sculpture among the Ancients* is published. In this book he takes issue with the "white as plaster" conception of the classical world, and shows that the Greeks lived in a world full of color.

1835 H. C. Rawlinson is transferred to Persia. Independently of Grotefend, he deciphers cuneiform script.

1835 Block by block, parts of the temple of Athena Nike are removed from the bastion into which they had been incorporated during the siege of the Acropolis and, under the direction of Ludwig Ross, are put together again to restore the temple.

1836 L. Chesney's attempt to use steam vessels on the Euphrates ends with the total loss of his ship, the *Tigris*. But his experiment is useful for all later archaeologists who wish to transport heavy sculpture.

1837 Colonel Howard Vyse uses gunpowder to blast entrances into the Egyptian pyramids.

1842 John L. Stephens publishes his *Incidents of Travel in Central America . . .* , the first extensive account of the discovery and excavation of Mayan cities.

1842 Paul E. Botta begins his excavations at Kuyun-

jik and Khorsabad. His work is crowned by extraordinary success; he uncovers the palace of King Sargon and the first masterpieces of Assyrian sculpture.

1842– Richard Lepsius conducts an Egyptian expedi-
1846 tion. He extends existing knowledge of the Egyptian Old Empire back to the fourth millennium B.C., brings the number of known pyramids to 67, and investigates some 130 of the hitherto unknown *mastabas*.

1843 Blind W. H. Prescott publishes his *History of the Conquest of Mexico*. This book is followed in 1847 by *The Conquest of Peru*.

1845 H. A. Layard begins his excavations in the vicinity of ancient Nineveh.

1846– F. C. Penrose draws the outline of the Parthe-
1847 non at Athens and proves the existence of the so-called "horizontal curves."

1849– Layard finds in Nineveh significant portions
1850 of King Assurbanipal's clay-tablet library.

1851– Jules Oppert investigates the ruins of Baby-
1854 lon.

1851– Near Memphis, Auguste Mariette excavates
1855 the Serapeum, the graves of the sacred Egyptian bulls. Later he founds the present Cairo Museum and thus helps protect Egypt against further looting excavations.

1852 Ernst Curtius gives a lecture in Berlin designed to arouse public interest and participation in an excavation of Olympia. His fund-raising brings in only 787 marks.

1852– Hormuzd Rassam digs in Nineveh and discov-
1854 ers more of Assurbanipal's library, including parts of the Gilgamesh Epic.

1853– Publication of H. Brunn's *Geschichte der
1859 Griechischen Künstler* (*History of the Greek Artists*). Brunn sets forth the fundamentals for understanding the laws of form in classic art. In 1888 he publishes the first number of *Denkmäler griechischer und römischer Skulptur in historischer Anordnung* (*Monuments of Greek and Roman Sculpture in a Historical Arrangement*).

1857 Publication in London of the pamphlet containing the translations of Rawlinson, Talbot, Hincks, and Oppert, proof that these men have correctly read the cuneiform script.

1857 C. T. Newton excavates the Mausoleum at Halicarnassus, one of the Seven Wonders of the ancient world. He completes the Amazon frieze, parts of which have already been taken to the British Museum in 1846.

1858 In Cnidos, Newton for the first time lays bare the ground-plan of an ancient city.

1859 C. Lenormant digs in Eleusis.

1861 Napoleon III acquires the Villa Farnese in Rome. Pietro Rosa uncovers the palaces of emperors. (In 1869 the wall paintings in the House of Livia are found.)

1861 Georges Perrot's Galatian Expedition starts. Although his task is to study inscriptions on the temple of Augustus in Ankara, he also undertakes explorations of Anatolia and brings back word of "Hittite" monuments.

1861 In Madrid, Brasseur de Bourbourg finds notes by Diego de Landa which provide a first key to a tentative understanding of Mexican hieroglyphs.

1865 Palma di Cesnola begins the excavation and collection of antiquities on Cyprus, which he exhibits in New York in 1872.

1865 Karl Humann pays his first visit to Pergamon.

1866 The centenarian Count Waldeck's account of the Mayan pyramids at Palenque is published.

1869 Schliemann goes to Troy for the first time. (See the tables on pages 34-6.)

1869– J. T. Wood locates the temple of Artemis
1874 near Ephesus, another of the Seven Wonders of the ancient world. Out of marshy terrain he brings to light marvelous remains of the temples.

1870 A. Conze determines the "geometric style" of vase ornamentation, thus revealing the importance of ceramics for chronology.

1872 W. Wright sends squeezes of the Hittite hieroglyphs in Hamath to the British Museum.

1872 George Smith announces that he has found in the British Museum, among the clay tablets assembled by Rassam, a pre-Biblical Flood legend, part of the Gilgamesh Epic.

1873 Smith searches the library of Kuyunjik for the tablets missing from the Gilgamesh Epic. After a week's search he finds them.

1873 A. Conze begins excavations at Samothrace. This is the first official archaeological undertaking on the part of Austria since Prince Metternich forbade all archaeological work.

1874 Foundation of the German Archaeological Institute in Athens.

1875 Beginning of the excavations in Olympia under Ernst Curtius. First excavation financed by a government in a foreign country (to the extent of 600,000 marks) in spite of the stipulation that all finds remain at the site. W. Dörpfeld distinguishes himself on this expedition. The Olympia excavation serves as a model for up-to-date field archaeology. The best-known single find of this excavation—noteworthy also for clarifying, by its position, the whole plan of the site—is the Hermes of Praxiteles.

1877– Théophile Homolle digs out the temple of
1879 Apollo on Delos. Under various directors the digging is continued until 1894, then resumed in 1902.

1877– In Tello, Ernest de Sarzec finds the first works
1881 of Sumerian art.

1878 K. Humann begins the excavations in Pergamon (continued 1880-1, 1883-6). In 1879 he excavates the last, ninety-seventh piece of the *gigantomachia*. The altar, packed in 462 boxes weighing a total of 35 tons, is shipped to Berlin and housed in a special museum.

1880 At Knossos, M. Kalokairinos uncovers the remains of walls which, it is supposed, were part of the Labyrinth.

1880 W. Flinders Petrie begins his work in Egypt, and continues until 1935. His work comprises the most extensive research in modern Egyptology.

1880 In London, A. H. Sayce gives a lecture asserting that an empire of the Hittites existed in the second millennium B.C.

1881 In a cave at Deir el-Bahri, Emil Brugsch finds the mummies of forty kings—Sethos I, Ramses II, and others.

1881 Gaston Maspero discovers the first inscriptions in the pyramids of Sakkara—some four thousand lines.

1882 W. Dörpfeld begins his collaboration with Schliemann. He introduces system into the excavations at Troy.

1882– Demetrios Philios digs at the sanctuary of the
1890 Mysteries in Eleusis.

1885– Marcel Dieulafoy brings sculptures from Susa
1886 to Paris.

1887 By chance, with no scientists present, the clay-tablet archives of Tell-el-Amarna are found.

1887– Eduard Seler explores Middle America, study-
1910 ing the archaeology, ethnology, religions, and languages of the region. He becomes the founder of modern Americanist studies.

1888 K. Humann and F. von Luschan begin excavation of the Late Hittite city of Zinjirli. By the second day of work they find twenty-six orthostats (carved slabs).

1888 Under direction of Peters the American Oriental Society expedition begins digging in Nippur. (Work continues 1889–90, 1893–6, 1898–1900.) Strictly scientific methods are not followed until the fourth excavation under Hilprecht. Rich finds of cuneiform inscriptions are made.

1891 H. Brugsch brings some three thousand rolls of Egyptian papyri to Europe.

1892– O. Puchstein and R. Koldewey investigate the
1894 temples of southern Italy and Sicily, in particular Selinunte.

1893 Adolf Furtwängler undertakes to classify by artists the vast amount of ancient sculpture which by now has been collected.

1893 Under T. Homolle's direction, excavations in Delphi begin.

1895 K. Humann begins to uncover the city of

Priene. (This work is continued by Wiegand and Schrader.) This excavation marks a shift in archaeological interest from single objects to relationships; archaeologists turn their attention from *finds* to *history*.

1899 Robert Koldewey begins his eighteen years of excavation at Babylon, one of the greatest excavations of all time. Germany grants a total of two million marks in support of this work.

1899 Max von Oppenheim devotes his own wealth to excavations at Tel Halaf and displays finds and sculptures of three millennia in a museum of his own in Berlin.

1899– Baalbek Expedition under O. Puchstein and
1904 B. Schulz.

1899– Theodor Wiegand, after purchasing sizable
1914 portions of the city, examines the remains of Miletus.

1900 Arthur Evans begins his quarter-century of work on Crete.

1900 A. Furtwängler publishes his *Antique Gems*, a first treatise on the *historical* as well as the artistic value of gems.

1900 Gustav and Alfred Körte open five mound graves in Gordion, the ancient capital of Phrygia.

1900 Sponge-divers discover near the island of Antikythera a sunken Roman ship with a cargo of bronze statues.

1900– Christian Blinkenberg and K. F. Kinch explore
1904 Lindos on the island of Rhodes. They find inscriptions that enable them to establish more precisely the dates of the sculptor Boethos and of the sculptors of the Laocoön group.

1902– Ludwig Borchardt deduces the general plan of
1904 the tremendous area of pyramids at Abusir.

1902– Rudolf Herzog digs on the island of Cos.
1904

1903 W. Andrae starts his excavations at Assur and charts the development of the city over a period of more than three thousand years.

1905 Hugo Winckler and T. Macridi-Bey travel in Anatolia. In 1906 they begin to uncover the clay-tablet archives of the Hittite city of Hattusas (Boghazköy).

1907 Sellin begins excavations near Jericho; his finds extend from the neolithic to the Byzantine age.

1910 John Garstang, after travels in Asia Minor, publishes *The Land of the Hittites*, the first important attempt to write Hittite history.

1911 Amadeo Maiuri begins to probe Pompeii and Herculaneum in a scientific manner.

1911– D. G. Hogarth, C. Leonard Woolley, and
1914 T. E. Lawrence begin excavations in the Late Hittite city of Carchemish.

1912 On the plateau around Cuzco, Peru, Hiram Hingham discovers the old Inca fortresses of Machu Picchu and Vitcos.

1912 Julius Jordan begins excavations in Warka (Uruk, Erech).

1914 Publication of *Mexican Archaeology*, by T. A. Joyce, the first handbook of Middle American archaeology.

1914 Ernst Buschor temporarily writes finis to the excavations at Samos. (Continuation, 1925–40.)

1915 Friedrich Hrozný publishes his decipherment of Hittite cuneiform script and announces that Hittite is an Indo-European language.

1915 S. G. Morley publishes his fundamental *Introduction to the Study of Maya Hieroglyphs*.

1917 The Carnarvon expedition, under the direction of Howard Carter, begins digging near Luxor in the Valley of the Kings.

1918 H. R. H. Hall starts excavations in Ur of the Chaldees.

1920 H. E. Winlock finds in Thebes the "mummy of Wah," of which X-ray photographs are prepared for the first time in New York; earlier Elliot Smith has examined mummies by fluoroscope.

1922 Leonard Woolley goes to Ur, where he succeeds in finding royal graves filled with golden treasures.

1922 Howard Carter discovers the entrance to the tomb of Tutankhamen.

1922– John Marshall digs in Mohenjo-Daro in India.
1927 He discovers the hitherto unknown Indus culture, as old as the Sumerian, possibly older.

1922 Elliot Smith revives the question, often raised earlier by amateurs, of a possible relationship between the cultures of the Mediterranean and Asia and those of Middle America.

1925 Publication in Germany of the fundamental work on *Attic Red-Figure Vase Painters*, by John D. Beazley, who has examined some ten thousand pieces of ceramic. The English edition does not appear until 1942, by which time Beazley has studied fifteen thousand pieces.

1926 H. E. Winlock finds at Deir el-Bahri on the Nile a mass grave containing sixty half-mummified soldiers of the period *circa* 2000 B.C.

1926– Oliver G. Ricketson investigates Mayan cities,
1937 especially Uaxactún.

1927 T. Wiegand resumes interrupted work at Pergamon.

1929– Claude F. A. Schaeffer digs in Ras Shamra,
1939 "Ugarit," the principal port city of Syria in the second century B.C. The many layers of the site afford significant information on the chronology of the Near East and Egypt. Schaeffer's *Stratigraphie comparée et chronologie de l'Asie occidentale* (1948) is a fundamental book on the subject. Schaeffer resumes excavations in 1948.

1930– The Semitic expert Hans Bauer performs an
1932 amazing feat of decipherment. He proves the alphabetic character of the clay-tablet script from Ras Shamra and immediately deciphers seventeen signs correctly.

1931 The Mexican archaeologist Alfonso Caso discovers on Monte Albán near Oaxaca the richest gold treasure ever found in Middle America. Almost all the pieces show a high degree of artistry.

1931 Kurt Bittel (with Rudolf Naumann) begins systematic excavations at the Hittite capital of

Hattusas, near present-day Boghazköy. He finds more than six thousand clay tablets, among them bilingual seals by which H. G. Güterbock is able to confirm a number of hypothetical readings of Hittite hieroglyphs.

1933 André Parrot begins his investigations of the ruins of Mari, which are to continue for some twenty years. His most important find is the state archives, including some twenty thousand clay-tablet inscriptions. Decipherment of these dictates a new date for the reign of Hammurabi.

1935 Sir Leonard Woolley digs up the capital of the Yarim Lim near Alalakh Atchana.

1936 Werner Jaeger publishes *Paedeia*.

1937 S. N. Kramer begins a study of the cuneiform finds from Nippur and discovers a hitherto unknown chapter of the Gilgamesh Epic.

1938 K. Lehmann resumes excavations at Samothrace (and again in 1947–8).

1941 The Carnegie Foundation completes its seven-year restoration work in Copán. The government of Honduras assumes the task of protecting the ruins.

1945 Helmut T. Bossert fixes his attention upon Karatepe, where in subsequent years he discovers numerous reliefs in a Late Hittite citadel, as well as a Phoenician-Hittite bilingual which enables him to decipher the Hittite hieroglyphic script.

1946 Dhorme in Paris offers a tentative decipherment of the protobyblic script that was used in Byblos, northern Phoenicia, around 1000 B.C.

1946 Photographer G. G. Healey, a member of a motion-picture expedition, is led by Lacandón Indians to a temple near Bonampak wherein are colored frescoes portraying the daily life of the ancient Maya.

1947 Out of fragments of cuneiform script brought from Nippur by H. V. Hilprecht around 1900, F. Steele pieces together a law book of King Pipit-Ishtar which is older than the laws of Hammurabi.

1947 A Bedouin finds in a cave near Kumran, north of the Dead Sea, Hebrew scrolls stored in clay vessels; among them is a scroll of Isaiah dating from the second century B.C. and the first century A.D. Since then numerous other finds seem to necessitate a revision of the existing text of the Bible, and throw new light on the sect of the Essenes and its relationship to New Testament origins.

1949 The Mexican archaeologist Alberto Ruz begins excavations at the Temple of the Inscriptions at Palenque. Inside the pyramid he discovers the tomb of a ruler, thus producing the first proof that the Mayan pyramids, like the Egyptian pyramids, *could be* used as mausoleums.

1950– Leonhard Schultze-Jena continues the work of
1952 Seler, retranslating the greater part of Sahagún's *Historia*.

1952 Willard F. Libby publishes his method of radiocarbon dating, a technique for determining the age of organic substances; this constitutes the most significant contribution physics has made to historical science.

1952– Homer Thompson completely excavates the
1956 Stoa on the Agora at Athens, and at a cost of two million dollars erects a mighty reconstruction.

1953 The architect Michael Ventris deciphers Cretan Linear Script B and finds that Old Cretan was a Greek dialect.

1953 Mme Halet Çambel, formerly assistant to H. T. Bossert at the Karatepe excavations, with the aid of Italian specialists begins restoration of the Late Hittite sculptures from Karatepe.

1954 Zakkaria Goneim discovers a new step pyramid near Sakkara, and in the interior of it an untouched sarcophagus—which, however, is empty.

1954 Zaki Nour, digging close to the pyramid of Cheops, turns up the 120-foot-long "death ship" of a Fourth Dynasty pharaoh.

1955 The Russian scholar Y. V. Knorosov publishes a tentative decipherment of the Mayan hieroglyphs.

BIBLIOGRAPHICAL NOTE

Many of the works consulted for this book are noted in the text or in the List of Sources for the Illustrations. The following selection has been deliberately restricted to a few basic, or more general, works which, in the author's opinion, will supply the essential background for anyone wishing to delve deeper into the history of archaeology. With these books as guides, moreover, the interested reader will be able to pursue the subject as far as he wishes.

The best general survey is *A Hundred Years of Archaeology*, by Glyn E. Daniel (London, 1950). Daniel devotes particular attention to prehistoric archaeology. A more specialized work, which tells the story of Mesopotamian exploration, is Seton Lloyd's *Foundations in the Dust* (London, 1947). A brief handbook of archaeological practice is Kathleen M. Kenyon's *Beginning in Archaeology* (London, 1953). Considerably more comprehensive is Sir Mortimer Wheeler's brilliantly written *Archaeology from the Earth* (London, 1954), which can be most warmly recommended. For

Middle American archaeology, acquaintance with William Prescott's histories is a prerequisite; then Sylvanus G. Morley's *The Ancient Maya* (London and Stanford, 1946) and George C. Vaillant's *The Aztecs of Mexico* (London, 1950) will serve as excellent introductions.

Among the many other books that can be suggested are I. E. S. Edwards's *The Pyramids of Egypt* (Harmondsworth, 1952); Sir Leonard Woolley's *Digging Up the Past* (Harmondsworth, 1950) and *Ur of the Chaldees* (London, 1950); J. Eric Thompson's *The Rise and Fall of the Maya Civilization* (Norman, Oklahoma, 1956); and Miguel Covarrubias's *Indian Art of Mexico and Central America* (New York, 1957). *The Testimony of the Spade*, by Geoffrey Bibby (New York, 1956), is useful as a study of northern Europe and of periods earlier than those covered in this book.

For the reader to whom German is no obstacle, the classical work on the history of archaeology remains, for all its restriction to "art archaeology," *Die archäologischen Entdeckun-*

gen des neunzehnten Jahrhunderts, by Adolf Michaelis (Leipzig, 1906). *Die archäologischen Entdeckungen im 20. Jahrhundert*, by Friedrich von Oppeln-Bronikowski (Berlin, 1931), can be regarded as its continuation. A survey of recent research is provided by Karl Schefold in his *Orient, Hellas und Rom in der archäologischen Forschung seit 1939* (Bern, 1949). The history of ideas is the subject of Max Wegner's *Altertumskunde* (Munich, 1951). Probably the best outline of the problems of decipherment for the reader who is already grounded in philology is Johannes Friedrich's *Entzifferung verschollener Schriften und Sprachen* (Berlin, 1954).

The list is brief, but the bibliographies in these books will lead the interested reader to the original sources.

List of Sources for Illustrations

All references followed by asterisks (*) are to illustrations photographed or drawn especially for this book.

Book I
Page

3 Body of girl. Drawing in a letter from B. Fonte to F. Sassetti. Collection of Professor Bernard Ashmole, Oxford. (*Photo Warburg Institute, University of London.*)

5 Laocoön. Marble group by Agesandros, Polydoros, Athenodoros. Vatican, Rome. (*Photo Alinari, No. 6591.*)

7 Pen drawing by G. Permoli, Parma. (*Photo Biblioteca Palatina, Parma.*)

8 J. J. Winckelmann. Oil painting by A. von Maron, 1768. Weimar, Palace Museum. (*Photo Staatliche Kunstsammlungen, Weimar.*)

9 Antinous. Marble relief, restored. Villa Albani, Rome. (*Photo Alinari, No. 27551.*)

10 Model of the ruins of Pompeii in 1900. (*Photo Mansell Collection, London.*)

13 Bronze horse from Herculaneum. Museo Nazionale, Naples. (*Photo Alinari No. 11213.*)

14 Cavaceppi's workshop. Copper engraving from *Raccolta d'antiche statue, busti, bassorilievi ed altre sculture restaurate de Bartolomeo scultore romano*, Vol. I, Rome, 1768, frontispiece.*

15A Pompeii: Via die Sallustio. Pen drawing by G. B. Piranesi. (*By permission of the Trustees of the British Museum.*)

Book I
Page

15B Hadrian's villa in Tivoli. Copper engraving by G. B. Piranesi, 1777. (*By permission of the Trustees of the British Museum.*)

16 Pompeii: Temple of Isis. Copper engraving by F. Piranesi after a drawing by L. Desprez, 1788. (*By permission of the Trustees of the British Museum.*)

17 Pompeii: skeleton in the laundry. Engraving from a drawing by F. Mazois in *Les Ruines de Pompeii, dessinées et mesurées par F. Mazois*, 2me Partie, Paris, 1824.*

18 Pompeii: plaster cast of dog. (*Photo Alinari, No. 11339.*)

19 Pompeii: plaster cast of victims. (*Photo Professor Maiuri.*)

20 Pompeii: excavation on the Via di Nola. Copper engraving from F. Mazois's *Les Ruines de Pompeii*: see 17.*

21 Pompeii: Greek bronze statue. (*Photo Professor Maiuri.*)

22 Pompeii: *Termopolium Asinellae*. Bar on the Via Stabiae. (*Photo Professor Maiuri.*)

23 Pompeii: advertising inscriptions on the house of Trebius Valens. (*Photo Professor Maiuri.*)

24 Pompeii: painted frieze on the Via dell'Abbondanza. (*Photo Professor Maiuri.*)

Book I
Page

25 Pompeii: triclinium in the Casa del Moralista. (*Photo Professor Maiuri.*)

26–7 Pompeii: murals at the Villa dei Misteri. (*Photo Professor Maiuri.*)

28A Portrait of Piaggio. Pastel drawing, Naples. (*Photo gift of the Director of the Biblioteca Nazionale, Naples.*)

28B The first papyrus unrolled by Piaggio. (*Biblioteca Nazionale, Naples.*)

29 Father Piaggio's unwinding machine. Engraving by A. de Jorio in *Reale Museo Borbonico. Officina de' Papiri,* Naples, 1825.*

30 Pompeii: magic square. Schematic drawing.*

31 Maiuri, director of excavations in Campania. (*Photo Professor Maiuri.*)

32 The hill of Hissarlik. Engraving after a drawing by Choiseul-Gouffier in V*oyage pittoresque de la Grèce,* Paris, 1809.*

33 H. Schliemann. Photo taken 1860, in possession of Schliemann's descendants. (*Photo Dr. Ernst Meyer. Published in Meyer: Schliemann, Briefwechsel I, Berlin, 1953.*)

37 Double page from Schliemann's diary. Source same as p. 33.

38 "Ilium's great tower." Drawing by Lempesis in the *Atlas Trojanischer Alterthümer* attached to Schliemann's *Trojanische Alterthümer,* Leipzig, 1874.

39 Sophia Schliemann in "Helen's" jewels. Photo from *Trojanische Alterthümer.*

40A Troy: Schliemann hands Sophia a vase. Detail from a drawing by Lempesis.

40B Troy: uncovering the remains of a house. Another detail from the same drawing by Lempesis.

41 Troy: excavations directed by Semple, 1937. (*Photo by permission of Professor Blegen; reproduced in Troy, by C. W. Blegen and others, Cincinnati, 1950.*)

42 Title page of pamphlet by Ernst Boetticher, Berlin, 1890.*

43 William Dörpfeld, William T. Semple, and Mrs. Louise Taft Semple at Troy, 1935. (*Photo courtesy of Professor Blegen.*)

44–5 Schliemann's letter to Gladstone. Photo of the original among the Gladstone papers in the British Museum. (*By permission of the Trustees of the British Museum.*)

47A Mycenae: the grave circle after Schliemann's excavation. Drawing from Schliemann: *Mycenae,* Leipzig, 1878.

47B Mycenae: the grave circle at present. Photo published in A. J. B. Wace: *Mycenae,* Princeton, 1939.

Book I
Page

48 Mycenae: plan of the grave circle and vicinity. Drawing by members of the British School at Athens, published in *Annual,* 1923. (*By permission of the British School at Athens.*)

50 Mycenae: dagger sheath with lion hunt, after E. Gilliéron's reconstruction.

51A Mycenae: The largest remaining parts of a silver rython. National Museum, Athens.

51B Mycenae: royal golden mask. National Museum, Athens.

51C Mycenae: stele with relief. Original restored. National Museum, Athens. From Schliemann: *Mycenae,* Leipzig, 1878.

51D "Lion Cup." 10.8 x 12.8 cm. National Museum, Athens. (*Photos on pp. 50–1 from Galvano; Ashmolean Museum, Oxford.*)

53 Sir Arthur Evans. Oil painting by Sir William Richmond, 1907. In the background, the "rython carrier" (drinking-horn) reconstructed by E. Gilliéron. (*Original and photo Ashmolean Museum, Oxford.*)

55 Knossos: part of the "Palace of Minos." (*Photo Hulton Picture Library.*)

56 Example of a reconstruction of a palace by Evans. (*Photo Multiphoto, Paris.*)

57A Knossos: fragment of a "miniature fresco." From Evans: *Palace of Minos at Knossos,* London, 1923–36. (*By permission of Macmillan & Co., Ltd.*)

57B Knossos: "The Queen's Megaron." Painted reconstruction. From Evans: see 57a. (*By permission of Macmillan & Co., Ltd.*)

58 Knossos: "Priest-King." Stucco relief. Museum of Herakleion, Crete. From Evans: see 57a. (*By permission of Macmillan & Co., Ltd.*)

59 Knossos: "Priest-King." Frontispiece from Evans: see 57a.

60A Knossos: stone seal from Achat; plaster cast. (*Photo Ashmolean Museum, Oxford.*)

60B Cup of Vaphio. National Museum, Athens. (*Photo from Galvano; Ashmolean Museum, Oxford.*)

61A Knossos: bull-dancer, fresco fragment, c. 30 cm. high. (*Photo Ashmolean Museum, Oxford.*)

61B Knossos: "snake goddess." Restored figure in glazed clay. Museum of Herakleion, Crete. (*By permission of Macmillan & Co., Ltd.*)

62A Knossos: rear view of "snake goddess," restored. (*By permission of Macmillan & Co., Ltd.*)

62B Knossos: front view of the "snake goddess," restored. (*Photo Mansell Collection, London.*)

62C Knossos: "dancing priestesses." Stone seal from Achat; plaster positive. (*Photo Ashmolean Museum, Oxford.*)

Book I
Page

63A Stone seal in form of an owl. Crete, Early Minoan III. (*Photo Ashmolean Museum, Oxford.*)

63B Knossos: bird with outspread wings. (*Photo Ashmolean Museum, Oxford.*)

63C Pitcher under crescent moons. Positive of a pearl-shaped stone seal, Middle Minoan I. (*Photo Ashmolean Museum, Oxford.*)

63D Pair of goats grazing. (*Photo Ashmolean Museum, Oxford.*)

63E Three clay votive figurines. From the Kiktaean Cave on Crete. (*Photo Ashmolean Museum, Oxford.*)

64 Four Cretan script signs interpreted by Michael Ventris. Drawing from Ventris.*

65 "Phaestos Disc." Photo from the original in Herakleion.

66 Part of an inscription in Cretan script, demonstrating the correctness of the decipherment proposed by Ventris.*

67 Baalbek: keystone of the lintel of the temple gate.

68A Baalbek: the temple gate during the restoration of 1900–1. Photo by T. Lüpke from T. Wiegand: *Baalbek: Ergebnisse der ausgrabungen und Untersuchungen in den Jahren 1898 to 1905*, Vol. II, Berlin and Leipzig, 1923.

68B Baalbek: the restored temple gate, seen from within. Photo in T. Wiegand: see 68a.

Book II

71 The Sphinx. Woodcut in J. Helffrich's travel book: *Kurtzer und warhafftiger Bericht von der Reis aus Venedig nach Hierusalen, von dannen in Aegypten, auff den Berg Sinai, Alcair, Alexandria und folgendes wiederumb gen Venedig . . .* (*Short and Truthful Account of the Journey from Venice to Jerusalem, from There into Egypt, to Mount Sinai, Alcair, Alexandria and Subsequently Back to Venice*), Leipzig, 1579.*

72 The Sphinx. From an engraving of a drawing by V. Denon in *Voyage dans la Basse et la Haute Egypte pendant les campagnes du général Bonaparte*, Vol. II, Paris, 1802.*

73 The Sphinx. Drawn and engraved for *Description de l'Egypte ou recueil des observations et des recherches qui ont été faites en Egypte pendant l'expédition de L'Armée française, publié par les orders de Sa Majesté l'Empereur Napoléon le Grand*. Vol. I was published in Paris in 1809; Vol. V, containing this plate, in 1822.*

75 The Sphinx. Photographed after the excavation of 1925–6. (*Photo Hulton Picture Library.*)

Book II
Page

76 V. Denon in General Belliard's camp. Engraving from his drawing, from Vol. II of his *Voyage*: see 72.*

77 Drawing of the temple of Ammon in Karnak, view from northwest. At the time it was called "Palace of Karnak." Vol. III of the *Description de l'Egypte*: see 73.*

78A Temple of Luxor. Main portal with obelisks. Copper engraving, 1812. Vol. III of the *Description de l'Egypte*: see 73.*

78B Remains of a colossal statue of Ramses III in the temple at Karnak, 1812. Vol. III of the *Description de l'Egypte*: see 73.*

79A Cornice and vault of the temple of Sethos I in Abydos. Pencil drawing by E. W. Lane, 1826–7. British Museum, Add. MS. 34084. (*By permission of the Trustees of the British Museum.*)

79B View of the interior of the cliff temple of Abu Simbel. Pencil drawing by E. W. Lane, 1826–7. British Museum, Add. MS. 34084, fol. 20. (*By permission of the Trustees of the British Museum.*)

80A "The wonderful stone statue of Memnon." Copper engraving in B. Picart: *Neueröffneter Musentempel*, Amsterdam and Leipzig, 1754.*

80B Colossal statue of Amenophis III, called Pillar of Memnon, Thebes. Drawing by F. Catherwood. British Museum, Add. MS. 29831, fol. 45–8. (*By permission of the Trustees of the British Museum.*)

81 Façade of the cliff temple of Abu Simbel. Pencil drawing by J. Bonomi. British Museum, Add. MS. 29840, fol. 8. (*By permission of the Trustees of the British Museum.*)

82 G. B. Belzoni directs the transportation of a fragmentary statue of Ramses II. From Belzoni: *Narrative of the Operations and Recent Discoveries within the Pyramids, Temples, Tombs and Excavations in Egypt and Nubia*, London, 1820.*

83 G. B. Belzoni, portrait lithograph of C. Hullmandel, after M. Gavei. Frontispiece of Belzoni's *Narrative*: see 82.*

85 J. F. Champollion. Oil painting by Léon Cogniet, Louvre, Paris. (*Photo Archives photographiques, Paris.*)

87 The Rosetta Stone. British Museum, London. (*By permission of the Trustees of the British Museum.*)

88 Plate I from Champollion: *Précis du système hiéroglyphique des anciens Egyptiens*, Paris, 1824.*

89 Plate II from Champollion: see 88.

90 The eastern obelisk of the temple of Luxor. Detail. (*Photo Multiphoto, Paris.*)

Book II
Page

91 Gizeh: the second pyramid. Infra-red photo. (*Photo Multiphoto, Paris.*)

92 Gizeh: interior of the Great Pyramid. Copper engraving from *Description de l'Egypte* (see 73), Vol. V., 1822.*

93 The "high corridor" of the Great Pyramid. Counterpart to the preceding plate in the *Description de l'Egypte.**

94A The pyramids of Gizeh. Woodcut, 1579, from J. Helffrich: see 71.*

94B The pyramids of Gizeh. Mosaic (*c.* 1250–1275) in the porch of St. Mark's, Venice. (*Photo Alinari: enlargement of a detail of the negative. Alinari No. 13731.*)

95 Belzoni enters the pyramid of Chephren. Lithograph from *Narrative*: see 82.*

96 Belzoni in Chephren's burial chamber. Lithograph from *Narrative*: see 82.*

97 Interior of the Cheops pyramid. Pencil drawing by E. W. Lane: see 79. British Museum, Add. MS. 34084, fol. 1.

98 E. W. Lane on the Nile. Drawn by himself. British Museum, Add. MS. 34088, fol. 45.

99 Pyramid of Chephren seen from the top of the pyramid of Cheops. Pencil drawing by E. W. Lane, 1825. British Museum, Add. MS. 34083, fol. 24.

100–1 The pyramid of Cheops. Lithograph from the camera-lucida drawing by E. W. Lane, 1827. First printing of a drawing prepared by the Robert Hay expedition. British Museum, Add. MS. 29812, fol. 64. (*Photos on pp. 98–101 by permission of the Trustees of the British Museum.*)

103 Sir Flinders Petrie and Lady Petrie bid farewell to the Megiddo expedition, 1935. (*Photo Hulton Picture Library.*)

104 Flinders Petrie, 1880/1882, in front of his "accommodation" at Gizeh. (*Photo by the kind permission of Miss Petrie.*)

105A The pyramid of Snofru in Medum: east-west cross-section. Drawing by L. Borchardt: *Die Entstehung der Pyramide*, Plates 3 and 4, 1928, in Vol. I of E. S. Edwards: *The Pyramids of Egypt*, New York, 1947.

105B Pyramid of Chephren. From U. Hölscher: *Das Grabdenkmal des Königs Chephren*, in Edwards: see 105a.

105C Pyramid of Cheops: north-south cross-section, from H. Vyse: *Operations Carried On at the Pyramids of Gizeh*, 1840, in Edwards: see 105a. (*Photos on p. 105 by permission of Mr. Edwards and Penguin Books, Ltd.*)

Book II
Page

106–7 Reconstruction of the pyramid field of Abusir by L. Borchardt. From: *Wissenschaftliche Veröffentlichungen der Deutschen Orient-Gesellschaft*, Vol. VII, Berlin, 1907.*

109 Alabaster sarcophagus in the pyramid of Sakkara. Fig. 43 from Zakaria Goneim: *The Buried Pyramid*, London, 1956. (*By permission of Mr. Goneim and Longmans, Green & Co., Ltd.*)

110 Entry to Pyramid of Unis. Photographed by E. Brugsch.

111 "Representation of a real Egyptian mummy." Woodcut from J. Strüppe: *Consensus celebriorum medicorum, historicorum et philosophorum, super secretissimis, ac preciosissimis quibusdam Medicinis fere exoticis, primumque super Mumia . . .* , Frankfurt, 1574.*

112A "Mummies." Copper engraving from P. Pomet: *Historie générale des drogues*, Paris, 1694.*

112B "Interior of a mummy pit . . ." Lithograph from Gardner Wilkinson: *Manners and Customs of the Ancient Egyptians*, London, 1837–42.*

113 Reconstruction of "Thais": mummy found in 1900 in Antinoë by A. Gayet. Color lithograph.*

114–15 Prints of four sketches by Le Heux from J. F. Champollion: *Monuments de l'Egypte et de la Nubie*, Vol. IV, Paris, 1843.*

116–17 Photo by H. Burton, showing the valley of Deir el-Bahri. (*By permission of the Metropolitan Museum, New York.*)

118 Professor Maspero, E. Brugsch, and the grave-robber Abd-el-Rasul at the entrance to the cave of royal mummies. Reproduction of a photo in the *Century*, New York, May 1887.

120 Mummy of Ramses II. (*Photo E. Brugsch, 1881.*)

121A Head of Sethos I. (*Photo E. Brugsch, 1886.*)

121B Mummy of Sethos I: see 121a.

122A Mummy of Amenophis I. (*Photo E. Brugsch, 1881.*)

122B Wig of Isimkhobiu. (*Photo E. Brugsch, 1881.*)

123A Mummy of Isimkhobiu. Left, innermost coffin; right, mummy in state of perfect preservation. (*Photo E. Brugsch, 1881.*)

123B Supplies provided for Queen Isimkhobiu for her journey to the hereafter. (*Photo E. Brugsch.*)

124 Upper part of body of Tau-a-quen, who died of wounds. (*Photo E. Brugsch, 1886.*)

125A Mummy of Nsitanebashru. (*Photo E. Brugsch, 1886.*)

125B The same mummy: see 125a.

126A Detail of Nsitanebashru: see 125a.

126B Profile of the head of Nsitanebashru: see 125a.

Book II
Page

127A Mummy of a Greek boy from Hawawa. Only the head painted on wood has hitherto been reproduced. (*By permission of the Trustees of the British Museum.*)

127B Mummy of child, from Roman times, probably found in Memphis. Hitherto unpublished. (*By permission of the Trustees of the British Museum.*)

128A Mummy of Wah, excavated by Winlock and sent to the Metropolitan Museum, New York, 1936.

128 B, C X-ray photos of mummy of Wah before unwrapping.

129A First stage of unwrapping of Wah, 1940.

129 B, C Second stage and third stage.

129D Last stage of the unwrapping. (Published in the *Bulletin* of the Metropolitan Museum, New York, 1940.) Jewelry revealed by the X-ray photographs was found. (*Photos on pp. 128–9 by permission of the Metropolitan Museum, New York.*)

130 Mummified cat.

130–1 A, B Two mummies of crocodiles, wrapped and unwrapped.

131 Mummified falcon, New Kingdom. (*Photos on pp. 130–1 by permission of the Trustees of the British Museum.*)

132 A woman excavator handles a newly found mummy. (*Photo Multiphoto, Paris.*)

133 Head of the mummy called "Thais." (*Photo Collection Musée de l'Homme, Paris.*)

134 Entrance to a vault in the Valley of the Kings. Gray-tinted drawing. British Museum, Add. MS. 29816, fol. 16. (*By permission of the Trustees of the British Museum.*)

135 Interior of the expedition camp. Pencil drawing by E. W. Lane. British Museum, Add. MS. 29816, fol. 132. (*By permission of the Trustees of the British Museum.*)

136–7 View of the Valley of the Kings showing site at which implements used for burial of Tutankhamen were found in 1908 by the Theodore Davis expedition.

136 One of the clay vessels in which these materials were placed. (*Photos on pp. 136–7 by permission of the Metropolitan Museum, New York.*)

139 Entrance shaft with steel grating to protect the antechamber to the tomb of Tutankhamen.

140–1 View of the antechamber (toward the south) of the tomb of Tutankhamen.

142 Carnarvon and Carter at the opening of the entrance to Tutankhamen's burial chamber.

Book II
Page

143 Small painted wooden portrait head of Tutankhamen.

145 Head of the innermost gold coffin of Tutankhamen.

146 Three of the four golden goddesses that protected the vessels containing the heart and organs of Tutankhamen.

148 The arms of Tutankhamen's mummy, with bracelets.

149 The bracelets worn by Tutankhamen in their original order. (*Photos on pp. 139–49 by permission of the Griffith Institute, Ashmolean Museum, Oxford.*)

151 Moving an alabaster statue at the time of the Middle Kingdom. From a painted relief reproduced in Frédéric Caillard: *Recherches sur les arts et métiers, les usages de la vie civile et domestique des anciens peuples de l'Egypte, de la Nubie et de l'Ethiope*, Paris, 1831.*

152 Two drawings by Sir Flinders Petrie, showing Egyptian techniques of raising stones. From his *Egyptian Architecture*, London, 1938. (*By the kind permission of Miss Petrie.*)

153 Sketches showing Egyptian stoneworkers at work. Reproduced in Champollion: *Monuments*: see 114–15.*

155 Painted wooden model of a granary. (*By permission of the Trustees of the British Museum.*)

156 Model of a death ship. Middle Kingdom, c. 2000 B.C. (*By permission of the Trustees of the British Museum.*)

157A One of Meket-Re's pleasure boats. (*By permission of the Metropolitan Museum, New York.*)

157B Reconstruction of the death ship found in 1954 near the pyramid of Gizeh. (*By permission of the Illustrated London News.*)

158–9 The Book of the Dead: Manuscript of Ani, British Museum. (*By permission of the Trustees of the British Museum.*)

Book III

163 Tower of Babel. Oil painting on wood by Pieter Brueghel, signed and dated 1563. Vienna Museum of Art History (from the collection of Rudolf II). (*Photo by permission of the Director of the Museum für Völkerkunde, Vienna.*)

164 The hill of "Babil." Drawing by Pietro della Valle, 1616. Published in A. Kircher's *Turris Babel*, Amsterdam, 1679.*

165 Erection of the Tower of Babel. Miniature from the Duke of Bedford's prayerbook, 1423, by an unknown Burgundian artist. British Museum, Add. MS. 18850, fol. 17 verso. (*By permission of the Trustees of the British Museum.*)

Book III
Page

166   Sitti Maani, Pietro della Valle's wife. Copper engraving after original portrait painted by Valle's "personal artist," published in the German translation of Pietro's travel book, *Eines vornehmen Römischen Patritii Reiss-Beschreibung in die orientalische Länder*, Geneva, 1674.*

167   Earliest depiction of the ruins of Persepolis. Called by English author Thomas Herbert: "Chil-manor or fourty Toures." Published 1634 in *A Relation of some years travaille, begunne 1626, into Afrique and the Greater Asia especially the Territories of the Persian Monarchie. . . .**

168   The ruins of Persepolis as depicted by Wenzel Hollars. Prepared for the third edition of Herbert's book (see 167), solely from the author's descriptions. Copper engraving, 1665.*

169   The first view of the Persepolitan ruins drawn from nature, prepared by A. Daulier des Landes in 1665 and published in *Les Beautez de la Perse . . .*, Paris, 1673.*

172   Sir John Chardin. Drawn and engraved from life by David Loggan, probably 1685/1686. Frontispiece from *Journal du voyage du Chevalier Chardin en Perse*, London, 1686.*

172–3   Festive reception of J. Chardin by Kanavas Khan, viceroy of Tiflis. Copper engraving after Joseph Guillaume Grélot, engraved 1673 for Chardin's *Journal* (first edition).*

174   Great portal of Persepolis. Engraving from a drawing by Engelbert Kämpfer. Published in *Amoenitatem exoticarum politico-physico-medicarum . . .*, Lemgov, 1712.*

175   First depiction of the winged bulls from Xerxes' gate in Persepolis. Sketched by Chardin at the site and engraved for his *Journal*, edition of 1711, Plate LVII.*

176   One of the two pillars shown on the preceding picture, engraving after drawing made by Cornelis de Bruin in Persepolis.*

177   The first cuneiform signs to be seen by Europeans. Pietro della Valle sent these to his friend Schipano.*

179   Kämpfer's copy of twenty-four-line Babylonian inscriptions (only twenty lines shown here). British Museum, MS. Sloane 5232, fol. 67, verso. (*By permission of the Trustees of the British Museum.*)

181   Six rows of cuneiform signs, with relief figures above, from Persepolis. Drawing by Carsten Niebuhr, 1763, published in *Reisebeschreibung nach Arabien und andern umliegenden Ländern*, Vol. II, Plate XXIII, Copenhagen, 1778.*

182   Schematic representation of the development of cuneiform script from a hieroglyphic script. After J. Fried-

Book III
Page

rich: *Entzifferung verschollener Schriften und Sprachen*, Berlin, 1954, Fig. 20, p. 31. The order of the signs in this figure has been slightly altered here. (*By permission of Mr. Friedrich and Springer Verlag.*)

183   G. F. Grotefend, decipherer of Persepolis cuneiform script. Ceramic medallion. (*By the kind permission of the owner, Siegfried Grotefend, Celle.*)

185A   De Bruin's copy of the text on the garment of Darius. From *Reizen van C. de Bruyn*, Vol. II, Fig. 135, Delft, 1698.*

185B   Grotefend's corrected and deciphered version of the inscription of Darius in Persepolis. *In Neue Beiträge zur persepolitanischen Keilschrift*, Hanover, 1837.*

187   C. J. Rich. Oil painting by an unknown hand. British Museum. (*By permission of the Trustees of the British Museum.*)

188   Map, sketched by Rich in December 1811 and executed by Abraham Lockett, of the area of ruins on the eastern shore of the Euphrates, the site of ancient Babylon. Frontispiece of his *Memoir on the Ruins of Babylon*, London, 1815, first published in *Fundgruben des Orients*, Vienna, 1812.*

189   Sir Robert Ker Porter. Engraving from a painting by J. Wright, 1806.*

190   Four different representations of the Naksh-i-Rustam relief. Sent by Olenin to Ker Porter as an example of imprecise copying. Pen drawing, British Museum, Add. MS. 14758, Vol. I, fol. 71.

191   Ker Porter in front of the cliff tombs of Naksh-i-Rustam. Wash drawing. British Museum, Add. MS. 14758, Vol. I, fol. 64, recto.

192–3   Birs Nimrud. Wash drawing by Ker Porter, done between 1818 and 1820. British Museum, Add. MS. 14758, Vol. II, fol. 124.

192   Reconstruction of the Tower of Babel by Ker Porter. Based on his drawing of Birs Nimrud. Partly tinted pen drawing. British Museum, Add. MS. 14758, Vol. II, fol. 139. (*Photos on pp. 190–3 by permission of the Trustees of the British Museum.*)

195A   F. R. Chesney travels in Arab disguise down the Euphrates in 1830. Lithograph from *Narrative of the Euphrates Expedition*, facing page 60, London, 1868.*

195B   Transportation of the knocked-down steamships during the Chesney expedition. From *Narrative* (see 195a), Plate 70.*

197   Sinking of the Tigris on May 21, 1836. Lithograph from Chesney's *Narrative* (see 195a), plate 90.*

199A   Excavation by Botta of one of the first Assyrian reliefs, 1844. Copper engraving from P. E. Botta: *Monuments de Ninive découverts et décrits par Botta, mé-*

Book III
Page

surés et dessinés par M. E. Flandin, Vol. I, Plate 49, Paris, 1849.*

199B Nineveh. Engraving from a drawing by Carsten Niebuhr, made 1766, published in *Reisebeschreibung*: see 181.*

200 Transporting a winged bull from Khorsabad.*

201 *Keleks* on which Place shipped his finds. Engraving from a drawing by Felix Thomas. From Place: *Ninive et l'Assyrie* (also source of 200), Plate 43.*

202–3 Reliefs from Kuyunjik (*c.* 21 inches high). Both reliefs taken by Layard from the gate of Assurbanipal in Nineveh and sent to London. (*By permission of the Trustees of the British Museum.*)

204 The cliff at Behistun. Wash drawing by Sir Robert Ker Porter, 1818. British Museum, Add. MS. 14758, fol. 123. (*By permission of the Trustees of the British Museum.*)

205 The cliff at Behistun. (*Photo "Negatif Citroën," Phototèque Musée de l'Homme, Palais de Chaillot, Paris.*)

206 Major General Sir H. C. Rawlinson. Mezzotint from the portrait by H. W. Phillips, 1850.*

207A Rawlinson's copy of the right uppermost cuneiform text above the head of Darius on the relief at Behistun.*

207B Lithograph from Rawlinson's drawing of the inscriptions and relief on the cliff at Behistun.*

208 Rawlinson's transcription and translation of the inscription reproduced on page 207. Photos on pp. 207–8 from *The Cuneiform Inscriptions of Western Asia.*

209 Pages 62–3 from *Inscription of Tiglath-Pileser I, King of Assyria, B.C. 1150, as translated by Sir Henry Rawlinson, Fox Talbot, Esq., Dr. Hincks and Dr. Oppert*, London, 1857.*

210 One of the eight-sided clay prisms in the British Museum. (*By permission of the Trustees of the British Museum.*)

211 H. A. Layard with his servant Saleh, the Lurian. After a sketch by J. Miner Kellogg. Frontispiece from Layard: *Early Adventures in Persia*, Vol. II, London, 1887.*

212 Layard at the age of sixty. Gernsheim Collection. (*Photo Lock and Whitfield.*)

213 Layard's acrobatic feat at the bas-relief of Bavian, 1846.*

214 Layard at the discovery of the first human-headed animal sculpture, the guardian of Nimrod's gate in Nineveh. From Layard: *Nineveh and Its Remains*, I, 66, London, 1849.*

Book III
Page

215 One of the guardians of the gate in the palace of Assurnasipal. Colossal alabaster sculpture, discovered in 1847 by Layard. (*By permission of the Trustees of the British Museum.*)

216A Hebrews bring tribute. Original photograph of a detail of the "Black Obelisk." (*By permission of the Trustees of the British Museum.*)

216B The "Black Obelisk" of Salmanassar III. From *Monuments of Nineveh*, Plate 55, London, 1849.*

217 The "Sleeping Lioness." Relief found by Layard in the palace of Assurbanipal. (*By permission of the Trustees of the British Museum.*)

218 Assurbanipal hunting lions. Bas-relief sent by Layard from Kuyunjik to London. Now in the "Assyrian Saloon" of the British Museum. (*By permission of the Trustees of the British Museum.*)

219 Bronze sheathing from wooden gate of the palace of Salmanassar III in Balavat. Discovered in 1877 by Hormuzd Rassan. (*By permission of the Trustees of the British Museum.*)

221 Clay tablet containing fragments of the Gilgamesh Epic, from Assurbanipal's clay-tablet library. British Museum, Neg. I D 48. (*By permission of the Trustees of the British Museum.*)

224 Rioting and fire at the "Citadel America" camp. Drawing in Persian miniature style by Ulrica Lloyd for Seton Lloyd's *Foundations in the Dust*, London, 1947. (*By the kind permission of Mrs. Seton Lloyd.*)

225 Robert Koldewey, the excavator of Babylon. Photo taken about 1900.

227 Babylon: the Ishtar Gate after the excavation of 1914. Painting by Elizabeth Andrae in the Near Eastern Division of the Staatliches Museum, Berlin.

228A Babylon: the Ishtar Gate at the beginning of the excavation. (*This photo and photo on p. 227 by permission of the Director of the Near Eastern Division of the Staatliches Museum, Berlin.*)

228B Babylon: cross-section of the Ishtar Gate. From Koldewey: *Das wiederestehende Babylon*, Leipzig, 1914.*

229 Babylon: model of the Ishtar Gate. Near Eastern Division of the Staatliches Museum, Berlin.

230A Babylon: first publication of the *sirrush* (*sir-ruššu*) in the *Mitteilungen der Deutschen Orient-Gesellschaft*, Berlin, 1902.*

230B Babylon: wall with animals on Ishtar Gate. Below: relief tiles without enamel. Above: enameled tiles without reliefs. (*This photo and photo on p. 229 by permission of the Director of the Near Eastern Division of the Staatliches Museum, Berlin.*)

Book III
Page

231A Koldewey's reconstruction of the Tower of Babel. *Mitteilungen der Deutchen Orient-Gesellschaft*, May 1918.*

231B Babylon: remains of the tower. From Koldewey: see 228b.*

233A Leonard Woolley and his wife doing one of the "subtle jobs" of an archaeologist. Excavation at Ur. From Sir Leonard Woolley: *Digging Up the Past*, Plate I, London, 1930.

233B Workmen wait for *baksheesh* as Sir Leonard Woolley lists their finds.

234 Sir Leonard and Lady Woolley with assistants preserving cuneiform tablets.

235A Drying, baking, and packing the cuneiform script bricks.

235B Cuneiform tablets before and after treatment.

237 View of the death-pit, taken while gold objects were being found. From Woolley: *Ur Excavations: The Royal Cemetery*, London, 1934.

239 The "death-pit of Ur." Pen drawing by the excavators, reproduced in *The Royal Cemetery* (see 237), Plate 71.

240 Three harps—the work of reassembling in various stages of completion.

241A Detail of the "bull-headed harp" found in Ur. British Museum, No. 121198.

241B Woolley and his wife (in the background) during excavation work on two of the harps.

242 The mosaic standard of Ur: section showing peaceful activities.

243 The mosaic standard of Ur: section showing military activities.

244 Life-size statue of a Sumerian ruler, perhaps Gudea or his son Ur-Ningursu. Green-flecked diorite.

246 Woolley's reconstruction of the ziggurat of Ur as it probably looked under the Third Dynasty.

246-7 The ziggurat of Ur. Aerial photograph. (*Photos on pp. 233-47 by permission of Sir Leonard Woolley and the Trustees of the British Museum.*)

Book IV

251 First meeting between Cortés and Moctezuma. From the facsimile printing of the *Lienzo di Tlascala*, 1892. (*By permission of the American Museum of Natural History, New York.*)

252A Cortés—medallion by C. Weiditz, representing the conqueror of Mexico at the age of forty-three, in 1529. (*By permission of the director of the coin collection, Museum am Kupfergraben, Staatliche Museen, Berlin-Dahlem.*)

Book III
Page

252B Cortés, from the Nuremberg copy of the Weiditz manuscript, 1529. (*By permission of the Germanisches Museum, Nuremberg.*)

253 Feather headdress of Moctezuma. (*By permission of the Museum für Völkerkunde, Vienna.*)

254 The original framework (restored) of the feather headdress (see 253). Photograph and restoration by Franz Heger, prepared in 1908 for the Vienna Congress of Americanists. (*By permission of the Museum für Völkerkunde, Vienna.*)

255 Human skull encrusted with fragments of turquoise, probably representing Tezcatlipoca (mirror smoke), the lord of heaven and earth. (*By permission of the Museum für Völkerkunde, formerly Staatliche Museen, Berlin-Dahlem.*)

256 Golden breastplate with the mask of the Mixtec god of death; four inches long. (*By permission of the Museo Regional de Oaxaca, Mexico.*)

257 Indian juggling a log. Three drawings from the Weiditz manuscript in Nuremberg: see 252b.

258A Two Indians playing with a rubber ball. From the Weiditz album: see 252b.

258B The first Indian woman in Europe. Wash drawing by Weiditz: see 252b. (*Photos on pp. 257-8 by permission of the Germanisches Museum, Nuremberg.*)

259 Autograph of Fray Bernardino de Sahagún: last page of the original manuscript of the Spanish version of his book on Mexican culture.

261 Several of Sahagún's illustrations for his chapter on the making of feather ornaments.

262 Four additional illustrations by Sahagún of the technique of feather work. (*Photos on pp. 259-61 by permission of the Biblioteca Lorenziana, Florence.*)

263A The Mexican god Omeyocan. Woodcut, from the adjacent drawing, by Lorenzo Pignoria, inserted in 1615 into his revision of *Le vere e nove Imagini de gli Dei delli Antichi*, by Vincenzo Cartari.*

263B The Mexican god Omeyocan. Water color from a Vatican codex, with Italian text by Fra Pietro del Ríos, after whom this manuscript is also called the Codex Ríos. (Fol. I, verso of this manuscript.) Ríos made his comments in 1566; the codex is older, about the middle of the sixteenth century. (*By permission of the Biblioteca Vaticana, Vatican.*)

265A Codex Ríos (see 263b), fol. 7. "Sochiquetzal." (*By permission of the Biblioteca Vaticana, Vatican.*)

265B "Sochiquetzal," according to Pignoria the diabolic imitation of the archangel Gabriel. Woodcut in Pignoria's revision of *Le vere*: see 263a.*

Book IV
Page

266A Human sacrifices, on the threshold of the *teocalli.* From the Codex Magliabbechiano, XIII 3, written by a native after the conquest of Mexico. (*By permission of the Biblioteca Nazionale Centrale, Florence.*)

266B Human sacrifices represented in the Codex Ríos (see 263b). Middle of the sixteenth century. (*By permission of the Biblioteca Vaticana, Vatican.*)

267 Sister Juana Inés de la Cruz in her library. Oil painting by Miguel Cabrera. (*By permission of the Museo Nacional de Historia, Mexico City.*)

269A Alexander von Humboldt. Lithograph by Jules Boilly, 1821. Represented as a *"membre de l'Institut."* *

269B The pyramid of Cholula, drawn in 1800 by Humboldt and engraved for him by Gamelin in Rome. *Vues des Cordillères, et monuments des peuples indigènes de l'Amérique,* Paris, 1816. *

270 The pyramid of Cholula as Mount Calvary. Hand-colored lithograph from a drawing by Luciano Castañeda, 1805. The lithograph was made in Paris in 1834 for the account of Captain Dupaix's expeditions. *

271 Facsimile from the Codex Mendoza, reproduced as a plate in A. Aglio: *Antiquities of Mexico,* edited by Viscount Kingsborough, London, 1830–48. *

273A The relief frieze of Xochicalco, from a drawing by Luciano Castañeda. Kingsborough (see 271), Vol. IV, Part 2, Lamina 15, No. 33. *

273B Photo of a part of the same relief frieze of Xochicalco. (*Photo Multiphoto, Paris.*)

274A Zapotek funerary urn, after a drawing by Luciano Castañeda. Kingsborough (see 271), Vol. IV, Part 2, Lamina 46, No. 103. *

274B Urn: modern photograph of a piece in the Museo Regional de Oaxaca, Mexico. (*Photo Musée de l'Homme, Paris.*)

275A Modern photograph of a relief from a pillar at the front of Palace D in Palenque. (*Photo Musée de l'Homme, Paris.*)

275B The same relief shown on the preceding plate. Lithograph after Dupaix. Kingsborough (see 271), Vol. IV, Part 3, Lamina 29, No. 34. *

276 Count Waldeck in a litter in the jungle. Colored lithograph from Comte de Waldeck: *Voyage pittoresque et archéologique dans le province d'Yucatan, Amérique Centrale, pendant les années 1834 et 1836,* Paris, 1838. *

277 Panorama of Palenque. Taken 1896–9. (*By permission of the American Museum of Natural History, New York.*)

278 The step pyramid of Uxmal. By Count Waldeck: see 276. *

Book IV
Page

279 Model reconstruction of the Temple of the Cross, Palenque. (*By permission of the American Museum of Natural History, New York.*)

281 One of the stelae of Copan: Monument "T." Lithograph from J. L. Stephens: *Incidents of Travel in Central America, Chiapas and Yucatan,* Vol. II, Plate 68, London, 1844. *

282 Reverse of one of the stelae of Copan: Idol "P." From Stephens (see 281), Vol. I, Plate 19. *

283 One of the stelae of Quiriguá. (*Photo Multiphoto, Paris.*)

284 Colossal mask on the exterior wall of the now badly decayed step pyramid of Izamal. Colored lithograph from F. Catherwood: *Views of Ancient Monuments in Central America, Chiapas and Yucatan,* London, 1844. *

285 Stephens directs the removal of a sculptured stone doorpost in Kabah (Yucatán). Lithograph from Catherwood (see 284), p. 312. *

287 Mayan chief kneeling in prayer. Detail of a relief stele from Yaxchilán (Chiapas), c. seventh to eighth century A.D. British Museum, London. (*By permission of the Trustees of the British Museum.*)

288 Two Aztec women's costumes. Page from the Codex Ríos: see 263b. (*By permission of the Biblioteca Vaticana, Vatican.*)

291 The sacred well at Chichén-Itzá. (*By permission of the American Antiquarian Society, Worcester, Mass.*)

292 Part of a gold mask found in the sacred well. (*By permission of the Peabody Museum, Harvard University, Cambridge, Mass.*)

293 Eduard Seler. Etching by Erich Heermann. Frontispiece of the anniversary volume published in his honor. *

295 A Mexican relief on the palace of Palenque which has been taken for a representation of an elephant. Drawing by Frédéric de Waldeck. (*By permission of the Newberry Library, Chicago.*)

296 Model of the pyramid of Tenayuca. In the American Museum of Natural History, New York. This model was made in 1931. (*By permission of the American Museum of Natural History, New York.*)

297 Temple of the Inscriptions, Palenque. (From a reconstructed model drawn by C. W. Ceram.)

298–9 Wall painting of the Lacandón Indians, Bonampak. From the copy in the Peabody Museum, Harvard University. (*By permission of the Peabody Museum, Harvard University, Cambridge, Mass.*)

Book V

303A G. Lancaster Harding, British director of archaeological research for the Hashemite Kingdom of Jordan,

Book V
Page

sorting fragments of the sacred scriptural scrolls of the Essenes in the Palestinian archaeological museum in Jerusalem. (*Photo Hulton Picture Library.*)

303B A skin diver bringing the neck of a Greek amphora from the sea bottom to the surface in the course of underwater researches conducted by M. Philippe

Book V
Page

Diolé, 1948–53. Jacket picture from Diolé: *Promenades d'archéologie sous-marine.* (*By permission of M. Diolé and the publishers, Albin Michel, Paris.*)

305 Aerial photograph taken by Père Antoine Poidebard in Syria in 1930. (*By permission of Université St. Joseph, Beirut.*)

INDEX

Abd-el-Rasul, 119
Achilles, 32
Adair, James, 272
Agamemnon, 45, 46, 51
Agesandros, 5
Aglio, Agostino, 272
Akerblad, 86
Alcubierre, Rocco Gioacchino de, 11, 12, 29
Alexander the Great, 163, 169
Amenophis I, 119, 121, 122
Amenophis III, 80, 121
Amenophis IV, 143
Amer, Mustapha, 108
Andrae, Elisabeth, 226
Andrae, Walter, 226
Andromache, 38
Antinous, 8–9
Antiochus I, 132
Anubis, 159
Apis Bulls, 130–1
Assurnasirpal II, 211–12, 214, 227
Assyria, 212–14, 216–20

Athenodorus, 5
Atreus, 45
Atrides, 45
Avilix, 288–9
Ayrton, Edward, 136
Aztec culture, 250–68; feather work, 253–4, 261–2; games, 258; human sacrifice, 265–8; calendar, 293

Babel, Tower of, 160–3, 226, 231–2, 270
Babylon, 162–6, 181, 186–94, 220, 225
Bacchus, 8
Bacchus, temple of, 66–7
Balbilla, 80
Baraize, 73, 74
Bellino, Carl, 186, 187, 190
Belzoni, Giovanni Battista, 82–4, 95–6, 135, 200
Berenice, 86, 89
Bible, 162, 165, 198, 202, 220–1, 227, 229, 231, 232, 245, 248, 270
Blegen, Carl W., 41
Boetticher, Ernst, 42

i

Bonaparte, Marie Caroline, 20
Bonomi, Joseph, 81
Borchardt, Ludwig, 107
Bossert, Helmuth T., 64
Botta, Paul Emile, 199–200, 212, 217
Brasseur de Bourbourg, Charles-Etienne, 286, 290
British Museum, 29, 82, 83, 159, 217, 220, 245, 272
Brueghel, Pieter, 162
Brugsch, Emil, 110–11, 119, 120
Brugsch, Heinrich, 110–11
Burnouf, Emile, 36
Burton, James (Haliburton), 135
Buschor, Ernst, 22, 62, 81–2

Caffery, Jefferson, 132
Çambel, Halet, 132
Cambyses, 169
Camera lucida, 98–9
Canart, Joseph, 12
Canning, Sir Stratford, 211
Carnarvon, George Herbert, Lord, 138
Carter, Howard, 108, 138–42, 144
Castañeda, Luciano, 271, 273–5
Catherwood, Frederick, 80, 280–4
Cavaceppi, Bartolomeo, 14
Caviglia, 73
Cerberus, 70
Champollion, Jean-François, 84–5, 88–9, 115, 183, 186
Chardin, Jean, 172–3, 175, 176, 189, 190
Charles III, 14
Chavero, Alfredo, 251
Cheops, 92, 93, 94, 95, 100, 102, 105
Chephren, 74, 84, 91, 92, 95, 99, 105
Chesney, Francis Rawdon, 194–7
Choiseul-Gouffier, Count of, 32
Cleopatra, 86, 88, 89
Cookson, M. B., 81
Corte, Mattio della, 30
Cortés, Hernán, 250–4, 257, 265, 279

Cotton, Sir Dodmore, 168
Cousteau, Jaques-Yves, 304
Crawford, Osbert Guy Stanhope, 306
cuneiform writing, 176–88, 201–10, 224, 235
Cyrus, 169

Darius I, 169, 184, 191
Darius III, 169
Davis, Theodore, 136
Davis Expedition, 138
Dead Sea scrolls, 302
De Bruin, Cornelis, 175–6, 184, 189, 190
Delitzsch, Friedrich, 164
Denon, Baron Dominique Vivant, 72, 76
Desprez, 16
Dessaix, 76
Diehl, Ludwig, 30
Dionysian Mysteries, 26
Dixon, Wayman, 103
Dörpfeld, William, 36, 41, 42, 225
Dumas, Alexandre, 31
Dungi, 247
Dupaix, Guillaume, 271, 273–5
Dürer, Albrecht, 255–7

Echidna, 70
Edwards, I. E. S., 105
Egypt, 70–160; sphinx, 70–4, 95; hieroglyphs, 77, 84–90, 182; pyramids, 91–110, 150, 296; mummies, 111–49; building methods, 150–4; tombs, 154–7
Ellis, I. C., 102
Euphrates, 194–7
Evans, Sir Arthur, 52–62, 63, 64, 66

Fiorelli, Giuseppe, 31
Fiorillo, 183
Flandin, Eugène Napoléon, 200
Flaubert, Gustave, 72
Fonte, Bartolommeo, 2–4
Fox Talbot, W. H., 209, 210
France, Anatole, 114

Freddi, Felice de', 5
Friedrich, Johannes, 186

Gayet, 113, 114
Gilgamesh Epic, 220–2, 224, 248
Gillérion, Edouard, 58
Gizeh, 71, 74, 84, 91, 92, 94, 98, 100, 104, 157
Gladstone, William, 45
Goell, Theresa, 132
Goethe, Johann Wolfgang, 11
Goldman, Hetty, 132
Goneim, Zakaria, 108, 153–4
Gorst, Sir Eldon, 136
Greaves, John, 95
Grélot, Guillaume Joseph, 175
Grotefend, Georg Friedrich, 176, 180, 183–6, 206, 208
Guimet, Emile Etienne, 113–14

Hacavitz, 288–9
Hadrian, 9, 80
Hamilton, Sir William, 17, 29
Hammurabi, 232
Harachte-Chepere-Re-Atum, 73
Hass, Hans, 304
Hatshepsut, Queen, 74
Hay, Robert, 78, 271
Hay Expedition, 78, 81, 135, 280
Healey, Giles G., 299
Hector, 32
Heeren, 183
Heger, Franz, 254
Heine-Geldern, Robert von, 294
Helffrich, Johannes, 70, 71, 93, 94, 98
Heliopolis, 66
Herbert, Thomas, 168
Herculaneum, 9–12, 28, 30, 31
Herodotus, 92, 100, 115, 150, 162, 178, 184, 227
Herzfeld, Ernst, 169
Hetepheres, Queen, 108, 109
Hincks, Edward, 208–10
Hissarlik mound, 41–2

Hollar, Wenzel, 168
Homer, 8, 32, 34, 38, 49, 64, 65
Horapollon, 86
Huizinga, 6
Humboldt, Alexander von, 268–71
Hydra, 71

Innocent VIII, 2
Ishtar, 220
Ishtar, Gate of, 226, 229–30
Isimkhobiu, 123
Isis, 123, 147, 148, 156, 159
Israel, Menasseh ben, 294

Jomard, François, 77
Juana Inés de la Cruz, 266–8
Junker, Hermann, 109

Kamal El-Malakh, 157
Kämpfer, Engelbert, 174, 176, 178, 190
Kanavas, Khan, 173
Karo, Georg, 49
Kerényi, Karl, 26
Khumbabam, 220
King, Edward (Lord Kingsborough), 271–2, 274, 276, 278, 294
Knorosov, Y. V., 300
Kober, Alice, 64
Koldewey, Robert, 163, 188, 225–32
Kramer, Samuel N., 224

Lado, 70
Lakshmi, 30
Landa, Diego de (Bishop of Mérida), 290
Landes, André Daulier des, 169–70
Lane, Edward William, 78–9, 98, 135
Lange, Kurt, 121
Laocoön, 5–6
Lawrence, T. E., 232
Layard, Sir Austen Henry, 135, 203, 211–17, 220
Lempesis, 41

Lepsius, Richard, 105
Lessing, Gotthold Ephraim, 5
Lion Gate, 46
Livia, 6
Lloyd, Seton, 224
Lloyd, Ulrica, 224
Lockett, Abraham, 188

Maani, Sitti, 166–7
Mainwaring, George, 166
Maiuri, Amadeo, 31
Maket-Re, 128, 156
Malcolm, Sir John, 206
Marduk, 162, 230
Mariette, Auguste, 105, 108, 110, 130
Marina (Malinche), 250–1
Maron, Anton von, 8
Maspero, Gaston, 73, 110, 119, 121, 122, 125
Mayan culture, 277–300; religion, 286; calendar, 290
Mazois, François, 20
Meissner, Bruno, 226
Memnon, 80
Meriggi, Piero, 64
Mérimée, Prosper, 278
Merlin, Maurice, 304
Mesopotamia, 171, 198, 223, 236–8, 269
Mexico, 250–300
Michelangelo, 5
Middle America, 250–300
Minos, King, 52–7
Mixtec culture, 255, 257
Moctezuma, 250, 253, 254, 257
Mommsen, Theodor, 306
Montezinos, Aaron Levi de, 294
Morier, 189, 190
Moritz, Emanuel (Prince d'Elboeuf), 11, 12
Mummies, 111–49
Münter, Friedrich, 182
Murat, Joachim, 20
Mycenae, 42–68
Mycerinus, 92

Nabupolassar, 163
Napoleon, 20, 27, 76, 77
Neb-hebet-Re, 116
Nebuchadnezzar, 163, 226, 227, 229
Nephtys, 123, 147, 156, 160
Newberry, Percy, 109
Niebuhr, Carsten, 179–80, 189, 190, 198
Nineveh, 181, 198, 211–14, 216–21
Nippur, 222, 223
Nour, Zaki, 157
Nsitanebashru, 125, 126

Oedipus, 71
Olenin, Alexis von, 189, 190
Omeyocan, 263
Oppert, Julius, 209–10
Osiris, 79, 123
Ovando, Juan de, 259

Paderni, Camillo, 28
Palazzo dei Conservatori, 2
Palenque, 275, 276–9, 297
Pausanias, 46
Pendlebury, J. D. S., 53
Permoli, Giovanni, 6–8
Persepolis, 167–70, 175, 178, 180, 181, 183, 189
Perseus, 45
Persia, 167–70
Peters, Reverend Dr., 223
Petrie, Sir William Flinders, 102–4, 105, 150, 152, 306
Phaestos Disc, 64–6
Philodemos, 28, 29
Piaggio, Antonio, 28–9
Picart, Bernard, 80
Pignoria, Lorenzo, 263–4
Piranesi, Francesco, 16
Piranesi, Giovanni Battista, 15
Place, Victor, 201
Pliny, 5
Pococke, Richard, 135
Poidebard, Antoine, 304–6

Polydorus, 5
Pomet, Pierre, 112
Pompeii, 9–31; destruction of, 17–18; life of, 22–6
Popul Vuh, 286–9
Porter, Maria, 189
Porter, Robert Ker, 189–94, 204
Praschniker, Camillo, 57
Prescott, William, 252, 272
Priam's treasure, 39, 41
Ptolemy V, 86, 88, 89
pyramids: Egyptian, 91–110; New World, 269, 284, 295–8

Quetzalcoatl, 273

radiocarbon dating, 306
Ramses II, 79, 81, 82, 83, 119–20, 135
Ramses III, 77
Rassam, Hormuzd, 219
Rauwolff, Leonhard, 165–6
Rawlinson, Henry Creswicke, 204–10
Re, 148
Re-Harachte, 74
Reisner, G. A., 108, 109, 110
Reuther, Oscar, 225, 226, 232
Rich, Claudius James, 186–8, 190, 193
Richmond, Sir William, 52
Ríos, Antonio del, 266, 276, 279
Rosetta Stone, 77, 84, 86–9
Royal Asiatic Society, 208–10
Ruz, Alberto, 297–8

Sachau, Eduard, 226
Sahagún, Bernardino de, 259–63, 267
Salmanassar III, 216, 219
Sangallo, Francesco di, 5
Sangallo, Giuliano, 5
Sassetti, Francesco, 2
Scharff, Alexander, 90
Schlegel, Friedrich, 302
Schliemann, Heinrich, 32–51, 52; life of, 34–6; marriage, 38–40
Schliemann, Sophia, 39–40, 42, 132

Schmidt, Erich F., 169
Schultze-Jena, Leonhardt, 260
Schulz, Bruno, 68
Sekhem-khet, 109
Seler, Eduard, 260, 293, 294
Selquet, 147
Semple, William T., 41, 42
Sennacherib, 212, 213
Serapion, 113–14
Sethos I, 79, 84, 112, 119, 121
Severus, Septimius, 73, 80
Sherley, Sir Robert, 168
Sittig, Ernst, 52, 64, 66
Sloane, Sir Hans, 174, 272
Smith, Georg, 220
Smith, Grafton Elliot, 124, 125, 294
Smyth, Charles Piazzi, 101–2, 103
Snofru, 105
Sphinx: Greek, 70–1; Egyptian, 70–4, 95
Stadiatis, Elias, 303
Stamatakes, Panagiotes, 46
Stephen, John Lloyd, 280–5
Suhle, A., 252
Sumerians, 241–8
Sundwall, 64

Tau-a-quen III, 124
Tavernier, Jean-Baptiste, 170
Thais, 113–14, 133
Thompson, Edward Herbert, 290–2
Thutihotep, 150
Thutmosis I, 119
Thutmosis III, 119, 125
Thutmosis IV, 73, 133
Tiglath-Pileser, 209
Tiryns, 52
Tohil, 288–9
Toltec culture, 270, 277, 278
Troy, 32–9, 42, 49, 52
Tsountas, Chrestos, 46
Tutankhamen, 136–49
Tychsen, Olav Gerhard, 182, 183

Unis, 110
Ur, 232–48
Urnammu, 247

Valle, Pietro della, 166–7, 177
Ventris, Michael, 64–6
Vesuvius, 10
Virchow, Rudolf, 36
Vyse, Richard Howard, 95

Wace, Alan B., 49
Wah, 128, 129
Waldeck, Jean-Frédéric-Maximilien, Comte de, 276–8, 280
Weiditz, Christoph, 252, 258
Weinlig, Christian Traugott, 9, 14

Wheeler, Sir Mortimer, 81
Wiener, Norbert, 64
Wilkinson, Sir J. Gardner, 112
Winckelmann, Johann Joachim, 8–9, 12–14, 29
Winckler, Hugo, 37
Winlock, H. E., 116, 128, 137
Woolley, Sir Leonard, 232–48

Xelhua, 270
Xerxes, 163, 174, 175, 184
Ximénez, Francisco, 286

Young, Thomas, 86, 89

Zoser, 92, 109
Zumárraga, 259

A NOTE ABOUT THE AUTHOR

C. W. Ceram is the pseudonym by which the author of the best-selling *Gods, Graves, and Scholars* is known to everyone anywhere in the world interested in archaeology and in classical antiquity. Ceram, who now lives in the United States, was born in Berlin in 1915. He was for many years connected with newspaper work and publishing, first as drama critic and book reviewer for Berlin newspapers and later, after the war, as editor of Rowohlt Verlag, a Hamburg publishing house. *Gods, Graves, and Scholars,* completed in 1949 after five years of research and published in the United States in 1951, brought world fame to Ceram as a writer on archaeology. Thereafter he was frequently invited to join expeditions in the field. He made two trips to Turkey to participate in excavations uncovering the Hittite past; one of the results was the publication of his next book, *The Secret of the Hittites,* in 1956. Since then he has been immersed in the long task of preparing *The March of Archaeology.*

A NOTE ON THE TYPE

This book is set in ELECTRA, *a Linotype face designed by* W. A. *Dwiggins (1880–1956), who was responsible for so much that is good in contemporary book design. Although much of his early work was in advertising and he was the author of the standard volume* LAYOUT IN ADVERTISING, *Mr. Dwiggins later devoted his prolific talents to book typography and type design, and worked with great distinction in both fields. In addition to his designs for Electra, he created the Metro, Caledonia, and Eldorado series of type faces, as well as a number of experimental cuttings that have never been issued commercially.*

Electra cannot be classified as either modern or old-style. It is not based on any historical model, nor does it echo a particular period or style. It avoids the extreme contrast between thick and thin elements which marks most modern faces, and attempts to give a feeling of fluidity, power, and speed.

This book was composed, printed, and bound by KINGSPORT PRESS, INC., *Kingsport, Tennessee. Black-and-white line and halftone engravings supplied by* CAPPER ENGRAVING COMPANY, INC., *Knoxville, Tennessee. Color plates supplied by* THAMES AND HUDSON LTD., *London, England. The paper was manufactured by* S. D. WARREN COMPANY, *Boston. Designed by* GUY FLEMING.